The Formation and
Stocks of Total Capital

NATIONAL BUREAU OF ECONOMIC RESEARCH

Number 100, General Series

The Formation and Stocks of Total Capital

John W. Kendrick
THE GEORGE WASHINGTON UNIVERSITY

Assisted by
Yvonne Lethem and Jennifer Rowley

NATIONAL BUREAU OF ECONOMIC RESEARCH

New York   1976

DISTRIBUTED BY Columbia University Press

New York and London

Library of Congress Cataloging in Publication Data

Kendrick, John W.
   The formation and stocks of total capital.
   (General series–National Bureau of Economic Research; no. 100)
   Bibliography: p. 241
   Includes index.
   1. Capital—United States. 2. Capital productivity—
United States. 3. Saving and investment—United States.
I. Lethem, Yvonne, joint author. II. Rowley, Jennifer,
joint author. III. Title. IV. Series: National
Bureau of Economic Research. General series; no. 100.
HC110.C3K452   332'.041   76-20790
ISBN 0-87014-271-2

Relation of the Directors to the Work and Publications of the National Bureau of Economic Research

1. The object of the National Bureau of Economic Research is to ascertain and to present to the public important economic facts and their interpretation in a scientific and impartial manner. The Board of Directors is charged with the responsibility of ensuring that the work of the National Bureau is carried on in strict conformity with this object.

2. The President of the National Bureau shall submit to the Board of Directors, or to its Executive Committee, for their formal adoption all specific proposals for research to be instituted.

3. No research report shall be published by the National Bureau until the President has sent each member of the Board a notice that a manuscript is recommended for publication and that in the President's opinion it is suitable for publication in accordance with the principles of the National Bureau. Such notification will include an abstract or summary of the manuscript's content and a response form for use by those Directors who desire a copy of the manuscript for review. Each manuscript shall contain a summary drawing attention to the nature and treatment of the problem studied, the character of the data and their utilization in the report, and the main conclusions reached.

4. For each manuscript so submitted, a special committee of the Directors (including Directors Emeriti) shall be appointed by majority agreement of the President and Vice President (or by the Executive Committee in case of inability to decide on the part of the President and Vice Presidents), consisting of three Directors selected as nearly as may be one from each general division of the Board. The names of the special manuscript committee shall be stated to each Director when notice of the proposed publication is submitted to him. It shall be the duty of each member of the special manuscript committee to read the manuscript. If each member of the manuscript committee signifies his approval within thirty days of the transmittal of the manuscript, the report may be published. If at the end of that period any member of the manuscript committee withholds his approval, the President shall then notify each member of the Board, requesting approval or disapproval of publication, and thirty days additional shall be granted for this purpose. The manuscript shall then not be published unless at least a majority of the entire Board who shall have voted on the proposal within the time fixed for the receipt of votes shall have approved.

5. No manuscript may be published, though approved by each member of the special manuscript committee, until forty-five days have elapsed from the transmittal of the report in manuscript form. The interval is allowed for the receipt of any memorandum of dissent or reservation, together with a brief statement of his reasons, that any member may wish to express; and such memorandum of dissent or reservation shall be published with the manuscript if he so desires. Publication does not, however, imply that each member of the Board has read the manuscript, or that either members of the Board in general or the special committee have passed on its validity in every detail.

6. Publications of the National Bureau issued for informational purposes concerning the work of the Bureau and its staff, or issued to inform the public of activities of Bureau staff, and volumes issued as a result of various conferences involving the National Bureau shall contain a specific disclaimer noting that such publication has not passed through the normal review procedures required in this resolution. The Executive Committee of the Board is charged with review of all such publications from time to time to ensure that they do not take on the character of formal research reports of the National Bureau, requiring formal Board approval.

7. Unless otherwise determined by the Board or exempted by the terms of paragraph 6, a copy of this resolution shall be printed in each National Bureau publication.

(Resolution adopted October 25, 1926, as revised through September 30, 1974)

Contents

Tables

Appendix C

Tables on Microfiche

Note: Tables B-2a through B-20b, Part 1 are on microfiche card 3, and the remainder, on card 4.

Charts

Preface

The following pages offer a somewhat personal account of this study's genesis, a brief outline of its overall plan and contents, and a sincere acknowledgment of the contributions made by all those who helped bring it to fruition.

Genesis

My work of the mid-1950s on total factor productivity resulted in the provocative finding that only about half of the long-term economic growth in the United States—and even less than that since World War I—could be explained by the growth of intangible human and nonhuman factor inputs. The other half or more was ascribed to increases in total tangible factor productivity, resulting largely from "technical change or innovation," "variations in the rate or scale of production," and "changes per factor unit in the services of immaterial capital accumulated in order to increase the efficiency of resources in future periods."[1] As I then noted, immaterial capital ". . . is largely the technical knowledge of individuals, accumulated by investment in education and research, and its services are manifested through the application of know-how by individuals directly in productive activity, or through the instruments of production."[2]

1. John W. Kendrick, "Productivity Trends: Capital and Labor," *Review of Economics and Statistics*, May 1956; reprinted as Occasional Paper 53, New York, National Bureau of Economic Research, 1956.
2. Ibid.

My subsequent book on productivity presented estimates of the major types of "hidden investments" (so called because they were not identified in the national income and product accounts as investment) in research and development, education, and health.[3] I noted their significant growth relative to national product and to tangible investments, but did not attempt at that time to estimate the growth of the associated intangible capital stocks and related services or inputs into production.

In his introduction to my book Solomon Fabricant noted that, if we included along with tangible resources the intangibles, broadly defined, ". . . it would probably follow that much (not all) of the increase in product would reflect increase in resources." He itemized the other factors, such as changes in scale and the degree of competition, which would affect the productivity "residue" in addition to the contributions of the several forms of intangible capital.[4]

Abramovitz, in a paper which appeared the same year as my earlier study, and making use of much the same estimates, also remarked on the significant rise in total factor productivity in the United States since 1870. He, challenging, called it a "measure of our ignorance" concerning the sources of economic growth other than the increases in tangible inputs, and "an indication of where we need to concentrate our attention."[5] Ever since the mid-1950s, an increasing amount of attention has been devoted by economists to exploring the areas of ignorance concerning growth and narrowing "the residual," as Domar later termed the productivity variable.

In his work on technical change and aggregate production functions, Solow stressed the importance of technological improvements embodied in tangible capital goods. By separately weighting the various vintages of capital goods used in production, he was able to estimate statistically the effect of the changing age-mix of tangible capital stocks on productivity advance.[6] He noted that changes in average age tended to be associated with changes in growth rates of tangible capital, and cited Johansen's argument that capital growth facilitated the adaptation of productive processes to technological change. Other investigators emphasized the importance of research and development outlays in producing the technical advances that are

3. John W. Kendrick, *Productivity Trends in the United States,* Princeton, Princeton University Press for NBER, 1961, Chapter 4.

4. Ibid., p. xlviii.

5. Moses Abramovitz, *Resource and Output Trends in the United States since 1870,* Occasional Paper 52, New York, NBER, 1956.

6. Robert M. Solow, "Technical Change and the Aggregate Production Function," *Review of Economics and Statistics,* August 1957, pp. 312–320.

largely embodied in tangible capital. Terleckyj, for example, established a significant positive correlation between R&D spending as a percentage of revenue and rates of productivity advance in manufacturing industries.[7] No one attempted to measure the intangible stock of productive knowledge resulting from R&D complementary to the tangible capital stocks, however.

Attention to human investments designed to increase the efficiency or "quality" of tangible labor inputs received a major impetus by the work of Schultz in the latter 1950s,[8] and particularly by his presidential address to the American Economic Association in December 1960, entitled "Investment in Human Capital."[9] Although recognition of the importance of human capital has long roots in the history of economic thought, Schultz's work resulted in what Blaug has called "a sudden acceleration of research . . . and . . . proliferation of publications" in the area of human investment and capital.[10]

An early result was the Exploratory Conference on Capital Investment in Human Beings of December 1961, sponsored by the Universities-National Bureau Committee for Economic Research. The eight papers presented there were published in an October 1962 supplement to the *Journal of Political Economy*, and covered investments in education, training, health, and selected aspects of mobility. Since then there has been much additional work in all of these areas, as well as in the R&D area noted earlier. As I stated at a 1963 OECD conference:

> Economic growth is now seen largely to result from investments. This perhaps should be obvious when investment is defined as current outlays designed to enhance future income. But progress has been made in identifying and exploring the various types of investments made by the several economic sectors.[11]

Yet no one undertook to assemble estimates of all types of investment, or of the stocks of all the types of capital, intangible as well as tangible, resulting from the investments. This would have been necessary, of course, for assessing the contribution of total capital to eco-

---

7. Referred to in Kendrick, 1961, pp. 177–188. See also the recent study by Nestor Terleckyj, "Effect of R&D on the Productivity Growth of Industries," Washington, National Planning Association, 1974.

8. See, for example, Theodore W. Schultz, "Human Wealth and Economic Growth," *The Humanist*, 2, 19, 1959, pp. 71–81.

9. *American Economic Review*, March 1961, pp. 1–17.

10. Mark Blaug, ed., *Economics of Education*, Vol. 1, Baltimore, Penguin Books, Inc., 1968.

11. John W. Kendrick, "Comments," in *The Residual Factor and Economic Growth*, Paris, OECD, 1964, p. 109.

nomic growth and ascertaining how much of a final residual was left to be explained by noncapital variables. A number of economists, beginning with Denison,[12] had attempted to partition the economic growth rate among various contributing factors, starting with the tangible factor inputs, but none had approached the task in terms of estimating the contributions of real intangible capital stocks and inputs in addition to the tangible ones.

To fill this gap, I began to develop estimates of total investment and capital in the academic year 1964–1965, aided by a grant from the National Science Foundation, with subsequent support from the National Bureau of Economic Research. Since then I published several papers which represented progress reports, summarizing tentative findings.[13] This volume represents the first publication of the full set of estimates, together with a reasonably comprehensive description of results. Owing to time limitations, the analysis is far from definitive, but I believe that the material presented here will be of use to others who seek to understand more fully the relationship of saving, investment, and the associated increases in capital of all types to the growth processes of real income and product.

Plan

The conceptual and statistical foundations of the study are explained in Chapter 1. Starting with basic definitions of investment and capital and their relevance to growth analysis, we go on to operational definitions of each of the major types of investment included in our totals. Chapter 2 describes the economic accounting framework within which the saving and investment estimates are presented in order to ensure consistency of the investment and associated capital estimates with the flows of income and product. The sources and methodology employed in preparing the total gross and net investment and capital estimates (by sector and type, in current and constant prices) are also briefly summarized.

12. Edward F. Denison, *The Sources of Economic Growth in the United States and the Alternatives before Us*, New York, Committee for Economic Development, 1962.

13. John W. Kendrick, "Restructuring Economic Accounts for Growth Analysis," *Statistisk Tidskrift*, Stockholm, 1966, 4; "The Treatment of Intangible Resources as Capital," *Review of Income and Wealth*, March 1972; and "The Accounting Treatment of Human Capital," *Review of Income and Wealth*, December 1974. The first section of chapter 2 was drawn from the last-mentioned article.

In Chapter 3 we look at the movements of total investment and saving in the national economy—overall, by type of investment, and by sector—from 1929 to 1969, across peak years of the business cycle as well as between peak years and following troughs. First we examine the trends in the ratios of total gross investment (or saving, saving being equal to investment, by definition, at the national level) to (adjusted) GNP and of total net investment to NNP, in current and constant dollars. Changes in the ratios of each major type of investment, and thus in the composition of investment, are also examined.

As to the ratios of sector investment to GNP, since changes here depend on those in the ratios of sector investment to sector disposable income as well as of disposable income to GNP, we examine both aspects. Changes in the composition of total investment in each sector are also presented.

Chapter 4 consists of an analysis of trends and movements in the stocks of capital and in capital coefficients, by type and by sector of use. Cross-tabulations of stocks by type within each domestic sector are also shown. In addition to the average capital coeffecients, we also calculate and discuss changes in incremental capital coefficients between business cycle averages.

In Chapter 5 we present some calculations concerning the contributions of total capital, by major type, to the economic growth of the United States during the 1929–1969 period, and identify the usual residual reflecting the net effect of noncapital variables. In the private domestic business economy, we examine not only capital coefficients but also the ratios of current dollar income to capital stocks, by functional category, in order to appraise trends and movements in average and incremental rates of return. In addition to using estimates of total capital stocks, gross and net, we also consider variant stock estimates adjusted to include only the employed portions of intangible capital.

Chapter 6 offers a summary of the study highlighting its major findings, as well as some suggestions for strengthening the estimates and extending the analysis.

Appendixes A and B contain detailed notes on the sources and methods used in preparing the estimates, together with basic tables containing time series for all or selected years of the period 1929–1969.

Late in 1975, when the manuscript was already in press, I had occasion to update some of the key investment and capital estimates through the year 1973 for publication by a Congressional committee.[14]

14. "Economic Growth and Total Capital Formation," a study prepared for the use of the Subcommittee on Economic Growth of the Joint Economic Committee, Congress of the United States (Washington: U.S. Government Printing Office, February 18, 1976).

These estimates, together with a brief discussion of recent trends, have been incorporated in the volume as Appendix C. This new material is particularly timely since it appears that the movements of total capital formation and stocks over the subperiods 1966–1969 and 1969–1973 have deviated significantly from the earlier trends.

Acknowledgments

Before this study came under the sponsorship of the National Bureau of Economic Research, my work was directly supported by two grants from the National Science Foundation for the period 1964–1968. At the Bureau it was grouped with several other studies in a project entitled "The Measurement of Economic and Social Performance," also supported by the NSF. (The findings and conclusions are, of course, those of the author and are not attributable to the National Science Foundation.) The project was under the supervision of Thomas Juster until mid-1973 and of Richard Ruggles and Robert Lipsey thereafter. I am indebted to them and to NBER's president, John Meyer, for their continuing encouragement.

During this volume's long gestation period I was assisted by quite a few individuals in preparing the basic estimates. The largest contributions were made by Jennifer A. Rowley and Yvonne Lethem, whose assistance is recognized on the title page. Jennifer Rowley was on the project staff full-time from 1965 to 1971. She prepared estimates of education and training outlays and stocks, was in charge of the computer work necessary for summarizing the entire set of estimates, and assisted in some other areas as well. Yvonne Lethem worked part-time on the study from 1966 to its completion in 1974. She was responsible for the mobility cost and stock estimates, and was instrumental in extending the other estimates from 1966 through 1969. Both wrote several sections of the appendixes and helped assemble the tables.

The tangible investment and stock estimates and the imputed rentals on nonbusiness capital were prepared by Anthony F. Japha, Raymond Sheppach, and Ralph R. Young. The research and development outlay and stock estimates were prepared and written up by Leonore Wagner, who also worked on the rearing cost estimates. The medical, health, and safety estimates were prepared by Ki-Hoon Kim, Kunio Hidaka, and Calvin Shelton. Dorothy Klein, Kilman Shin, and Hi-Whoa Moon worked in several areas in the early stages of the project. Eric Howe was helpful in the final stages.

My research assistant at NBER, Elizabeth Simpson Wehle, rendered substantial assistance in preparing the manuscript for review by the reading committees. The NBER editor, Hedy D. Jellinek, readied the manuscript for publication with care and understanding. Irving Forman drew the charts with his customary skill.

The staff reading committee consisted of Michael Boskin, Robert Eisner, and Michael Gort; the directors' reading committee, of Thomas D. Flynn, Robert M. Solow, and Willard L. Thorp. All of them contributed constructive comments.

Thus, like most major research undertakings, this study is the product of many people, to whom I am grateful.

John W. Kendrick

1

Conceptual Foundations of the Study

The foundation of this work is the concept of capital as capacity to produce output and income (including nonmarket income) over a succession of accounting periods. Investment, in turn, comprises outlays that maintain or increase output- and income-producing capacity. It follows from these definitions that the growth of real stocks of capital, broadly and inclusively defined, resulting from real net investment should be a major element in the growth of real income and product. As Johnson well stated at the 1963 OECD conference mentioned in the Preface, "The conception of economic growth as a process of accumulating capital in all the manifold forms that the broad Fisherian concept of capital allows is a potent simplification of the analytical problem of growth, and one which facilitates the discussion of growth policy by emphasizing the relative returns from alternative investments of currently available resources."[1] And since the saving that releases resources for investment depends importantly on income, the growth of capital is reciprocally related to the growth of income.

In his famous AEA presidential address, Schultz went so far as to suggest that the ratio of income to a comprehensive measure of capital stocks has been roughly constant through time.[2] He based this hypothesis on the observation that, while total tangible factor productivity had risen, intangible human capital also appeared to have risen relative to tangible capital stock and input. This suggested that the relative growth of intangible capital might largely explain the growth in the productiv-

1. Harry G. Johnson, "Comments," *The Residual Factor and Economic Growth*, Paris, OECD, 1964, p. 221.
2. Theodore W. Schultz, "Investment in Human Capital," reprinted in E. S. Phelps, *The Goal of Economic Growth*, New York, Norton & Co., 1969, p. 106.

1

ity of tangible factors (measured without allowance for increased efficiency due to education and other human investments), and that total capital growth might largely explain economic growth generally. Schultz's views were quite similar to those expressed in the latter 1950s by Fabricant and the present writer, as noted in the Preface. Although Schultz had measured the stock of educational capital, comprehensive measures of total capital were not available to permit him to test his hypothesis.

Unfortunately, the official national income and product accounts of most nations define and estimate investment exclusively with respect to tangibles—new construction, durable equipment outlays, and inventory accumulations—plus net foreign investment. The U.S. Department of Commerce domestic investment estimates are largely restricted to this day to tangible capital outlays of the private business sector. It is not yet standard practice in any country that we know of to include education and other intangible or human investments in the capital accounts. Yet the concept of human capital has an ancient and honorable lineage. As Kiker has documented: "Economists who considered human beings or their skills as capital include such well-known names in the history of economic thought as Petty, Smith, Say, Senior, List, von Thünen, Roscher, Bagehot, Ernst Engel, Sidgwick, Walras, and Fisher. Basically, two methods have been used to estimate the value of human beings: the cost of production and the capitalized earnings procedures."[3] But Marshall's dictum that capital should include only those classes of wealth that can be bought and sold in the marketplace constricted subsequent work on human capital, just as his emphasis on value theory under static equilibrium conditions tended to divert attention from the dynamics of economic growth analysis. Concern with capital formation was further narrowed by Keynes, who focused largely on tangible business investment, which he cast as the crucial volatile variable in his theory of the determination of national income in a market economy, again under largely static conditions.

Keynes's *General Theory* had the favorable effect of providing an impetus for the development of national income accounts in most countries of the world during the subsequent quarter century. But the structure of the national accounts, including the initial standard system of the United Nations (1953), reflected the Keynesian approach to explaining income determination, and incorporated a correspondingly narrow definition of saving and investment.

3. B. Frazier Kiker, "Human Capital: In Retrospect," University of South Carolina Bureau of Business and Economic Research, *Essays in Economics* 16, June 1968, p. 112.

The revised U.N. standard system of national accounts (1968) does provide capital accounts for each sector accommodating estimates of tangible nonhuman capital formation in each sector alongside those for the economy as a whole. It thus represents a considerable improvement over the more restricted U.S. official national income accounts. But what is needed now is a further restructuring of economic accounts to include human tangible (rearing costs) and human and nonhuman intangible investments in order to yield total investment of the nation, by sector. Further, the associated balance sheets and wealth statements must be developed to show the total tangible and intangible stocks of capital, human and nonhuman, by sector. Only this way can the economic growth theories of Schultz and the others cited above be tested and a more adequate empirical basis for growth policies developed. The present work may be regarded as a pilot study for determining the feasibility and usefulness of such restructuring of economic accounts and of developing estimates of total investment and capital stocks by type and sector.

An indispensable element of this endeavor consists of identifying and defining all of the significant constituents of total investment and capital. It is easy to define capital as output- and income-producing capacity and to theorize that the growth of real capital, so defined, should be the chief element in explaining the growth of real income and product. It is more difficult to define the components of total investment, distinguishing carefully between consumption and capital formation, and to specify the various types of investment in operational terms as a basis for estimation. This task is undertaken in the remainder of this chapter, and the relevant estimating methodology summarized in the following chapter. No attempt is made here to review the literature on the various types of investment and capital, although a number of references to basic works relating to the various areas will be given.

The Scope and Composition of the Investment and Capital Estimates

Delineated below are all the types of investment and associated capital that conform to our general concept, classified by the major categories in terms of which the estimates are presented—tangible (nonhuman and human) and intangible (nonhuman and human). The intangible investments (R&D, education, training, medical, and mobility expenditures) are, of course, generally embodied in the tangible capital, nonhuman or human, so an alternative classification may be couched in terms of the human-nonhuman categories.

It will be noted that we include all investments made by all sectors and the resulting capital stocks financed or used by each in productive processes. This contrasts with the current Commerce Department approach, which counts as investment only the tangible capital outlays of the enterprise sector, including private nonprofit institutions, and new residential construction for owner-occupancy as well as rental (on the fiction that the homeowner is in the "business" of renting to himself). Inclusion of outlays by all sectors that yield a flow of services extending over more than one annual accounting period conforms not only to our comprehensive definition of investment, but also to a basic economic accounting rule that the estimates should be invariant to institutional changes. It is desirable that the investment, capital, and income totals remain unaffected as sources of financing the various investments shift among sectors (as in the case of public versus private education, for example), or as practices change as to ownership by nonbusiness sectors versus leasing from the business sector. Also, as one type of investment is substituted for another the total should be unaffected, which is only true if capital formation embraces all types of forward-looking outlays that may be substituted for each other at the margin.

TANGIBLE INVESTMENT AND STOCKS

Tangible investments, as distinguished from intangible ones, are material; they have body (human or nonhuman) and thus are "touchable." They are the carriers in which intangible investments are "embodied" and contribute to the quality, or productivity, of the tangible factors.

NONHUMAN TANGIBLES. These comprise what is traditionally considered "wealth"—structures, land and other natural resources, machinery and other durable equipment, and inventory stocks. It is this category that has been traditionally classified as investment, if made by the enterprise sector. But these outlays, and the resulting capital stocks, also yield a return when undertaken by the nonbusiness sectors, even though the return is generally nonpecuniary. In the household sector, residential real estate, automobiles, and other durable goods produce utilities either in furnishing direct pleasure or in aiding with household work. The latter is the case also with household inventories, which reduce shopping time. In the case of government, some of the structures, equipment, and inventories are required for the governmental functions of producing services for the community. As in private industry, the cost savings resulting from investments in new capital goods can be calculated. But much of the public capital represents "infrastructure," which provides direct utilities to the public, or facilitates production by the private sector. Some public capital (highway construction, for example) does both. The present value of future benefits to the public can be frequently at least roughly estimated.

Because of the economic value of the nonbusiness capital we impute a rental value to it by techniques described in Appendix B. This makes for consistency with the business sector, since the earnings of business capital are included in national income. Without imputed rental values the accounts would not be invariant to changes in institutional structure and practices. This is recognized by the Commerce Department in its treatment of new residential construction: it is all treated as investment, whether undertaken by real estate firms for rental purposes or by contractors or individuals for owner-occupancy. In the latter case, a rental value is imputed to the residences by the Commerce Department, so that income flows will not be distorted by changes in ownership patterns. But the same logic applies to all durable goods and other capital, as pointed out by Juster and others.[4]

For example, if governmental units lease equipment from private firms, the equipment purchased by those firms shows up as investment, and the rentals are included in income and product. If, on the other hand, the government purchases the equipment, these purchases are not identified as investment, and the rental value is not included in income and product (except for the maintenance and repair costs). Or, if households lease equipment or buy equipment services from private firms (e.g., laundromats), the capital outlays of those firms show up as investment, and the depreciation and net return on the investments are part of income and product. But if households buy the equipment, the purchases do not appear as investment (although they are part of consumer outlays), and the implicit interest and depreciation portions of the rental values are not included in income and product.

Logic and consistency require that purchases of structures and equipment, inventory accumulation, and outlays for natural resource development by governments and households also be termed investment; that the accumulated net investment enter capital stocks (or "tangible wealth") estimates; and that the rental value of capital be included in the income and product flows. This is merely an extension

4. F. Thomas Juster, *Household Capital Formation and Financing, 1897–1962*, New York, NBER, 1966.

of the treatment presently accorded owner-occupied residential structures and may be justified by the argument cited above—that shifts in sector ownership patterns should not affect investment, capital, or the associated income estimates.

HUMAN TANGIBLES. It is not yet conventional in estimating human investment and capital to include either the outlays required to produce the physical human being or those designed to enhance his productivity. For example, Bowman writes: "Training man's mind aside, the costs of forming human capital are primarily those involved in building his physical condition. But many of the outlays that have this effect are also consumption priorities of the first order, and in the minor exceptions any assessment of return on such outlays viewed as investment in producer capital is meaningless unless the men are slaves."[5]

Yet, it seems inconsistent to count the costs of educating a man as investment but not the cost of producing the physical being whose mind and reflexes are being educated and trained. As Fisher wrote: "The 'skill' of a mechanic is not wealth in addition to the man himself; it is the 'skilled mechanic' who should be put in the category of wealth."[6] And it does make sense to estimate rates of return on human capital at its total cost of production, as we do in Chapter 5, as well as on the capital created by education alone, as do Becker and others.[7] Indeed, these economists, who estimate the capital value of human beings by discounting future labor compensation less maintenance costs, are implicitly valuing the entire bundle of human attributes, physical and mental.[8]

Official national income estimates generally do not treat man as a means of production, only as the end. That is, neither rearing costs nor the intangible outlays that increase the productivity of human beings are counted as investments. Accordingly, no deductions from income are made for "maintenance" or "depreciation" of human capital, although this would be consistent with the treatment of nonhuman capital as advocated by Irving Fisher. In our accounts we follow his lead and include "rearing costs" and "intangible human investments" (discussed below) as capital formation, and deduct depreciation on

5. Mary Jean Bowman, *Economics of Higher Education*, HEW Bulletin 5, 1962, Chapter 6.

6. Irving Fisher, *The Nature of Capital and Income*, New York, Macmillan and Co., 1930, p. 9.

7. Gary Becker, *Human Capital*, New York, NBER, 1975.

8. Herman P. Miller and Richard A. Hornseth, "Present Value of Estimated Lifetime Earnings," Technical Paper 16, Bureau of the Census, U.S. Dept. of Commerce, 1967.

human capital from gross income. Further, in estimating net returns on total and human capital, we also deduct estimated maintenance costs from income. By so doing (as we shall see in Chapter 5), we arrive at average rates of return on total human capital that are quite similar to those on nonhuman capital.

Another argument for counting rearing costs as investment is that such expenses compete not only with consumption but also with other forms of investment in expanding capacity. Apparently the cost of rearing children reduces consumption of parents through an "abstinence effect," although the reduction is less than one for one.[9] It also results in a reduction in saving, and thus in the resources that would have been available for other types of investment. Most directly affected would be household investments in durable goods and in the extent of education and health care—although tangible and intangible human investments are also complementary to some degree. But since financial saving is affected, other types of investment, by other sectors, are also affected. Thus, since rearing costs are an alternative use of funds, they should be included with other forms of investment in studies of aggregate investment and its mix, by sector and type. This is particularly important for less developed countries with high birth rates, where rearing costs obviously reduce funds available for other investments, which quite likely promise higher rates of return.

Once the decision is made to estimate rearing costs, several key aspects of the variable must be defined. Should all children be included, or only those destined to enter the labor force? Until what age or stage of life should the living costs be included? Just what family costs should be allocated to the children being reared? On the first score, our decision is to include the rearing costs of all children. Some die before working age, and some never enter into productive activity. But in order to obtain a certain proportion of eventual labor force entrants from a given crop of babies, it is necessary for the parents and society to bear the cost of the entire cohort. Just as the cost of unfruitful mineral exploration or research must be spread over the successful output, so it seems reasonable to include the rearing costs of all children.

The human rearing span may be defined as the period from birth up to working age. Age fourteen has somewhat arbitrarily been chosen as the upper age limit, since the official U.S. labor force estimates included persons fourteen years of age and older at the time the

9. See William F. Ogborn, "The Financial Cost of Rearing a Child," in William L. Chenery, ed., *Standards of Child Welfare*, Sec. 1, Children's Bureau Conference Series No. 1, Washington, D.C., 1919.

estimates were made. Most states now designate sixteen as the upper age limit on compulsory school attendance, but work permits may be issued for youths under the legal working age. In some states school attendance is compulsory through the eighth grade, completion of which normally comes at age fourteen. Also, at age fourteen most children have attained their physical growth and have entered adolescence. As good a case, or possibly a better one, could be made for using age sixteen (now used in U.S. labor force data), or even eighteen, but statistically fourteen is better, since various population statistics are collected and tabulated in terms of age groups that end or begin with that level.

As to coverage, it should first be noted that we are trying to estimate the cost of producing the physical human being. Intangible investments affecting the quality or productivity of labor, such as costs of education and health care, are separately estimated and therefore not included in rearing costs in order to avoid double counting. The intangible investments have to be added to rearing costs to obtain total human investment.

Basically, we include the average variable costs of raising children to working age. This does not mean marginal costs, based on budget studies of families of varying sizes, since the "abstinence effect" of additional children causes marginal costs to fall below actual costs. Rather, consumption patterns based on studies of different age-sex groups have been used, as explained in the technical notes. Certain types of consumption, such as tobacco and spirits, have been excluded altogether, since their consumption is not usual among children under fourteen. Variable costs include increases in "fixed" costs incurred as families grow larger (as in the higher value of larger dwelling units and household furnishings and equipment), but tangible household investments are excluded to avoid double counting.

Finally, while fourteen is the approximate start of working age in this country, the actual commencement of regular work activity or labor force participation is occurring at increasingly higher average ages as the period of education is extended. But beginning with age fourteen we estimate the opportunity cost in terms of foregone earnings of students, as explained below. In terms of total human investment, the age selected to end the rearing period is not very important, since the opportunity costs of youths between fourteen and eighteen is little more than their subsistence cost.

The real gross stock of tangible human capital represents the accumulated rearing costs (in constant prices) at age fourteen for each cohort on a per capita basis, multiplied by the population in each cohort, and summed for all cohorts fourteen years of age and over. This approach automatically takes care of retirement from the national population through death or emigration, and immigration is provided for by imputation of the same rearing costs as those used for the corresponding domestic cohort. Depreciation on tangible human capital is calculated on the same basis as that on fixed nonhuman capital goods to provide for comparability. But the estimates of retirement and depreciation can be better for human than for nonhuman capital because reasonably good actual population estimates are available for the former, while the latter are based largely on assumed lives.

INTANGIBLE INVESTMENT AND CAPITAL

The intangibles embrace the investments made primarily to improve the quality or productivity of the tangible human and nonhuman factors in which they are embodied. Like the tangibles, they must have a lifetime of more than one year—i.e., improve the quality of the tangible factor over two or more annual accounting periods. The accumulated intangible investments over their lifetimes (which may differ from those of the tangible carrier) represent the gross capital stock. Net stock estimates are obtained after depreciation rates consistent with those for the tangibles are applied to each year's gross investment and the resulting accumulated depreciation on each vintage of investment remaining in stock is summed and subtracted from gross stock.

While economists have been increasingly treating the various forms of intangible outlays enhancing tangible factor productivity as investments, estimates of the resulting capital stocks are a unique feature of the present study. The combined real tangible and intangible capital estimates, for each factor separately and in combination, represent the output-producing capacity resulting from the increase in both quantity and quality of the factors. The relative increase in the real intangible stocks provides a means of quantifying quality improvements and indirectly provides a means of measuring technological and organizational advance to the extent that this is associated with capital formation.

NONHUMAN INTANGIBLES. This category refers to the expenditures required to advance productive knowledge and know-how, including that incorporated in new or improved consumer and producers' goods and in productive processes and systems. In recent decades most of such investment has been included in the statistics on research and development (R&D) expenditures. R&D outlays eminently qualify as investment, since the part that results in cost reductions increases productivity and the part that results in new and improved consumer goods increases satisfaction. However, it is often difficult to quantify quality change, and real product and productivity estimates are generally considered to understate growth to the extent that there have been net improvements in the quality of goods and services.

The National Science Foundation, the chief source of R&D estimates in recent years, uses the following definitions for the three major components that can usefully be distinguished.[10] (1) *Basic research* is that "in which the primary aim of the investigator is a fuller knowledge or understanding of the subject, rather than a practical application thereof." (2) *Applied research* is "directed toward practical application of knowledge." (3) *Development* is "systematic use of scientific knowledge directed toward the production of useful materials, devices, systems or methods, including design and development of prototypes and processes."

In some cases it may be difficult for respondents to demarcate the cutoff points between phases, particularly since R&D is not only a flow process but is also characterized by feedbacks from one phase to another. Further, different respondents may classify and report data using somewhat different criteria. Nevertheless, the NSF categories are broadly useful for analytical purposes.

While basic research is not directed toward practical applications, it clearly enlarges the pool of scientific knowledge which is continually drawn upon (and contributed to) by those engaged in practical invention and engineering development. As a whole, it seems fair to count basic research as well as related development activities as investment, with the cost of the "useless" research being borne by that which has an economic payoff—just as unsuccessful mineral exploration is part of the cost of the discoveries.

The real costs of R&D may be regarded as an input, resulting in an output of knowledge, ideas, and know-how, some of which may be incorporated in designs, prototypes, et cetera. The R&D output, in turn, becomes an input in the further investment process, whereby the ideas are translated into practical and commercially feasible products (consumer and producer), processes, methods, and systems which expand income-producing capability.

The sector estimates of R&D are based on the sources rather than the use of funds. Measured R&D includes only the formal activities of the various sectors. Some informal research and development, such as that of the lone inventor of the household sector, is not included. With informal activities becoming less important, the estimates would tend

10. *Reviews of Data on Research and Development,* No. 33, National Science Foundation, April 1962, p. 8.

to have some upward bias as a measure of all R&D activity, but this is probably of minor importance for recent decades. A possibly more important source of bias is a tendency for organizations to include more of their costs as R&D as this group of activities has become more clearly recognized and prestigious.

The pool of productive knowledge and know-how drawn on by producers is the capital resulting from R&D, which we measure at cost revalued to constant and current prices. Basic research results in accumulation of knowledge, which continues to be drawn on through the ages. But the applied research and productive knowledge and know-how developed through engineering has a finite life and is eventually supplanted by new applied research and related development. We take account of the finite lives of new products and technologies in preparing the estimates of the stocks of productive knowledge resulting from R&D, as explained later.

EDUCATION AND TRAINING.   The dissemination of knowledge has long been recognized as an important form of intangible investment. The stock of knowledge and know-how embodied in human beings is an important source of income, both psychic and monetary. Increases in the knowledge of individuals, other things being equal, tend to increase their income-earning capacity. Thus, the costs of knowledge dissemination may be termed investment—they are associated with increased income and yield a return.[11]

Much education is general in nature, producing what Machlup has called "intellectual" and "spiritual" knowledge. Intellectual knowledge refers to the kind of general understanding of the natural world and human society and culture that is imparted by a "liberal" education. Spiritual knowledge concerns man's place in the universe and the basic values of life, as taught by philosophy and religion.[12] General knowledge is an important part of human knowledge, in part because it trains the mind and forms a basis for more practical knowledge, but, more importantly, because the understanding imparted by a liberal

11. See Gary Becker, *Human Capital*, for a discussion of the costs of and return to education; also Mark Blaug, *Economics of Education*, Vol. I, Baltimore, Penguin Books, Inc., 1968.

12. A portion of both religious and secular intellectual knowledge at any given time may not be provable, of course, or even demonstrable. This has always been so; it would be an impossible task to try to distinguish between the portion of education and knowledge that is "true" and that which is "untrue," or even to apply a pragmatic test as to what works and what does not. Presumably the latter is gradually weeded out, though perhaps not as rapidly as new errors take the place of old! See Fritz Machlup, *The Production and Distribution of Knowledge in the United States*, Princeton, Princeton University Press, 1962.

education enhances one's appreciation and possibly enjoyment of life. That the return to general education may be largely a psychic income does not invalidate the designation of the produced knowledge as capital, although it does mean that a portion of education is consumer rather than producer capital or wealth.

Some education and most training result in what Machlup calls "practical knowledge," or know-how. Most of this is designed to prepare people for particular types of productive activity—professional, managerial, production work, and so on. Obviously, practical education and training are expressly designed to enhance income-producing ability.[13] One might also throw in Machlup's additional category of "pastime knowledge," insofar as it increases one's skills in games and other recreational and social activities that yield a psychic income.

There is undoubtedly some pleasure associated with the educational process, as well as the pains that come from stretching the mind. The current net pleasure is generally adjudged to be small compared with the enhancement of future income, however, and most investigators have not attempted to reduce the investment cost by an imputed payment for current services; nor do we.[14]

Learning results not only from formal schooling and other more or less structured forms of education and training, but also from experience, both at work and in leisure-time activities and reflective periods. This type of unstructured, informal learning must elude the estimator. In what follows we shall discuss only the chief structured educational activities and their costs.

The main type of formal education is that carried on in the specialized institutions we broadly term "schools," not only the primary and secondary schools, but also colleges, universities, technical institutes, et cetera. The revenues of the private (nonprofit) schools are generally taken as a measure of the value of their services. In the case of the larger sector of public schools and private, nonprofit educational institutions,

13. As was stated by one of the early modern investigators in the field: " . . . the more advanced and prolonged the education, the more exclusively vocational its purpose, the more probable it is that the guiding principle will be that of ordinary economic gain. If this is true, it would seem clear that the abilities acquired through strictly professional education resemble capital very closely. These are cultivated for gain; and the investment is made in a market where competing savings will tend to force the returns on the cost of training to repay that cost with a profit, equal to that obtainable in other uses. Otherwise, the investment would take some other profitable form." (J. R. Walsh, "Capital Concept Applied to Man," *Quarterly Journal of Economics*, February 1935.)

14. See Theodore W. Schultz, "Investment in Human Capital," *American Economic Review*, March 1961.

the measure is the costs of their services, including imputed rental values of the structures and equipment.

An even larger cost than that of the educational institutions is the foregone earnings of students of working age (here taken as fourteen years and over, for consistency with the rearing cost estimates). This element, which, most economists agree, should be included as part of the educational investment, might also be viewed as an imputed compensation for the schoolwork of students in terms of opportunity costs. The complex assumptions and procedures for estimating foregone earnings are summarized in the next chapter and detailed in Appendix B-4a.

An important part of preparing workers for specific jobs is the training provided by the firm, governmental agency, nonprofit institution, or other organization employing labor. Some of the training or educational programs are formal, such as apprenticeship programs and management courses, requiring part or all of the employee's time for periods of varying length. Here the costs include the direct costs to the firm of providing the instruction, plus the compensation of the worker during the periods when he is not producing.

There is also informal training, sometimes called "breaking in."[15] Costs comprise the pay for the time spent by supervisors and others who assist in breaking in new employees, plus the expenses due to substandard production by new employees learning their new job assignments.

It may be noted that our approach of measuring training investment in terms of cost contrasts with that of Jacob Mincer, who estimates the value of on-the-job training indirectly via the human capital approach, using life-cycle earnings data.[16] The cost approach is, however, required for consistency with our other investment estimates.

In addition to more or less formal education in schools and workplaces, there are a number of structured, but more informal, means of learning. First, there are libraries and museums (other than those associated with schools), which are available to those seeking useful knowledge as well as immediate pleasure. Next, a portion of radio and television programs is educational in character; that portion of the imputed rental value of these household durable goods must be charged to education, as well as the direct cost of such programs. Some part of the contents of newspapers and periodicals impart "intellectual" or "practical" knowledge, to use Machlup's terminology. Teaching aids

15. See Grant W. Canfield, "Plan to Compute Your Labor Turnover Costs," *Personnel Journal*, August 7, 1959.

16. See Jacob Mincer, "On-the-Job Training: Costs, Returns and Some Implications," *Journal of Political Economy*, Supplement, October 1962.

such as phonograph records, moving pictures, and the like used in schools would be included in the direct costs of education, but some aids are bought for home use. Finally, there is frequently some education content in the programs of lectures and discussions sponsored by various organizations at their regular meetings, conventions, or other assemblages. Although precise estimates of these "incidental" types of education are not possible, some allowances are made for their costs.

The real gross capital stock resulting from general education and training can be viewed as the cumulative real costs per capita for each cohort, multiplied by the population in each. This can be revalued from constant to current dollars. In estimating net stocks, allowance can be made for "learning by doing" by not beginning depreciation allowances on the revalued costs of education and training until several years after completion of the education period (see Appendix B-4a). As with other human capital, that portion incorporated in the employed labor force can be segregated for production function analysis.

In the case of narrow, specific job training, our judgment is that these costs should be retired when the worker leaves the job, and depreciated over the average period workers retain given jobs (analogous to our treatment of mobility costs described below).

HEALTH AND SAFETY.   Like education outlays, investments in health produce both monetary and psychic returns over future periods. The returns are associated with reductions in three factors: mortality, disability, and debility. The additions to labor compensation and national income from decreasing mortality as it prolongs working life have been shown to be very great.[17] Likewise, reductions in time lost at work (and at school) due to illness yield a quantifiable increase in income, although available man-day data are fragmentary. Decreased debility as a result of better health, or, conversely, increased levels of vitality undoubtedly increase productivity as well as psychological well-being, although this effect of better health would be most difficult to measure at all adequately. In general, the economic effect of health investment is chiefly on quantity of labor input rather than on quality.

While much of the expenditure on health and safety is genuine investment, it is also true that some medical outlays are useless, if not positively harmful, and that some are largely for current maintenance without longer-term benefit. Although we consulted a number of experts in the field, there was no consensus on the portion that represents investment. In the absence of firm evidence, we have taken half of all outlays for health and safety as representing investment. This ratio

17. See Selma Mushkin, "Health as an Investment," *Journal of Political Economy*, Supplement, October 1962.

makes it easy for those who favor a different proportion to adjust our estimates accordingly.

In counting half of health outlays as investment, we posit that both the prevention and cure of disease and other ailments produce benefits with respect to both productivity and well-being that extend beyond the year in which the outlays were made. One's general health in the future is usually better following expenditures for the avoidance or treatment of disorders than in the absence of such measures. Basic maintenance of human beings is performed by nature; to the extent that man is able to improve health and extend life compared with what the situation would be without medical programs, the costs of such programs are an investment with benefits that extend beyond the current accounting period.

We refer to both health and medical outlays, since environmental (usually public) health programs are an important part of health improvement, along with direct medical treatment. Other environmental factors affect health, particularly the adequacy of food, shelter, and working conditions. In a country as wealthy as the United States has been for some decades, improvement in those factors have probably not been of major health significance, certainly far less so than would be the case in poor countries. We do not count as investment any portion of those expenditures which have only an indirect and uncertain effect on health.

Our approach to the gross capital stocks resulting from investments in health and safety is the same as that regarding rearing costs, education, and general training. That is, we estimate the cumulative real investments per capita for each cohort, and sum for the population. Consistently with the other types of capital, depreciation is estimated by the double-declining balance method. Levels of net stocks would not be comparable if different depreciation curves were used. The stocks can be revalued to current replacement costs and reduced to the portion embodied in the active labor force. In the case of health, it should be noted that the stock relates to the condition of health over and above what it would be without the outlays, valued in terms of the cumulative costs at constant or current prices.

MOBILITY.   Less systematic work has been done in this area of intangible investment than in the others. Therefore, the concepts advanced here are more tentative, and the estimates more exploratory in nature. In a dynamic economy individual incomes, and social income and efficiency, are increased as resources are shifted from industrial and geographical areas of declining relative demand to areas where the demand for inputs is increasing. The costs of transferring resources are a form of investment, for investment in mobility results in an increase in the future income stream beyond what incomes would be if the shifts were not made.[18]

The costs of transferring nonhuman capital—in the form of obsolescence as well as of direct physical transfer costs (transportation and installation)—are already included in tangible capital outlays, but additional calculations have to be made for human mobility costs. These may be viewed as consisting of three components. First, there are the costs of periodic unemployment associated with dynamic changes resulting from shifts in tastes, technology, and resources. Next there are the direct costs of job search and hiring. Finally, there are the costs of migration and immigration, either as part of job search or as a step in taking jobs that are already found.

1. *Unemployment costs.* Apart from cycle-related unemployment, some unemployment is voluntary, chosen in the expectation of finding a better job (in which the monetary or psychic income is higher than in the previous one); but much of it is forced on the worker. The period of unemployment is one of search for new jobs, by definition. Some search for better jobs goes on while workers are employed, but we assume there is no significant opportunity cost of this time. However, we do count the opportunity cost of frictional unemployment as a social cost of the mobility required by a dynamic economy.

Frictional unemployment (including "structural" unemployment but excluding that due to insufficient demand) can be approximated by examining the unemployment rate in years of high-level demand. On this basis we have used 3 per cent (or the actual rate if less, as in the war years) to approximate the rate required for adequate mobility of labor in a dynamic, high-growth economy.

To the extent that imputed unemployment costs are not covered by either government unemployment compensation benefits or severance pay by former employers, they are counted as an imputed cost of the household sector. In addition to unemployment insurance benefits paid by government, the appropriate fraction of operating expenses of the unemployment insurance system are charged to mobility costs. Likewise, separation costs of employers, over and above special severance payments, are included as part of unemployment costs charged to the business sector.

2. *Job-search and hiring costs.* Private household costs of job search comprise payments of fees to private employment agencies and direct "job wanted" advertising and related costs.

---

18. For a theory of migration viewed as human investment, see R. F. Wertheimer, *The Monetary Rewards of Migration within the U.S.*, Washington, The Urban Institute, 1970. See also George Stigler, "Information in the Labor Market," *Journal of Political Economy*, Supplement, October 1962.

The hiring costs of employers, public and private, have been described as follows by the source of our data on average costs per new hire: " . . . A total of all direct and indirect costs specifically chargeable as expenses brought about by the procurement, selection, and placement of the employees. Typical expenses would include advertising, recruiting, testing materials, stationery supplies, wages and salaries of all employees exclusively engaged in employment activity and the appropriate percentage of wages and salaries of employees who spent a portion of their time on employment activities, pre-employment physical examinations, and appropriate allocation for departmental overhead."[19] An additional cost borne by governments is that of the appropriate portion of the expenses of the U.S. Employment Service and of other public programs that seek to facilitate worker mobility. One must be careful not to include any training costs in the hiring costs.

3. *Moving expenses.* In recent years estimates of the number of migrants, interstate and intrastate (between counties of the same state), and of the number of immigrants have become available. With respect to· migrants, one must first determine how many are members of the labor force, employed or unemployed. We would assume that the unemployed bear their own moving costs. A portion of the moving costs of employed persons and their families is borne by the individuals; the rest, by their employers, private or public. The costs cover (a) transportation of persons and (b) moving of furniture and other household effects. Unfortunately, available data permit only crude estimates of these components of moving expenses.

In the case of immigration, the chief relevant cost is that of the Immigration and Naturalization Service. The travel costs of the immigrants are largely borne by themselves, prior to their inclusion in U.S. income as "residents." Once the immigrant becomes a resident his mobility costs are included in those described below.

With regard to the stocks of capital resulting from mobility costs (investments), it is necessary first to derive estimates of the average time elapsing between periods of unemployment, job search, and migration. To derive real gross stock estimates, the real mobility investments of each year are held in stock for the relevant periods of time, then retired. Likewise, depreciation is computed over the relevant time periods. The real stocks can be revalued to current prices by the deflators used to convert current dollar costs into real terms. It is not necessary to estimate the portion of stocks embodied in the active labor force, since the estimates are confined to labor force members in the first place.

19. *The National Underwriter*, August 7, 1959, p. 6.

Notes on the Capital Stock Estimates

Since market values are not available (nor could they be for human capital), stocks of capital are here estimated, as will have been noted, in terms of their real costs, revalued to current prices. This approach is followed in preference to estimating the present value of future income streams through discounting, which involves circularity when the capital estimates are used as a base for estimating rates of return, or productivity, as we do in Chapter 5. Further, it is much more practical to estimate capital stocks based on investment estimates; this approach can be used consistently for the nonbusiness sectors as well as for the business sector, and for human as well as nonhuman capital.

Also, the real investment and stock estimates do not include adjustments for changes in "quality" or output-producing capacity of new capital goods models from that of old models, except to the extent that real costs per unit differ. This approach is preferable for the purpose of estimating changes in factor productivity, as has been argued by Denison.[20] Nor do the constant dollar estimates represent the real factor costs of the capital, reflecting changes in productivity of the capital goods industries. Rather, they represent what it would have cost to produce the capital at base period prices and technology, exclusive of accumulated depreciation reserves in the case of net capital stocks.

We are aware of the objections that have been raised to aggregation in general and to aggregation of stocks of capital assets in particular.[21] Even if it were possible to obtain current market values of all capital goods, these would reflect future income-producing capacity imperfectly due to imperfect foresight, market imperfections, taxes, and so forth. For much the same reason, market values also fail to reflect the relative factor costs of production perfectly in the case of reproducibles (allowing for depreciation in the case of depreciable assets). In constant prices, the real stock estimates through time are subject to the index number problem to the extent that relative changes in prices and quantities are significantly correlated.

But the same objections apply to the national income and product

20. Edward F. Denison, "Theoretical Aspects of Quality Change, Capital Consumption, and Net Capital Formation," in *Problems of Capital Formation*, Studies in Income and Wealth 19, NBER, 1957.

21. See, for example, J. R. Hicks, *Capital and Time*, Oxford University Press, 1973; and, for an earlier summary of the discussion, M. Ishaq Nadiri, "Some Approaches to the Theory and Measurement of Total Factor Productivity: A Survey," *Journal of Economic Literature*, December 1970.

accounts, which are tremendously useful nevertheless for macroeconomic analysis. We believe the same to be true of wealth estimates: although they are imperfect, they are useful as scalars of broad historical trends in aggregates, structure, and relationships with associated flows and other variables. The very reasonableness of the analytical results attests to the value of the estimates. And as far as the index number problem is concerned, to the extent that the movements of real stocks and real product are affected in the same direction (which is likely), the capital-output ratios would be less affected by alternative weight bases than either variable separately.

Our net capital estimates in current prices ("depreciated reproduction costs," for fixed assets) approximate market values, assuming reasonably good foresight by the businessmen who made the investment decisions. The annual depreciation estimates are designed to approximate the decline in value of the capital goods as they age due to deterioration, obsolescence, and the shortening of the remaining useful economic lives. The part of gross investment needed to offset depreciation is required to maintain the net income-producing value of the capital intact. The net capital stocks, representing net income-producing capacity, are appropriate for use in net-of-return computations. They may also be used in constant dollar form for comparison with the associated real net product estimates in productivity calculations.

The net stock and net product estimates are, of course, sensitive to the depreciation formula chosen. Evidence assembled by Terborgh and others[22] on market prices of second-hand durable goods strongly indicates that values decline at a faster rate in the early years of life. Accordingly, we have used double-declining balance rather than straight-line depreciation. Although the evidence on depreciation relates chiefly to nonhuman tangible reproducibles, we have also used the same formula for depreciating human capital. Some evidence on this is cited in Appendix B-2a. Also, for purposes of aggregation it seemed important to us to use the same depreciation formula for all types of depreciable assets since the levels are substantially affected; straight-line depreciation results in higher levels of net asset value than declining-balance formulas. Growth rates of real net capital stocks, however, do not appear to be particularly sensitive to the depreciation formula used, so long as the same formula is applied to the components of aggregates.[23] Growth rates of both net and gross stocks are more

22. George Terborgh, *Realistic Depreciation Policy*, Chicago, Machinery and Allied Products Institute, 1954.

23. See John W. Kendrick, *Postwar Productivity Trends in the United States, 1948–1969*, New York, NBER, 1973, Appendix, Part I, pp. 159–162.

sensitive to length-of-life assumptions for the nonhuman depreciable assets.[24] Fortunately, in the case of human capital, demographic statistics provide quite accurate mortality information.

It has been argued that the depreciated replacement cost of fixed capital understates its true value as a discounted future income stream due to "externalities ... uncertainty, information costs, risk aversion, and imperfect capital markets. . . . This would suggest, even apart from unmeasured capital inputs and (unexplained) 'residual factors,' we would find the value of capital growing through systematic capital gains which make capital at any point of time tend to exceed in value its original cost, adjusted both for depreciation and changes in price levels."[25]

In some firms and industries, however, the present value of capital is less than depreciated replacement cost, and there are capital losses. But even if Eisner is right in his view that, on net balance, present values exceed depreciated replacement cost, it does not necessarily follow that the differential increases over time. And even if it did his point relates to current dollar values, not to the real stocks in terms of which most of our capital-output comparisons are made. Nevertheless, his argument with regard to current values deserves further empirical investigation.[26]

For productivity analysis, it is generally preferable to relate real product to the comparable real capital stock estimates on a gross basis rather than a net basis. The real gross stocks represent output-producing capacity; gross depreciable stocks are maintained intact by the portion of gross investment that offsets retirements, and they grow to the extent that gross investment exceeds retirements. Their output-producing capacity will grow even more, of course, as their quality, or productive efficiency, improves through innovation, which is what the productivity calculations are intended to measure. Maintaining the output-producing capacity of structures and equipment as they age, of course, requires adequate maintenance and repair expenditures.

Some analysts believe that even with adequate maintenance the gross output-producing capacity of depreciable assets declines somewhat with age, and therefore they adjust their real gross stock estimates

24. See Robert C. Wasson, "Some Problems in the Estimation of Service Lives of Fixed Capital Assets," in *Measuring the Nation's Wealth*, Studies in Income and Wealth 29, New York, NBER, 1964, Appendix I, pp. 367–369.

25. Comments by Robert Eisner, member of the NBER staff reading committee, on the initial draft of this study, dated March 4, 1974.

26. An interesting approach comparing stock market valuations with original costs was taken by Vernon L. Smith, "The Measurement of Capital," in *Measuring the Nation's Wealth*, 1964.

accordingly for productivity comparisons.[27] We have not done so, preferring, instead, to consider changes in the average age of real depreciable assets as a possible factor in the explanation of productivity change.

Gross stock estimates in current prices may also be used as a base for estimating gross rates of return (net income plus depreciation allowances). The more interesting calculation, however, would seem to be the net rate of return, obtained by relating net income from depreciable assets, after allowance for depreciation, to the value of those assets as approximated by the depreciated reproduction cost.

27. See the BEA estimates of total factor productivity in the nonfinancial corporate sector of the U.S. economy, which average the real gross and net stock estimates as a basis for estimating capital input. (John A. Gorman, "Nonfinancial Corporations: New Measure of Output and Input," *Survey of Current Business*, 52, March 1972.)

2

The Accounting Framework and the Estimates

The estimates of total capital formation and stocks in the United States, by sector, presented in this study were made within an economic accounting framework. Using a systematic framework of economic accounts ensures consistency with the national income and product and sector income and outlay estimates, and facilitates analyses of investment and stocks in relation to income and product and to the components of the accounts on a similarly consistent basis. Although it does not eliminate errors from the estimates, it reduces the likelihood of errors because of the double-entry nature of accounts.

Our expansion of the concepts of saving, investment, and wealth beyond those underlying the official U.S. national income accounts necessitated our modifying the latter to a considerable extent. These modifications will be described in the first section of this chapter with reference to the set of accounts presented in the tables. The sources and methods underlying the capital formation and stock estimates and price deflators relative to the Appendix B tables are summarized in the second section.

The Accounting Framework

Our economic accounts involve three major modifications of the U.S. Department of Commerce system. First, the broad concept of investment developed in Chapter 1 requires the expansion of the national saving-investment account and its deconsolidation by major sector. That is, since we include nonbusiness tangible capital formation as well as the intangible investments of all sectors, investment is no longer confined largely to the tangible capital formation of the business sector. Accordingly, capital accounts are set up for each sector, and the income-outlay account of each sector is limited to the current outlays, including rental values of capital used by the nonbusiness sectors but excluding the formation of capital, which is shifted to the capital accounts. By including intangible and human investments in the capital accounts we depart from the paradigm of business accounting. Research and development financed by business is typically charged off as a current expense. So are the human investments, as for training and health. In part, this is done because—to the extent these are embodied in workers and accrue to their benefit—they do not "belong" to the firm and are removed whenever the workers decide to change jobs. But from the broader socioeconomic viewpoint, it is clear that all outlays that expand monetary or nonmarket income over several accounting periods should be capitalized.

Second, the scope of the income and product accounts has to be broadened to include not only rental values of nonbusiness capital, but also the imputed portions of capital formation which are charged to current expense or are otherwise not included in the official estimates.

Finally, the capital stock estimates of the Commerce Department, which do not yet cover all sectors and all types of capital, have been expanded for our purposes to include all wealth, tangible and intangible, human and nonhuman, resulting from the total investments of all sectors. In order to implement financial analysis, the capital accounts could also be expanded to include flows of funds, and the wealth statements enlarged into complete balance sheets. We do show a combined national balance sheet below in order to demonstrate its relationship to the wealth estimates. But since our emphasis is on "real" rather than financial analysis, we confine the capital accounts and wealth statements to productive capital outlays and stock. But the financial flows and levels could easily be added to the capital accounts and balance sheets, respectively, for those who wish to do so.

Our system is close to the United Nations revised standard system of national accounts, except that we include, and they exclude, intangible capital formation and stocks. And, with the same exception, it is closer to the Federal Reserve Board's flow-of-funds accounts than it is to the Commerce Department system, although the Federal Reserve Board does not yet include public capital formation in the capital account for the governments sector.[1]

1. For discussions of various systems of economic accounts, see Richard and Nancy Ruggles, *The Design of Economic Accounts*, New York, NBER, 1970; and John W. Kendrick, *Economic Accounts and Their Uses*, New York, McGraw-Hill Book Co., 1972.

The main features of the seven basic sets of accounts are reviewed below, with detailed notes on the derivation of the various entries in the tables provided in Appendix A. Contra-entries to each line in the accounts are indicated in the tables by the table and line numbers in parentheses.

THE PRODUCTION ACCOUNT

Before looking at the sector accounts, it is useful to examine the expanded national income and product account (Table 2-1) in order to get an overview of the adjustments made to the conventional accounts. With respect to GNP, it will be noted that the domestic investment components are much larger than in the official accounts—43.1 per cent against 15.7 per cent in 1929, and 50.6 per cent against 16.2 per cent in 1966. In large part, the greater absolute and relative size of gross investment was due to reclassifications of items from current consumption to investment. In the case of gross tangible nonhuman investment (line 31), the Commerce Department still includes only business and institutional investment, plus new residential construction for owner-occupancy, whereas we also include the tangible investments by the nonbusiness sectors (households and governments) in new structures, durable equipment, additions to inventories, and natural resource development. Gross tangible human investment (line 37), the cost of rearing children to working age, is also a deduction from the Commerce Department's personal consumption expenditure estimates.

Gross intangible investment (line 38) consists of outlays for education and training, health and safety, labor mobility, and research and development (lines 39–42). All of these are human investment except R&D, which is largely directed toward new and improved products and processes. We therefore classify R&D as nonhuman intangible investment, although it also acts to improve the productivity of human investment and capital by adding to knowledge and know-how. To the extent that R&D and certain other investments are charged to current expense by business, our investment estimates require an upward adjustment to the official GNP estimates (see Table 2-la).

Net exports (line 43) are the same as in the official accounts, comprising net foreign investment and unilateral transfer payments.

Both personal and government consumption (lines 29 and 30) begin with the official estimates, less the categories reclassified as investment, plus imputed rental values of the services provided by the tangible nonhuman capital stocks owned by each of the two nonbusiness sectors. The adjusted consumption estimates are below the official

U.S. estimates to the extent that the imputed rentals are less than the tangible capital outlays of each sector, and because of the deduction of the intangible capital outlays. But GNP and gross national income are enlarged by the imputed rental values which are not now included except for owner-occupied residences. As shown in the reconciliation table (2-1a), the aggregate estimates are also larger to the extent of foregone earnings of students and of the frictionally unemployed, which are counted as part of intangible investments in education and in labor mobility, respectively.

As a result of the various additions, our adjusted GNP estimates are 23.5 per cent higher than the official estimates for 1929, and 34.3 per cent higher for 1969. (See Table 2-1a and Chart 2-1.) Note, however, that the adjustments were made purely for the sake of consistency with the expanded investment and capital estimates. In another project we have imputed values for all nonmarket production (indicated by parenthetical stub entries in the sector accounts). Other investigators have made further adjustments in an attempt to provide a still closer approximation to NEW (net economic welfare), as Samuelson has dubbed it in the latest edition of his textbook.[2] That was not our objective in making the adjustments shown in Table 2-1a, although these items make a modest contribution to broader welfare-oriented measures.

Turning to the debit side of the production account, which comprises factor costs (national income) and other charges against product, adjustments were made for the additions to product just noted. Thus, labor compensation is increased by the imputed value of nonmarket services involved in eduation and mobility (line 7), and net rental income includes the net rental value of household tangible wealth (line 10) and of public sector wealth (line 12). We have also imputed the labor value of proprietors' work (line 6) on the basis of the average wage-salary of employees in the various industries, in order to isolate the profit portion of proprietors' net income to be included with corporate profits (line 11). This is necessary in order to estimate returns on human and nonhuman capital separately, as shown in Table 2-1b. Net interest was modified by deducting from the official estimates consumer interest on brokerage loans and the excess of interest paid by the federal government over and above the net rental value of that sector's real wealth. (See Appendix A for a more detailed discussion.)

It should be noted that we have not imputed a rental income for the human capital stock, tangible and intangible, since our view is that the labor compensation estimates already represent the return on total

2. See William Nordhaus and James Tobin, "Is Growth Obsolete?," *Economic Growth*, Fiftieth Anniversary Colloquium V, New York, NBER, 1972.

Table 2-1. *National Income and Product Account* (billions of current dollars)

Line No.		1929	1948	1966
	DEBITS			
1.	Labor compensation	67.42	182.81	547.58
2.	Wage and salary disbursements (IIA-13)	50.44	135.34	394.50
3.	Wage accruals less disbursements (IIB-73)	0.00	0.04	0.00
4.	Employer contributions for social insurance (IVA-19)	0.10	3.04	20.29
5.	Other labor income (IIA-14)	0.56	2.71	20.71
6.	Imputed labor compensation of propietors (IIA-15)	9.11	21.51	38.86
7.	Additional labor compensation imputations (IIA-16)	7.21	20.17	73.22
8.	Net rental income of persons and institutions	6.96	9.80	28.13
9.	From auxiliary business activities (IIIA-10)	3.08	5.36	8.72
10.	From owner-used capital (IIA-22)	3.88	4.44	19.41
11.	Profits of business enterprises (IIIA-11)	16.30	51.95	116.52
12.	Net rental income of government (IVA-20)	0.78	1.95	6.17
13.	Net interest	6.61	6.07	45.79
14.	Personal interest income (IIA-28)	7.22	7.88	43.64
15.	Less: Unproductive interest paid by consumers (IIA-11)	0.95	0.03	0.19
16.	Government interest income (IVA-21)	0.52	1.36	4.15
17.	Less: Unproductive interest paid by government (IVA-11)	0.18	3.14	1.81
	NATIONAL INCOME	98.07	252.58	744.19

18. Less: Human capital consumption (IIA-33)	14.57	34.57	101.15
NET NATIONAL INCOME	83.50	218.01	643.04
19. Capital consumption allowances	35.07	91.30	272.57
20. Personal (IIB-57)	24.33	54.53	169.44
21. Nonhuman	9.77	19.97	68.29
22. Human	14.57	34.57	101.15
23. Business (IIIB-38)	9.02	19.45	71.26
24. Government (IVB-41)	1.72	17.32	31.87
GROSS NATIONAL INCOME	118.57	309.31	915.61
25. Current business transfer payments (IIA-30)	0.59	0.70	2.99
26. Indirect tax and nontax charges (IVA-16)	7.34	20.51	67.60
27. Less: Subsidies less current surplus of government enterprises (IVA-12)	−0.14	0.86	2.62
28. Statistical discrepancy (VI-18)	0.70	−1.99	−1.01
CHARGES AGAINST GROSS NATIONAL PRODUCT	127.34	327.67	982.57

(continued)

27

Table 2-1. *National Income and Product Account (billions of current dollars)* (concluded)

Line No.		1929	1948	1966
	CREDITS			
29.	Personal consumption (IIA-2)	64.84	146.04	381.57
30.	Government consumption (IVA-1)	6.43	35.30	98.48
31.	Gross tangible nonhuman investment (VI-1)	29.47	76.63	244.36
32.	Structures	11.48	27.80	78.27
33.	Private residential	3.95	14.44	25.04
34.	Other	7.53	13.36	53.23
35.	Durable goods	15.46	43.80	144.02
36.	Change in inventories	2.53	5.03	22.07
37.	Gross tangible human investment (VI-2)	9.77	18.28	54.62
38.	Gross intangible investment (VI-3)	15.69	44.98	198.26
39.	Education and training	11.00	30.78	136.60
40.	Health	1.90	5.22	21.47
41.	Mobility	2.53	6.61	17.41
42.	Research and development	0.25	2.37	22.77
43.	Net exports of goods and services	1.15	6.44	5.28
44.	Exports (VA-1)	7.03	16.79	43.36
45.	Less: Imports (VA-2)	5.89	10.35	38.08
	GROSS NATIONAL PRODUCT	127.34	327.67	982.57

NOTE: Detail may not add to totals due to rounding.

28

Table 2-1a. Reconciliation of Adjusted GNP and Commerce Department GNP, 1929, 1948, and 1969 (billions of current dollars)

Line No.		1929	1948	1969
1.	GNP, Commerce concept	103.095	257.562	929.095
	Plus			
	Households and institutions:			
2.	Imputed student compensation (less unemployment adjustment)	5.141	15.660	92.265
3.	Imputed compensation of frictionally unemployed (less subsidies)	2.072	4.506	16.048
4.	Imputed rentals (excl. maintenance and insurance) on HH durables and inventories	10.405	20.499	100.057
5.	Imputed rentals (excl. maintenance) on institutional plant and equipment and land, over OBE depreciation and interest paid	0.337	0.544	5.711
	Business:			
6.	Tangible investment conventionally charged to current account	0.282	0.899	2.340
7.	Intangible investment conventionally charged to current account	2.187	6.953	35.387
	General government:			
8.	Imputed rentals (excl. maintenance) on land, durables, and inventories	3.825	21.048	66.967
9.	Equals: GNP, adjusted	127.344	327.671	1,247.870
10.	Ratio: Adjusted to Commerce GNP	1.235	1.272	1.343

29

Chart 2-1. *Relation of Adjusted to Official GNP Estimates, 1966*

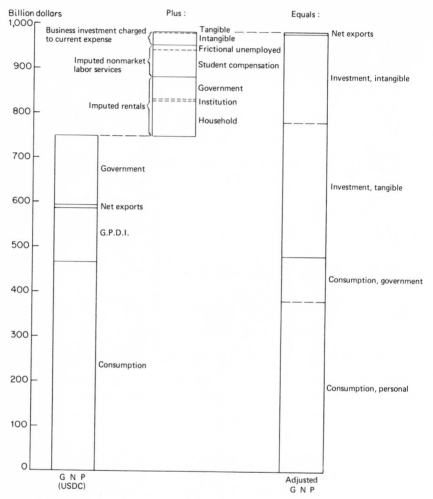

human capital employed. The official national income estimates are asymmetrical, however, in that property income is net of capital consumption allowances, while labor income is gross of human capital consumption. Accordingly, in line 18 we deduct human capital consumption allowances to arrive at "net national income" estimates which are symmetrical in that respect. The allowances represent that portion of gross income which, from a theoretical social accounting viewpoint, must be invested in human capital in order to maintain its productive capacity intact.

Table 2-1b. *Factor Compensation, Gross and Net* (billions of current dollars)

Line No.		1929	1948	1969
	A. U.S. Domestic Economy			
1.	Gross domestic factor compensation	117.764	308.332	1161.365
2.	Capital consumption (nonhuman)	20.503	56.727	223.874
3.	Adjusted domestic income (factor compensation)	97.261	251.605	937.491
4.	Human maintenance	33.974	83.425	216.145
5.	Adjusted gross domestic income less maintenance	63.287	168.180	721.346
6.	Human depreciation	14.566	34.568	126.376
7.	Adjusted net domestic income less maintenance	48.722	133.608	594.952
8.	Employee compensation	51.098	141.131	565.548
9.	Imputed proprietors' labor compensation	9.110	21.509	47.081
10.	Imputed compensation of students and frictionally unemployed	7.213	20.166	108.313
11.	Total gross labor compensation	67.421	182.806	720.942
12.	Total gross labor compensation excluding maintenance	33.447	99.381	504.797
13.	Total net labor compensation	18.881	64.813	378.421
14.	Gross capital compensation	50.344	125.522	440.405
15.	Net capital compensation	29.841	68.795	216.531
	B. Private Domestic Business Economy			
1.	Gross factor income	83.476	213.532	694.338
2.	Human maintenance	29.291	69.275	162.057
3.	Gross income less maintenance	54.185	144.257	532.281
4.	Capital consumption, nonhuman	9.016	19.446	95.557
5.	Human depreciation	12.558	28.705	94.752
6.	Net compensation excluding maintenance	32.611	96.106	341.972
7.	Gross labor compensation	52.251	137.253	469.772
8.	Gross labor compensation excluding maintenance	22.960	67.978	307.715
9.	Net labor compensation excluding maintenance	10.402	39.273	212.963
10.	Gross property compensation	31.225	76.279	224.566
11.	Net property compensation	22.209	56.833	129.009

It could be argued that even our net national income estimates are asymmetrical, since property income is considered net of maintenance expenditures while labor income is not. Most, but not all, economists believe that, since the portion of current consumption representing maintenance affords satisfaction, no deduction should be made if a welfare criterion is observed. We have followed this line in Table 2-1, recognizing a possible inconsistency with our treatment of human capital consumption, although it can be argued that the current utility portion of human investment is negligible in relation to the flow of income, psychic as well as monetary, deriving from human capital creation over future accounting periods. We do estimate maintenance outlays, as shown in Table 2-1b, as a basis for estimating rates of return on human and nonhuman capital in a consistent manner, as discussed in the final section of this volume.

Once deducted, human capital consumption can be neatly combined with nonhuman capital consumption (line 19) and added to net national income to obtain gross national income. Then the usual reconciliation items, chiefly indirect business taxes less subsidies, can be added to arrive at total charges against GNP at market prices.

THE SECTOR ACCOUNTS, CURRENT AND CAPITAL

The basic design of sector accounts is well known. (See Tables 2-2 through 2-5.) On the credit side, "primary" income flows from current production plus transfer payments received (including tax revenues) are entered. To the official U.S. estimates we have added, in the appropriate sector accounts, the rental values of capital goods owned by the household and government sectors, the imputed values of nonmarket time spent by persons on investment-in-self, and the several lesser items discussed earlier. Note that we follow the Commerce Department in crediting total proprietors' profits to the personal sector, since there is no basis for estimating the proportion retained for investment in unincorporated firms. Also, human capital consumption is deducted from personal income to arrive at "net personal income," so that personal saving will be net of human as well as of nonhuman depreciation allowances.

In the business sector account (which the Commerce Department does not explicitly develop), we credit profits (before taxes) after the various valuation adjustments. Our foreign sector account is the same as that of the Commerce Department.

On the debit side of the current accounts, both personal and government consumption estimates are adjusted as described earlier; to these are added transfer payments (including tax and nontax payments in the case of the personal sector) and "unproductive interest" payments. In using the term "government consumption" we follow U.N. usage, and include noninvestment purchases presumably designed to produce services for collective consumption. In the business sector, the debits are for dividends, entrepreneurial withdrawals, and corporate tax liabilities. In all sectors, net saving is the balancing item obtained as the residual after subtracting the various debits just described from the net sector incomes.

In the sector capital accounts, net saving becomes the initial credit item as a source of funds. Since the capital accounts are gross, in order to explain the sources of funds to finance gross investment, capital consumption allowances—tangible and intangible—are credited to the sector accounts from the gross production account.

The final category of credits, intersectoral net capital transfers, requires some explanation. Whereas initial new investment is entered according to the sector that finances it, we wish to show capital accumulation and stocks by the sector that controls and reaps the primary benefit from the capital. Thus, we posit that the personal sector controls all human capital, so the intangible human investments financed by business and governments are transferred to the personal sector. Transfers are not necessary for rearing costs, which are both incurred by and accrue to the benefit of households. We also posit that applied R&D accrues to the benefit of the business sector, so nonbusiness R&D is transferred to business. Net capital transfers from abroad represent the change in net human stock, calculated by age groups and adjusted for accumulated depreciation, resulting from net immigration (immigration less emigration). To simplify the estimation procedure, we assume that immigrants represent the same amounts of capital, in dollars, as persons of the same age groups already in the United States.

In this treatment, we have adopted the approach of the revised SNA, although the capital transfers provided for there are intended to be primarily financial. As a result of the productive capital transfers, sector stock estimates relate to the capital controlled, and it is on this basis that depreciation is estimated.

On the debit side of the domestic sector capital accounts, there are three chief groupings of entries. First comes the productive tangible and intangible investment financed, by type. Next, the capital accumulation from net capital transfers is detailed by type rather than by sector of origin (as on the credit side). The third category, "net financial investment," is the balancing item in the capital accounts as the difference between total credits and the sum of the other debits. If the capital account were elaborated to show financial transactions, it would repre-

Table 2-2. *Personal Sector Accounts* (billions of current dollars)

Line No.		1929	1948	1966
	A. CURRENT ACCOUNT (Cash Basis)			
	DEBITS			
1.	Personal tax and nontax payments (IVA-14)	2.31	20.64	73.41
2.	Personal consumption (I-29)	64.84	146.04	381.57
3.	Imputed rentals for services of capital	18.47	35.30	138.41
4.	Owner-occupied residences	6.41	10.80	46.28
5.	Institutional plant	0.41	0.75	5.50
6.	Consumer durable goods and inventories	11.38	23.54	85.65
7.	Institutional equipment	0.26	0.20	0.99
8.	Less: Imputed rentals allocated to intangible and human investment	2.84	5.43	22.75
	(Consumption provided by business to employees)			
	(Current consumption transfers from business to general public)			
9.	Other consumption expenditures	49.22	116.18	265.91
10.	Personal transfer payments to rest of world (net) (VA-3)	0.34	0.70	0.56
11.	Unproductive interest paid by consumers (I-15)	0.95	0.03	0.19
12.	Net personal savings (IIB-56)	11.12	30.07	111.22
	DISPOSAL OF NET PERSONAL INCOME	79.56	197.48	566.95
	CREDITS			
13.	Wages and salary disbursements (I-2)	50.44	135.34	394.50
14.	Other labor income (I-5)	0.56	2.71	20.71

15.	Imputed labor compensation of proprietors (I-6)		9.11	21.51	38.86
16.	Additional labor compensation imputations (I-7)		7.21	20.17	73.22
17.	Students		5.14	15.66	60.89
18.	Frictionally unemployed		2.07	4.51	12.34
	(Household members)				
	(Volunteers)				
	(Employees for business provided consumption)				
19.	Withdrawals of proprietors' profits (IIIA-2)		5.47	18.54	21.92
20.	Net rental income		6.96	9.80	28.13
21.	From auxiliary business activities (IIIA-1)		3.08	5.36	8.72
22.	From owner-used capital (I-10)		3.88	4.44	19.41
23.	Residences		2.13	0.98	8.33
24.	Institutional plant		0.11	0.27	2.82
25.	Consumer durable goods and inventories		1.61	3.18	8.06
26.	Institutional equipment		0.02	0.02	0.20
27.	Dividends (IIIA-4)		5.80	7.04	20.80
28.	Personal interest income (I-14)		7.22	7.88	43.64
29.	Current transfers to persons		1.50	11.24	44.06
30.	From business (I-25)		0.59	0.70	2.99
	(Cash)				
	(Consumption provided to general public)				
31.	From government (IVA-9)		0.91	10.54	41.08
32.	Less: Personal contributions for social insurance (IVA-18)		0.14	2.18	17.74
	PERSONAL INCOME		94.13	232.05	668.10

(continued)

Table 2-2. *Personal Sector Accounts* (billions of current dollars) (completed)

Line No.		1929	1948	1966
33.	Less: Human capital consumption (I-18)	14.57	34.57	101.15
	NET PERSONAL INCOME	79.56	197.48	566.95
	B. CAPITAL ACCOUNT (Accrual Basis)			
	DEBITS			
34.	Gross personal investment (VI-7)	33.26	81.20	260.38
35.	Tangible nonhuman investment	12.95	34.14	99.41
36.	Land (net purchase)	0.01	−0.17	−1.63
37.	Residential structures	2.21	11.74	18.67
38.	Institutional plant	0.43	0.71	3.82
39.	Consumer durable goods	9.21	22.68	70.75
40.	Institutional equipment	0.27	0.20	0.80
41.	Change in household inventories	0.82	−1.02	7.00
42.	Tangible human investment	9.77	18.28	54.62
43.	Intangible investment	10.54	28.78	106.35
44.	Education and training	6.85	19.37	75.29
45.	Health	1.47	3.82	15.37
46.	Mobility	2.20	5.55	14.83
47.	Research and development	0.02	0.04	0.86
48.	Accumulation through capital transfers (VI-11)	5.85	15.10	75.22
49.	Tangible nonhuman capital	0.00	0.00	0.00
50.	Tangible human capital	0.47	0.51	1.68
51.	Education and training	4.59	12.10	64.84
52.	Health	0.46	1.44	6.38

53.	Mobility	0.33	1.06	2.58
54.	Research and development	-0.00	-0.01	-0.25
55.	Net financial investment (VI-15)	2.19	3.44	20.28
	GROSS ACCUMULATION	41.30	99.74	355.88
	CREDITS			
56.	Net personal saving (IIA-12)	11.12	30.07	111.22
57.	Personal capital consumption allowances (I-20)	24.33	54.53	169.44
58.	Tangible nonhuman capital	9.77	19.97	68.29
59.	Residential structures	1.51	4.10	11.74
60.	Institutional plant	0.17	0.33	1.69
61.	Consumer durable goods	7.87	15.39	54.20
62.	Institutional equipment	0.21	0.15	0.65
63.	Tangible human capital	5.10	9.84	17.42
64.	Intangible capital	9.46	24.73	83.73
65.	Education and training	5.28	15.55	54.67
66.	Health	1.21	3.16	13.26
67.	Mobility	2.98	6.02	15.80
68.	Net capital transfers	5.85	15.10	75.22
69.	Capital transfers from business (IIIB-48)	2.02	5.92	19.94
70.	Capital transfers from government (IVB-46)	2.90	7.94	50.05
71.	Capital transfers from rest of world (VB-8)	0.93	1.25	5.48
72.	Less: Capital transfers to business (IIIB-45)	0.00	0.01	0.25
73.	Wage accruals less disbursements (I-3)	0.00	0.04	0.00
	FINANCE OF GROSS ACCUMULATION	41.30	99.74	355.88

Table 2-3. *Business Sector Accounts* (billions of current dollars)

Line No.		1929	1948	1966
	A. CURRENT ACCOUNT			
	DEBITS			
1.	Withdrawals of net rental income from auxiliary business activities (IIA-21)	3.08	5.36	8.72
2.	Withdrawals of proprietors' profits (IIA-19)	5.47	18.54	21.92
3.	Corporate profits tax liability (IVA-15)	1.37	12.52	34.28
4.	Dividends (IIA-27)	5.80	7.04	20.80
5.	Net business saving (IIIB-37)	3.66	13.86	39.52
6.	Unincorporated business nonwithdrawn profits before adjustment	NA	NA	NA
7.	Corporate undistributed profits before adjustment	2.82	15.63	29.15
8.	Amortization adjustment	0.22	0.78	12.55
9.	Inventory valuation adjustment	0.61	−2.56	−2.17
	DISPOSAL OF NET BUSINESS INCOME	19.38	57.30	125.25
	CREDITS			
10.	Net rental from auxiliary business activities (I-9)	3.08	5.36	8.72
11.	Profits of business enterprises (I-11)	16.30	51.95	116.52
12.	Unincorporated business profits before adjustment	5.47	18.54	21.92
13.	Corporate profits before adjustment	9.99	35.19	84.22

14.	Amortization adjustment	0.22	0.78	12.55
15.	Tangible capital	-1.83	-5.05	-0.67
16.	Intangible capital	2.05	5.84	13.22
17.	Inventory valuation adjustment	0.61	-2.56	-2.17
	NET BUSINESS INCOME (BEFORE INCOME TAX)	19.38	57.30	125.25

B. CAPITAL ACCOUNT

DEBITS

18.	Gross business investment (VI-8)	15.78	41.22	127.03
19.	Tangible investment	13.60	34.27	99.98
20.	Land (net purchase)	0.00	0.00	0.00
21.	Residential structures	1.74	2.70	6.37
22.	Nonresidential structures	4.53	8.11	24.67
23.	Producers' durable equipment	5.61	18.75	54.14
24.	Change in inventories	1.71	4.71	14.80
25.	Intangible investment	2.19	6.95	27.04
26.	Education and training	1.64	4.84	17.50
27.	Health	0.07	0.22	0.58
28.	Mobility	0.31	0.86	1.86
29.	Research and development	0.16	1.03	7.10
30.	Accumulation through capital transfers (VI-12)	-1.95	-4.60	-4.88
31.	Tangible human capital	0.00	0.00	0.00
32.	Education and training	-1.64	-4.84	-17.50
33.	Health	-0.07	-0.22	-0.58

(continued)

Table 2-3. *Business Sector Accounts* (billions of current dollars) (completed)

Line No.		1929	1948	1966
34.	Mobility	-0.31	-0.86	-1.86
35.	Research and development	0.07	1.32	15.07
36.	Net financial investment (VI-16)	-3.11	-7.92	-16.24
	GROSS ACCUMULATION	10.72	28.70	105.91
	CREDITS			
37.	Net business saving (IIIA-5)	3.66	13.86	39.52
38.	Business capital consumption allowances (1-23)	9.02	19.45	71.26
39.	Tangible capital	8.88	18.33	57.44
40.	Residential structures	1.11	1.59	3.89
41.	Nonresidential structures	3.05	5.21	14.76
42.	Producers' durable equipment	4.72	11.53	38.79
43.	Intangible capital, research and development	0.14	1.12	13.82
44.	Net capital transfers	-1.95	-4.60	-4.88
45.	Capital transfers from persons and institutions (IIB-72)	0.00	0.01	0.25
46.	Capital transfers from government (IVB-47)	0.07	1.31	14.81
47.	Capital transfers from rest of world (VB-9)	0.00	0.00	0.00
48.	Less: Capital transfers to persons (IIB-69)	-2.02	-5.92	-19.94
	FINANCE OF GROSS ACCUMULATION	10.72	28.70	105.91

Table 2-4. *Government Sector Accounts* (billions of current dollars)

Line No.		1929	1948	1966
	A. CURRENT ACCOUNT			
	DEBITS			
1.	General government consumption (I-30)	6.43	35.30	98.48
2.	Imputed rentals for services of capital	4.93	26.28	60.73
3.	Public land	0.76	0.73	2.83
4.	Structures	3.42	9.23	31.09
5.	Equipment and inventories	0.75	16.32	26.81
6.	Less: Imputed rentals allocated to intangible investment	0.55	1.71	12.00
7.	Other consumption expenditures	2.05	10.73	49.75
8.	Government transfer payments	0.94	14.37	43.35
9.	To persons (IIA-31)	0.91	10.54	41.08
10.	To rest of world (net) (VA-4)	0.03	3.83	2.28
11.	Unproductive interest paid by government (I-17)	0.18	3.14	1.81
12.	Subsidies less current surplus of government enterprises (I-27)	−0.14	0.86	2.62
13.	Surplus or deficit (−) on current account (IVB-40)	5.15	8.53	77.39
	DISPOSAL OF GOVERNMENT INCOME	12.56	62.20	223.65
	CREDITS			
14.	Personal tax and nontax receipts (IIA-1)	2.31	20.64	73.41
15.	Corporate profits tax accruals (IIIA-3)	1.37	12.52	34.28

(continued)

Table 2-4. *Government Sector Accounts* (billions of current dollars) (completed)

Line No.		1929	1948	1966
16.	Indirect tax and nontax charges (I-26)	7.34	20.51	67.60
17.	Contributions for social insurance	0.24	5.22	38.04
18.	Personal (IIA-32)	0.14	2.18	17.74
19.	Employer (I-4)	0.10	3.04	20.29
20.	Net rental income of government (I-12)	0.78	1.95	6.17
21.	Government interest income (I-16)	0.52	1.36	4.15
	GOVERNMENT INCOME	12.56	62.20	223.65

B. CAPITAL ACCOUNT

DEBITS

Line No.		1929	1948	1966
22.	Gross government investment (VI-9)	5.89	17.47	109.83
23.	Tangible investment	2.92	8.23	44.97
24.	Land (net purchase)	-0.01	0.17	1.63
25.	Structures	2.57	4.55	24.74
26.	Equipment	0.36	2.17	18.33
27.	Change in inventories	0.00	1.34	0.27
28.	Intangible investment	2.96	9.24	64.86
29.	Education and training	2.51	6.56	43.81
30.	Health	0.36	1.18	5.52

31.	Mobility		0.02	0.20	0.71
32.	Research and development		0.07	1.31	14.81
33.	Accumulation through capital transfers (VI-13)		−2.96	−9.24	−64.86
34.	Tangible nonhuman capital		0.00	0.00	0.00
35.	Education and training		−2.51	−6.56	−43.81
36.	Health		−0.36	−1.18	−5.52
37.	Mobility		−0.02	−0.20	−0.71
38.	Research and development		−0.07	−1.31	−14.81
39.	Net financial investment (VI-17)		0.98	8.38	−0.57
	GROSS ACCUMULATION		3.91	16.61	44.40
	CREDITS				
40.	Surplus or deficit (−) on current account (IVA-13)		5.15	8.53	77.39
41.	Government capital consumption allowances (I-24)		1.72	17.32	31.87
42.	Structures		1.20	4.77	13.76
43.	Equipment		0.52	12.55	18.11
44.	Net capital transfers		−2.96	−9.24	−64.86
45.	Capital transfers from rest of world (VB-10)		0.00	0.00	0.00
46.	Less: Capital transfers to persons (IIB-70)		2.90	7.94	50.05
47.	Less: Capital transfers to business (IIIB-46)		0.07	1.31	14.81
	FINANCE OF GROSS ACCUMULATION		3.91	16.61	44.40

Table 2-5. Foreign Sector Accounts (billions of current dollars)

Line No.		1929	1948	1966
	A. CURRENT ACCOUNT			
	DEBITS			
1.	Exports of goods and services (1-44)	7.03	16.79	43.36
	RECEIPTS FROM FOREIGNERS	7.03	16.79	43.36
	CREDITS			
2.	Imports of goods and services (1-45)	5.89	10.35	38.08
3.	Personal transfer payments to rest of world (net) (IIA-10)	0.34	0.70	0.56
4.	U.S. Government transfer payments to rest of world (net) (IVA-10)	0.03	3.83	2.28
5.	Surplus of nation on current foreign account (VB-6)	0.77	1.92	2.45
	CURRENT DISBURSEMENTS AND SURPLUS ON FOREIGN ACCOUNT	7.03	16.79	43.36
	B. CAPITAL ACCOUNT			
	DEBITS			
6.	Surplus of nation on current foreign account (VA-5)	0.77	1.92	2.45
7.	Net capital transfers from rest of world	0.93	1.25	5.48
8.	To persons (IIB-71)	0.93	1.25	5.48
9.	To business (IIIB-47)	0.00	0.00	0.00
10.	To government (IVB-45)	0.00	0.00	0.00
	SOURCE OF ACCUMULATION	1.70	3.17	7.92
	CREDITS			
11.	Accumulation through net capital transfers from rest of world (VI-4)	0.93	1.25	5.48
12.	Net foreign investment (VI-5)	0.77	1.92	2.45
	ACCUMULATION ON FOREIGN ACCOUNT	1.70	3.17	7.92

Table 2-6. *Consolidated Capital Formation Account* (billions of current dollars)

Line No.		1929	1948	1966
	DEBITS			
1.	Gross tangible nonhuman investment (I-31)	29.47	76.63	244.36
2.	Gross tangible human investment (I-37)	9.77	18.28	54.62
3.	Gross intangible investment (I-38)	15.69	44.98	198.26
4.	Accumulation through net capital transfers from rest of world (VB-11)	0.93	1.25	5.48
5.	Net foreign investment (VB-12)	0.77	1.92	2.45
	GROSS ACCUMULATION	56.63	143.05	505.16
	CREDITS			
6.	Gross domestic investment	54.93	139.89	497.24
7.	By persons and institutions (IIB-34)	33.26	81.20	260.38
8.	By business (IIIB-18)	15.78	41.22	127.03
9.	By government (IVB-22)	5.89	17.47	109.83
10.	Accumulation through capital transfers	0.93	1.25	5.48
11.	By persons (IIB-48)	5.85	15.10	75.22
12.	By business (IIIB-30)	-1.95	-4.60	-4.88
13.	By government (IVB-33)	-2.96	-9.24	-64.86
14.	Net financial investment	0.07	3.90	3.46
15.	By persons and institutions (IIIB-55)	2.19	3.44	20.28
16.	By business (IIIB-36)	-3.11	-7.92	-16.24
17.	By government (IVB-39)	0.98	8.38	-0.57
18.	Statistical discrepancy (I-28)	0.70	-1.99	-1.01
	SOURCE OF GROSS ACCUMULATION	56.63	143.05	505.16

45

Table 2-7. *Disposable Receipts and Expenditures, by Sector* (billions of current dollars)

Line No.		1929	1948	1966
1.	Net personal income (IIA-Credits total)	79.56	197.48	566.95
2.	Plus: Personal capital consumption (IIB-57)	24.33	54.53	169.44
3.	Wage accruals over disbursements (IIB-73)	0.00	0.04	0.00
4.	Equals: Gross personal income accruals	103.89	252.05	736.39
5.	Less: Personal tax and nontax payments (IIA-1)	2.31	20.64	73.41
6.	Personal transfer payments to rest of world (net) (IIA-10)	0.34	0.70	0.56
7.	Unproductive interest paid by consumers (IIA-11)	0.95	0.03	0.19
8.	Equals: Disposable personal income*	100.29	230.68	662.23
9.	Disposal: Tangible nonhuman investment (IIB-35)	12.95	34.14	99.41
10.	Tangible human investment (IIB-42)	9.77	18.28	54.62
11.	Intangible investment (IIB-43)	10.54	28.78	106.35
12.	Personal consumption (IIA-2)	64.84	146.04	381.57
13.	Net financial investment (IIB-55)	2.19	3.44	20.28
14.	Net business income before income tax (IIIA-Credits total)	19.38	57.30	125.25
15.	Plus: Business capital consumption (IIIB-38)	9.02	19.45	71.26
16.	Excess wage accruals over disbursements (I-3)	0.00	0.04	0.00
17.	Equals: Gross business income	28.40	76.79	196.51
18.	Less: Withdrawals of auxiliary business income (IIIA-1)	3.08	5.36	8.72
19.	Withdrawals of proprietors' profits (IIIA-2)	5.47	18.54	21.92
20.	Corporate profits tax liability (IIIA-3)	1.37	12.52	34.28
21.	Dividends (IIIA-4)	5.80	7.04	20.80
22.	Wage liability over disbursements (I-3)	0.00	0.04	0.00

23.	Equals: Gross retained earnings accruals[a]	12.68	33.29	110.79
24.	Disposal: Tangible investment (IIIB-19)	13.60	34.27	99.98
25.	Intangible investment (IIIB-25)	2.19	6.95	27.04
26.	Net financial investment (IIIB-36)	-3.11	-7.92	-16.24
27.	Government income (IVA-Credits total)	12.56	62.20	223.65
28.	Plus: Government capital consumption (IVB-41)	1.72	17.32	31.87
29.	Equals: Gross government receipts or accruals	14.28	79.52	255.52
30.	Less: Government transfer payments (IVA-8)	0.94	14.37	43.35
31.	Unproductive interest paid by government (IVA-11)	0.18	3.14	1.81
32.	Subsidies less current surplus of government enterprises (IVA-12)	-0.14	0.86	2.62
33.	Equals: Disposable government income[a]	13.30	61.15	207.74
34.	Disposal: Tangible interest (IVA-23)	2.92	8.23	44.97
35.	Intangible investment (IVB-28)	2.96	9.24	64.86
36.	General government consumption(IVA-1)	6.43	35.30	98.48
37.	Net financial investment (IVB-39)	0.98	8.38	-0.57
38.	Net foreign transfers (VA-3 + 4)	0.38	4.53	2.83
39.	Less: Net exports (I-43)	1.15	6.44	5.28
40.	Equals: Net foreign claims	-0.77	-1.91	-2.45
41.	Total current income (lines 8 + 23 + 33 + 38)	126.65	329.65	983.59
42.	Plus: Statistical discrepancy (I-28)	0.70	-1.99	-1.01
43.	Equals: Adjusted GNP	127.34	327.67	982.57

[a]Gross of capital consumption and capital transfers, but net of current transfers to other sectors.

sent the difference between net acquisition of assets (lending) and net incurrence of liabilities (borrowing), each of which could be detailed by type of financial instrument. But our interest here is not in the flow of funds.

In the foreign sector capital account (Table 2-5), note that we add the net capital transfers from the rest of the world (line 7), by recipient sector, to the surplus of the nation on current account (line 6).

The consolidated capital formation account (Table 2-6) contains the contra-entries to the various investments and capital transfers of the sectors, and summarizes national investment, by sector and major type. Note that the capital transfers among the domestic sectors plus net capital transfers from abroad sum to zero. So do net financial investment of the domestic sectors plus net foreign investment, after allowance for the statistical discrepancy. Or, to state it alternatively, the sum of net financial investment for the domestic sectors (line 14) equals net foreign investment (line 5) less the statistical discrepancy (line 18).

Another useful summary is provided in Table 2-7, showing disposable income and its disposition, by sector. The disposable income for each sector is derived as its gross income less transfers to other sectors, and it sums to GNP less statistical discrepancy. Disposable income is allocated by each sector to consumption, productive tangible and intangible investments, and net financial investment. Although saving equals investment for the nation, they are unequal for each sector to the extent of net financial investment. The sector disposable income series, and the channels of disposition, are necessary for an analysis of consumption, saving, and investment functions.

BALANCE SHEETS AND WEALTH STATEMENTS

The combined national balance sheets show the condition of the economy at the end of a period as a result of saving and borrowing, investing and lending, and (if stated in current prices) revaluations of assets since the beginning of the period. In the balance sheet, productive wealth, hitherto confined to tangibles, is added to the financial assets to obtain total assets, which are conventionally shown on the left-hand side. On the opposite side are liabilities (including stock and other equity if these are also carried on the asset side, as is usual in national and sector balance sheets).

Table 2-8 below presents a combined national balance sheet for the United States for the end of the year 1968. The financial assets and liabilities are taken from Goldsmith, who based them largely on Fed-

Table 2-8. *Combined Balance Sheet of the United States, 1968, Including Human Capital (billions of current dollars)*

Financial assets	4,349		Liabilities—total	2,791
Monetary reserves	22		Monetary reserves	5
Currency and demand deposits	209		Currency and demand deposits	211
Short-term claims	1,136		Short-term debt	1,061
Long-term claims	1,343		Long-term debt	1,337
Corporate shares	1,107		Other	177
Equity in unincorporated business	392			
Miscellaneous assets	140			
			Equity—Noncorporate business	1,489
Productive assets—total	6,296		and corporate shares	
Nonhuman capital	2,952			
Tangible	2,783		Net worth	6,365
Land	623			
Structures	1,250			
Equipment	570			
Inventories	340			
Intangible	169			
Human capital	3,344			
Tangible	1,063			
Intangible	2,281			
TOTAL ASSETS	10,645		TOTAL LIABILITIES AND NET WORTH	10,645
Addendum: Net foreign assets	69			

49

Table 2-9.   *Net National Wealth of the United States, by Sector and Type, 1929* (billions of current dollars)

	Nation	Persons	Business	Governments
Nonhuman	392.0	122.0	222.2	47.9
Tangible	390.3	121.7	221.2	47.4
Land	111.5	14.3	80.1	17.1
Structures	157.2	52.4	77.6	27.3
Equipment	60.0	33.5	23.6	3.0
(Military)	(4.3)			(4.3)
Inventories	61.5	21.5	39.8	0.1
Intangible	1.7	0.3	0.9	0.5
Human	390.7	327.3	15.6	47.8
Tangible	204.0	204.0	—	—
Intangible	186.7	123.3	15.6	47.8
Education	164.1	105.2	14.7	44.2
Health	18.1	14.2	0.4	3.5
Mobility	4.6	3.9	0.5	0.1
Total—domestic	782.8	449.3	237.7	95.7
Net foreign assets	16.5			
Total—national	799.2			

eral Reserve Board estimates.[3] The productive assets estimates (net of depreciation reserves), human as well as nonhuman, are those presented in this study. The estimates are intended to represent market price or proxies, notably depreciated replacement cost in the case of the depreciable assets. The latter concept is not only far easier to implement statistically than the economic concept of present value, but also makes possible the calculation of historical rates of return without the circularity inherent in relating compensation to a discounted future income stream, actual or expected.

The nonhuman reproducibles were obtained by use of the perpetual inventory method, generally with a double-declining balance method of depreciation. Estimates for the private business economy are largely extensions of earlier Goldsmith estimates. The human capital estimates were prepared in large part by cumulating human investments over the lifetimes of successive cohorts of individuals and summing each year for all cohorts.

It can be seen from the balance sheet that net worth is equal to the

3. Raymond W. Goldsmith, ed., *Institutional Investors and Corporate Stock: A Background Study*, Studies in Capital Formation and Financing 13, New York, NBER, 1973.

Table 2-10. *Net National Wealth of the United States, by Sector and Type, 1948* (billions of current dollars)

	Nation	Persons	Business	Governments
Nonhuman	892.5	298.7	378.1	215.8
Tangible	879.2	297.7	372.8	208.8
Land	197.9	44.7	123.6	29.6
Structures	365.2	134.7	110.8	119.7
Equipment	175.6	65.5	53.6	56.5
(Military)	(65.6)			(65.6)
Inventories	140.6	52.7	84.9	3.0
Intangible	13.3	1.0	5.3	7.0
Human	908.8	715.9	37.3	155.6
Tangible	396.9	396.9	—	—
Intangible	511.9	319.0	37.3	155.6
Education	457.8	278.1	35.2	144.5
Health	43.5	32.0	1.0	10.5
Mobility	10.6	8.9	1.2	0.5
Total—domestic	1,801.4	1,014.6	415.4	371.4
Net foreign assets	37.6			
Total—national	1,838.9			

Table 2-11. *Net National Wealth of the United States, by Sector and Type, 1969* (billions of current dollars)

	Nation	Persons	Business	Governments
Nonhuman	3,220.5	1,103.0	1,306.5	811.1
Tangible	3,035.6	1,091.5	1,252.1	692.0
Land	686.8	174.3	393.7	118.8
Structúres	1,376.1	515.9	423.0	436.3
Equipment	617.4	284.0	230.7	102.7
(Military)	(146.8)			(146.8)
Inventories	355.3	117.3	203.8	34.2
Intangible	184.9	11.5	54.4	119.1
Human	3,699.9	2,695.9	169.5	834.5
Tangible	1,146.9	1,146.9	—	—
Intangible	2,553.0	1,549.0	169.5	834.5
Education	2,267.3	1,334.1	162.4	770.9
Health	241.7	175.0	5.0	61.7
Mobility	43.9	40.0	2.0	1.9
Total—domestic	6,920.4	3,798.9	1,476.0	1,645.6
Net foreign assets	69.2			
Total—national	6,989.6			

value of the productive assets plus net foreign claims. This is, in effect, the result of *consolidating* sector balance sheets, with domestic assets and liabilities canceling out. Since our interest here is in *wealth*, the Appendix B tables show domestic productive wealth, by sector and type, with net foreign claims added for those who prefer to work with the national wealth aggregate. Changes in the statements of wealth are directly related to net investments in our capital accounts, plus revaluations.

Tables 2-9 through 2-11 show that inclusion of human capital more than doubles the national wealth of the United States as conventionally measured. The proportion of human to total wealth did not increase significantly between 1929 and 1969, however. In fact, nonhuman capital increased significantly in relation to tangible human wealth. But the intangible human wealth increased much faster. In Chapter 5 we suggest that the growth of intangible capital generally in relation to tangible factors is a primary explanation of the increase in total tangible factor productivity.

Summary of Methodology and Sources

The behavior of time series and their interpretation depend not only on the underlying concepts, but also on the methodology used in their estimation and the reliability of the basic data sources. This summary of sources and methods is provided for the general reader who is not interested in perusing the detailed description contained in the appendixes (particularly since much of it is on microfiche) but wants to grasp the general approach. The data sources are referred to here only in general terms; for specific references the appendixes must be consulted.

Our summary starts with the current dollar gross investment series, tangible and intangible. Next we look at the price indexes used for (1) deflating the various categories of investment to obtain the real investment estimates on the basis of which the associated real stocks are estimated, and (2) reflating real reproducible stocks to current prices. Finally, the methodology for estimating the real stocks, by category, is set forth.

CAPITAL FORMATION

TANGIBLE NONHUMAN INVESTMENT. This category covers expenditures for new construction, equipment, and inventory accumulation. In the U.S. national income accounts, only gross private domestic investment by businesses and institutions is identified as such. We include the comparable outlays for households and governments.

Personal sector residential construction consists of BEA's farm residential construction and our estimates of that portion of expenditures on nonfarm residential construction destined for owner-occupancy. Institutional plant and equipment outlays as well as expenditures on consumer durable goods come from BEA. Inventory stocks and the net change are estimated roughly on the basis of methods developed by Lenore Epstein.

Business sector figures on residential and nonresidential construction, outlays on producers' durable equipment, and the change in business inventories are based on BEA, but outlays pertaining to other sectors are deducted. The old BEA estimates of producers' durable equipment conventionally charged to current expense are resurrected and extended.

For *government sector* outlays on new construction, BEA estimates are used for federal, state, and local governments, including military as well as civilian construction. Estimates of government outlays on civilian and military equipment and inventories are based primarily on the work of Raymond Goldsmith.

Since we assume the national land stock constant over time, overall investment is zero. This assumption is somewhat arbitrary, but changes do take place in farmland, mineral land, and siteland, and a residual category of vacant and nonclassified land was introduced to offset these changes. Estimates of intersectoral land transfers are based on information from BEA. Net foreign investment estimates are taken directly from BEA.

TANGIBLE HUMAN INVESTMENT. This category embraces the portion of personal consumption expenditures allocated to rearing children to working age, that is, age fourteen, corresponding to the official U.S. labor force definition at the time the estimates were made (subsequently changed to age sixteen). All rearing costs are considered financed by the personal sector.

Estimates of average annual costs per child are by age groupings, based on surveys of family consumption patterns. Basically, BEA personal consumption expenditures by category are used, but some items are left out, either because they are not attributable to rearing children or because they are included elsewhere, such as expenditures on education. Population is divided into age groups, and the corresponding proportions of personal consumption expenditures are assigned to each group.

For the estimates of personal consumption expenditures prior to

1929 we relied upon Dewhurst, Kuznets, and Gallman. Rearing costs for the period 1830 to 1929 were estimated on the assumption that the 1929 ratios of per capita rearing costs for each age group to per capita consumption expenditures were true for the 1830–1928 period.

The opportunity costs of parents' time devoted to rearing were not included, since in this study we have not undertaken imputations for unpaid work, with the exception of schoolwork.

INTANGIBLE NONHUMAN INVESTMENT (R&D). Research and development outlays result in the production of new knowledge and its commercial application in the development of new or improved consumer and producers' goods and methods of production. While basic research, about 10 per cent of total R&D, is not directed toward practical application, it progressively enlarges the pool of scientific knowledge continually drawn upon (and contributed to) by those engaged in applied research, invention, and engineering development. It seems fair to count basic research as well as development activities as investment, with the cost of the "useless" research being borne by that which eventually has an economic payoff.

Measured R&D includes only the formal activities of the various sectors; some informal activity, such as that of the "lone wolf" inventor, is not included. As informal inventive activity has become relatively less important with the spread of the industrial laboratory, the estimates tend to have some upward bias as a measure of total R&D. This is accentuated by a tendency for more complete reporting of such costs with R&D gaining in prestige. In real terms, however, this possible upward bias is offset by the upward bias of the price deflators, which are based on input prices due to the difficulty of defining and measuring R&D outputs.

National Science Foundation estimates of R&D outlays are used for the period from 1953 onward, broken down into basic research and applied research and development. (It was not possible to subdivide the latter category.) The National Science Foundation estimates are available by sector of finance according to the sectoring used in this study, except that the relatively scanty funds provided by state and local governments are merged by NSF with those of private nonprofit institutions and had to be disentangled from fragmentary data. The R&D estimates were also distributed by broad product fields as a basis for developing the stock estimates.

The NSF estimates were carried back from 1953 to 1921 in a Conference Board study for selected years by Nestor Terleckyj.

INTANGIBLE HUMAN INVESTMENT. The *education and training* series cover expenditures on formal, informal, and special education, as well as costs of employee training.

Formal education costs for the personal sector consist of BEA's personal consumption expenditures on private education and research, plus our estimates of the net rental for this sector's educational plant and equipment. Students' expenditures on supplies and rentals of books and equipment are estimated as a percentage of imputed student compensation (opportunity costs). The latter forms an important part of educational costs in the personal sector, and is estimated by level of education, adjusted downward for unemployment (BLS rates). Government sector-financed formal education expenditures are basically BEA figures on federal, state, and local purchases for education and for veterans' education and training. Gross public educational structure and equipment rentals are added, with public educational capital derived from public construction figures and educational capital outlays estimated by HEW.

Informal educational outlays by the government sector are estimated from BEA data as the total purchases for state and local libraries and recreation, the Library of Congress, and the Smithsonian Institution. Personal sector informal education consists of parts of consumer costs for radio, TV, records, books, periodicals, libraries, museums, et cetera. For most of these items the proportions ascribed to informal education are derived from estimates developed by Fritz Machlup. For book rentals similar assumptions are made, while for libraries and museums net rentals as well as direct costs are based on BEA figures. Business and institutional expenditures on public education are estimated as percentages of media advertising expenditures, based on Machlup's proportional allocations to intellectual and practical topics of media time and space.

Special (religious) education expenditures are derived from BEA totals in the religious activity expenditures personal sector. The allocation to religious education uses a ratio based on numbers of students in Sunday schools times expenditures per pupil, with a portion of imputed interest on plant and equipment of religious organizations added. Military education and training is estimated from government expenditure series.

Employee training is estimated separately for each sector. Several cost components are included. The cost of initial nonproductive time is estimated by converting nonproductive hours of employees and supervisors to standard hours. The occupational standard hours are weighted by occupational distributions of employment, and training time is derived as a proportion of annual hours worked, applied to annual compensation of new hires. Training hours are based on *Personnel Journal* data, and occupational distributions of workers and average annual hours worked, on BLS data. Government new hire rates are from the U.S. Civil Service Commission, private sector rates, from BLS, and employee compensation, from BEA. Besides initial training time lost there is additional time lost, estimated as a percentage of the former. Nonwage production costs are also taken into account. Formal training costs for the business sector are the numbers of trainees by type of training, based on a U.S. Department of Labor survey, times cost per employee, based on a sample survey. The direct costs of formal training of federal government employees are estimated from Civil Service Commission data, and state and local costs, as a percentage of federal costs.

One-half of the expenditures on *medical, health,* and *safety* objectives is considered as investment, the other half as maintenance that does not increase future productive capacity. The personal sector's expenditures on health and medical care are based mainly on BEA estimates of this category of personal consumption expenditures, with imputed rental values of ophthalmic products and orthopedic appliances added. An imputed net interest on nonprofit hospital structures and equipment is derived by applying interest rates to stock estimates. Business sector outlays for in-plant medical care are derived from HEW estimates, and safety costs are based on Brookings Institution estimates of expenditures for safety programs. Government sector expenditures on health, sanitation, and medical care consist of the BEA estimates of total federal, state, and local outlays on goods and services for health and hospitals, sanitation, and veterans' hospital and medical care. Hospital construction and equipment outlays are deducted, but gross rentals on public hospital structures and equipment are added. The latter consist of depreciation and net interest (a percentage of total net interest on structures).

Mobility costs include job search and hiring, frictional unemployment, and migration costs. Job search costs are incurred by persons and are included in BEA's personal consumption expenditures (we used part of the group of expenditures which includes employment agency fees). The business sector also has costs linked to job changes. A cost estimate per new hire was multiplied by the number of new hires derived from BLS data. Hiring costs are estimated along the same lines for the government sector, using government new hire rates. To this sector's outlays for mobility are added the administrative costs of the U.S. Employment Service, based on Department of Labor and U.S. Government Budget data. These costs are allocated half to hiring and half to unemployment costs. Of the assumed employment costs, however, only part is retained in the frictional unemployment group, since frictional unemployment is assumed to be 3 per cent of the labor force. For the personal sector, frictional unemployment costs are the product of the number of frictionally unemployed and average annual wages and salaries. Although the opportunity cost of the unemployed may be less than the average pay of those employed, no adjustment is attempted. In recent years a deduction has been made for severance pay. The latter is included in business sector frictional unemployment costs along with separation costs incurred by firms because of layoffs.

Another important component of mobility costs is the outlay linked to work-oriented travel and moving of household items. We worked with a cost-per-mile estimate for each of these categories, applied to an estimated average mileage of work-oriented travel and moving for interstate and intrastate migration. Numbers of migrants are based on Census Bureau data, adjusted for work-oriented migration. For moving costs, numbers of families moving are derived. One-half of the estimated moving and travel costs is charged to the personal sector, the other half, to the business and government sectors in proportion to the number of persons employed by each. Besides internal migration, an estimate is made of the federal government's investment in international migration, i.e., the administrative costs of the Immigration and Naturalization Service.

PRICE DEFLATORS

NONHUMAN TANGIBLES.   For most categories of personal sector investment we use BEA deflators, supplemented by detailed consumer price indexes for selected components. For the business sector, all deflators are from BEA, and for the government sector, from BEA plus several other sources. Land deflators are based on prices of various land categories as compiled by Manvel and Goldsmith for the nonfarm sector, and the U.S. Department of Agriculture for farm lands.

HUMAN TANGIBLES.   Rearing cost estimates were made directly in constant dollars: most of the categories were either available in constant dollars from BEA. or deflators could be constructed from the underlying BLS consumer price indexes. However, to reflate constant dollar stock figures an implicit deflator for total rearing costs was calculated.

HUMAN INTANGIBLES.   Personal sector formal education costs in constant dollars are estimated directly, by the same method as that used for the current dollar estimates. Associated costs are deflated by a composite index including transportation and supply costs. For constant dollar foregone earnings of students, average compensation is held at the 1958 level. Organized education and training outlays for the government sector are deflated by BEA's implicit price deflator for state and local purchases of goods and services. The same deflator is used for

this sector's *informal* education expenditures. Direct outlays on libraries and museums are deflated by a BEA deflator for religious and
welfare outlays. The deflator for institutional and business public education costs is based on the cost of the various media per person
reached. *Religious* education expenditures are deflated by the BEA
deflator for religious and welfare activity. *Military* education costs are
deflated by the BEA deflator for federal government purchases of goods
and services.

Finally, for *training* costs all compensation is converted into 1958
dollars by an index of average compensation adjusted for quality
change. Nonwage training costs are deflated, for the personal and
business sectors, by BEA's private fixed nonresidential investment
price deflator, and for the government sector, by the price deflator for
government purchases of goods and services. The latter is also used to
deflate the government sector's formal training costs. For business
sector training costs we used a composite index including the compensation deflator and the nonresidential private fixed investment deflator.

Turning to *medical care* costs, deflators for both personal and
business sectors come from the American Medical Association. Government sector expenditures on health, sanitation, and medical care are
deflated by BEA's price index for government purchases of goods and
services. Hospital depreciation and net interest in real terms are
derived by applying base period ratios to constant dollar stock estimates.

In the area of *mobility* costs, job search costs in the personal sector
are estimated via the implicit BEA price deflator corresponding to the
personal consumption expenditures category used to get the costs. For
business sector hiring costs a composite index is applied based on
BEA's average industry labor compensation adjusted for quality
changes. The same index is used for frictional unemployment costs
other than governmental. For government sector hiring costs, frictional
unemployment costs and immigration costs are deflated by the price
index of government purchases of goods and services. For moving costs
the BLS transportation services price index is used, and for travel costs
a composite price index for costs of owner-operated and other transportation charges is developed.

CAPITAL STOCKS

TANGIBLE NONHUMAN STOCKS.   The estimates of tangible nonhuman capital were prepared via the perpetual inventory method. Both
current and constant dollar stock figures for the business sector are

those published by the BEA, adjusted to our sector definitions. Of the variants estimated by BEA for private structures and equipment, we chose those based on Treasury Bulletin F service lives less 15 per cent, and the Winfrey S-3 retirement curve. This curve is based on studies of the age distribution of retirements for various types of producers' durable goods in the 1930s. It seemed more accurate to apply a mortality curve than to assume retirement of assets at the end of their average life. The Bulletin F minus 15 per cent lives were adopted because structures and equipment since World War II have had a somewhat shorter life than before. Real nonfarm structures were adjusted for the well-known upward bias of construction cost deflators by using BEA's "constant cost 2" variant, which results in a higher growth of fixed capital.

Net stocks in all sectors are calculated by using double-declining balance depreciation, which is believed to give a more accurate representation of the decline in values of fixed assets as they age than the straight-line method.[4] A switch was made to straight-line depreciation in all stock calculations when it exceeded that obtained by the declining balance method.

The depreciable stock estimates for the personal and government sectors were calculated from investment estimates. Gross investments were retired at the end of their average lives and depreciated within these periods, by type. The price indexes used for deflating gross investment were generally adopted also for reflating real stocks.

Farm and nonfarm gross stocks of residential structures were accumulated in constant dollars, using 70-year average lives and 25-year flat-top retirement patterns centered on average life. Net stocks for this category, as well as for institutional plant and equipment and consumer durable goods, were derived by using double-declining balance depreciation. For household inventories we relied on methodology developed by Epstein.

Government sector real capital stocks, federal as well as state and local, are based on Goldsmith's estimates.

The value of total U.S. land in constant dollars has been kept unchanged apart from additions to territory. For most land categories we relied on Goldsmith. Siteland for all sectors is estimated as a constant proportion of the corresponding real stocks of structures.

Net foreign assets for recent years are from BEA, but are carried backward following estimates by Goldsmith. Monetary metals are included with net foreign assets. The gold component is compiled from

---

4. See, for example, George Terborgh, *Realistic Depreciation Policy*, Chicago, Machinery and Allied Products Institute, 1954.

Federal Reserve Board figures, the silver component, from Treasury data.

TANGIBLE HUMAN STOCKS. To estimate the stock of tangible human capital we cumulated the average constant dollar rearing costs per child up to age fourteen and multiplied the cumulative cost by the number of persons in each cohort up to age ninety-five plus. Retirements are thus automatically accounted for. Summing the total real costs for all cohorts each year yielded the annual real gross tangible human capital estimates.

Depreciation is calculated by the declining-balance formula, for the sake of consistency of the net investment and stock estimates with the nonhuman categories. Real gross and net human stocks can be revalued to current prices by the implicit deflator for rearing costs. Stock calculations required getting investment estimates as far back as the 1830s.

INTANGIBLE NONHUMAN STOCKS. Capital stock calculations for basic research are kept fairly simple: annual constant dollar expenditures are cumulated without regard to length of time needed for completion (since each step taken adds to new knowledge) and without regard to obsolescence or retirement (in view of the cumulative nature of the advance of knowledge). To the extent that these assumptions are exaggerations the portion of applied research that might be treated as basic research is considered as a tradeoff.

Stocks of applied research and development are estimated by the perpetual inventory method. To this end, R&D is divided into process and product innovations. The latter, in turn, are disaggregated into nondurable and durable, producers' and consumer, defense and nondefense goods.

Since information on process-product innovation breakdowns, time lags between R&D and commercial application, and lifespan of innovations was unavailable to us, a small survey was made of companies conducting research. Some of these were engaged in business-oriented research and others in government contract work, so that the results could be applied to all R&D expenditures.

As to product versus process innovations, the results of our survey were averaged by major product field and weighted by R&D product field expenditures. Durable goods had a high product-process innovation ratio; for nondurable goods the ratio was lower. For government sector defense goods the business durable goods ratios were used; other government R&D expenditures, as well as personal sector R&D, were allocated half to process and half to product innovations.

The next problem was that of retiring R&D from stock. It was subdivided into projects in process and completed projects, the latter being retired. Here again the survey gave some information as to the percentage of expenditures attributable to projects of different duration and the distribution of the expenditures within projects. These data were applied for all years to durable and nondurable goods R&D expenditures. The survey also gave some indication of the time lag between the end of R&D and the application of the innovation, which enabled us to estimate the amount of R&D ready to enter stock each year. Constant percentages were used to derive these magnitudes throughout the whole period, except for durable goods, where percentages varied between prewar and postwar years. Average lifespans of product and process innovations were derived from the same survey.

Separate stock estimates were made for producers' and consumer durable goods innovations based on BEA input-output data, using estimated lifespans for various categories of durable goods. Flat-top retirement patterns were constructed, centered at the average life expectancy.

To obtain net stocks and depreciation for applied research and development the double-declining balance switched depreciation method was used: at the point where straight-line depreciation of the net stock balance gives a larger annual depreciation we switch to staight-line for the remaining net stock balances.

INTANGIBLE HUMAN STOCKS. For education, general training, and health expenditures, the stock accumulation and depreciation methods used are analogous. We first estimated the average annual real expenditures per head by single age groups up to age ninety-five, then accumulated per capita lifetime expenditures for each cohort for each year covered in the stock calculation, then multiplied this by the number of persons in each age group each year and summed across age groups. This means we had to push the investment estimates back ninety-five years prior to 1929, the first year for which stock estimates exist. Our procedure automatically provides for the retirement of investment in persons who die during the year: expenditures are only accumulated into gross stock for survivors. Basic population figures by single years of age are from the Bureau of the Census.

For formal education, whether financed by the personal or government sector, constant dollar direct costs are broken down into elementary, secondary, higher, and other education, and allocated to age groups within these educational levels. This allocation is based on proportions by age in the enrollment series for each level. Informal education follows the same general procedure. For the portion financed by the personal and business sectors, it is assumed that all ages benefit equally. Government sector costs are allocated equally to persons of age five and over, and special education investment is traced only to ages five to seventeen. Military training costs are split between specific training and general training, the former cumulated over the period of active plus reserve duty, the latter spread over the total male population, with different ages receiving different weights. Employee training is broken down into the same subcategories, with specific training costs included in stock for the average duration of job tenure, and general training costs allocated to age groups according to the estimated age distribution of employment (developed from labor force participation rates, with a deduction for unemployment).

While all of the medical and health investment financed by the personal and government sectors is allocated by age groups, business sector investment is only partly treated that way. Fifty per cent of the investment outlays of this sector are considered "general" investment and are accumulated as stock, as in the case of other human categories. The other half is assumed to be "specific" investment, yielding benefits only as long as an employee stays with the original firm. This investment is considered part of stock for the average duration of job tenure only.

Medical, health, and safety outlays had to be allocated among age groups as a basis for cumulative real per capita outlays from which gross stocks were calculated. Personal and government expenditures are on a per capita basis and are distributed over various age groups according to data from *Vital and Health Statistics*. Business sector general health and safety expenditures are divided by the population (ages fourteen to seventy).

As to mobility stocks, lives are different for each cost category. Since these costs are estimated only for a fraction of persons in a group, life is estimated as the reciprocal of the percentage of people in the group. Thus, if in a given year mobility costs are incurred for 20 per cent of the employed, the life of these costs is assumed to be five years. Changes in the yearly percentages are taken into account. Hiring cost lives are the reciprocal of new hires rates; frictional unemployment cost lives are based on layoff rates; and moving and travel costs use the ratios of work-oriented migrants to the labor force.

Net capital stocks embodied in humans are derived by depreciating investment units from maturation ages (or the ages at which outlays are made if later) through age seventy-five. This is done for each investment unit and each age. Per capita accumulations are the next step, multiplied by corresponding population figures. The net stocks for those persons who die before age seventy-five are dropped out at the time of death.

Double-declining balance switched (to straight line) depreciation is used, constructed so as to approximate depreciation factors published by the Internal Revenue Service. Depreciation of rearing and medical costs is started at age eighteen, education and training, at age twenty-eight. This later age for education and training is derived from lifetime earnings curves: our depreciation reflects the decline in the lifetime earning capacity of the human capital. Discounted future earnings curves were obtained from a U.S. Census Bureau study which assumed an annual 3 per cent productivity increase and discount rates of 8 to 10 per cent per year.[5] It indicated appreciation in value of individuals through the late twenties, and a pattern of decline thereafter that seemed to be approximated by our declining-balance switched (to straight line) depreciation methods.

The real gross and net capital stock estimates, by type, are reflated to current prices with the same price indexes that are used to deflate current dollar investments, by type. The annual depreciation charges, in constant and current prices, are subtracted from the corresponding gross investment series to obtain net investment estimates.

STOCK VARIANTS.   It is assumed that all of the nonhuman capital is productively employed. But clearly much human capital is embodied in persons not employed. To estimate employed human capital stocks we applied ratios of employment to population by age group to the total stock estimates, by type and by age groups. Sector proportions of persons engaged were then applied to the productive stocks to obtain sector breakdowns. This treatment does not make allowance for the human capital devoted to unpaid economic activity (other than school-work), and the real product estimates are likewise unadjusted for the nonmarket outputs of unpaid labor.[6]

For organized education the basic method for calculating employed stock is the same, except that cost differentials are used. The differentials adjust for differences, by age group, in the stock of organized education embodied in employed persons relative to the total population.

All employee training, military education and training, and business medical stocks are considered employed during estimated average job tenures; that is, for the time span that specific investment is retained in stock. After average job tenure, only general investment is carried in stock. Stocks resulting from mobility costs, job search and hiring costs, and moving and travel costs are considered totally employed.

5. Herman P. Miller and Richard A. Hornseth, Technical Paper 16, Bureau of the Census, 1967.

6. The author is currently engaged in a study involving the expansion of imputations for nonmarket economic activity in the national income accounts, but the results were not ready for inclusion in this volume.

Besides employed stocks we also estimate stocks *utilized* by the private domestic business economy by applying a utilization rate to human stock employed by the private domestic economy. Utilization factors are calculated as the ratio of average weekly hours worked to hours awake, assumed to be 112 per week (7 times 16 per day). The real nonhuman capital stocks are adjusted only for cyclical variations in rates of capacity utilization, relative to selected high-level years taken as 100. Information is not available to determine whether there has been a significant trend in composite utilization rates of nonhuman capital.

3

Total Capital Formation and Saving, by Type and Sector, Relative to Income and Product

Although unequal at the sector level, saving and investment are equal at the national level. Note, therefore, that our description of the movements of total investment in relation to (adjusted) GNP in the initial section applies equally to saving. In the sector discussions, of course, investment and saving are treated separately.

Trends in Total Gross and Net Investment

Between 1929 and 1969 growth rates in total investment were higher than those in national product according to all four measures shown in Table 3-1. In current dollars, both gross and net total investment measures showed much the same growth rates as GNP and NNP, respectively, from 1929 to 1948 and then accelerated relatively between 1948 and 1969. In constant prices, both investment measures grew somewhat less rapidly than the corresponding product measures over the 1929–1948 period due to relative increases in the investment price deflators, but from 1948 to 1969 the real investment measures also showed distinctly higher growth rates than the real product measures.

The results of the relative trends in investment and product in

Table 3-1. *Total Investment and Product* (billions of current and 1958 dollars and average annual percentage rates of change)

Line No.		1929	1948	1969
	A. Billions of Dollars			
	Current dollars			
1.	Gross National Product	127.3	327.7	1,247.9
2.	Total gross investment	55.7	141.8	617.1
3.	Net National Product	92.3	236.4	897.6
4.	Total net investment	20.6	50.5	266.8
	Constant (1958) dollars			
5.	Real Gross National Product	252.4	420.6	957.2
6.	Real gross investment	119.0	185.6	474.7
7.	Real Net National Product	177.2	297.6	680.6
8.	Real net investment	43.9	62.7	198.1

Line No.		1929–69	1929–48	1948–69
	B. Average Annual Percentage Rates of Change			
	Current dollars			
1.	Gross National Product	5.9	5.1	6.6
2.	Total gross investment	6.2	5.0	7.3
3.	Net National Product	5.9	5.1	6.6
4.	Total net investment	6.6	4.8	8.2
	Constant (1958) dollars			
5.	Real Gross National Product	3.4	2.7	4.0
6.	Real gross investment	3.5	2.4	4.6
7.	Real Net National Product	3.4	2.8	4.0
8.	Real net investment	3.8	1.9	5.6

Table 3-2. *Total Investment as Percentage of National Product*

Line No.		1929	1948	1969
	Current dollars			
1.	Total gross investment/GNP	43.7	43.3	49.5
2.	Total net investment/NNP	22.3	21.4	29.7
	Constant dollars			
3.	Total gross investment/GNP	47.2	44.1	49.6
4.	Total net investment/NNP	24.8	21.1	29.1

terms of the percentages of national product saved and invested, according to our definitions, are shown in Table 3-2. Two major conclusions emerge from studying that table. The first is the high proportion of adjusted GNP devoted to gross saving and investment reached by 1969. In that year almost half of GNP represented total investment (according to our definition), compared with a less than 15 per cent ratio of gross private domestic (tangible) plus net foreign investment to GNP (according to official Commerce Department definitions and estimates).

The second major finding is the significant increase in the share of total investment in adjusted GNP—from around 43 per cent in both 1929 and 1948 to 49.5 per cent in 1969. This contrasts with some decline in the ratio of gross private domestic plus net foreign investment to GNP as conventionally defined—from 16.5 per cent in 1929 and 18.6 per cent in 1948 to 14.2 per cent in 1969.

The increase of net saving and investment in relation to adjusted NNP is even more pronounced—from a bit over and under 21 per cent in 1929 and 1948, respectively, to almost 30 per cent in 1969 (see Chart 3-1). Actually, the growth of capital consumption allowances closely parallels the growth of GNP. As a fraction of GNP, NNP remained relatively stable, at 72.5 per cent in 1929 and approximately 72.0 per cent in both 1948 and 1969. But since gross investment was growing faster than GNP after 1948, the ratio of capital consumption allowances to gross investment fell, and the ratio of net to gross investment rose— from 36 per cent in 1948 to 43 per cent in 1969. The drop in the capital consumption-gross investment ratio occurred entirely in the intangibles, reflecting their more rapid growth and the time lags between investment and the beginning of depreciation following maturation of the capital, particularly in the education category. The ratio of capital consumption to gross intangible investment also fell somewhat

Chart 3-1. *Gross and Net Investment-Product Ratios Based on Current Dollars, 1929–1969*

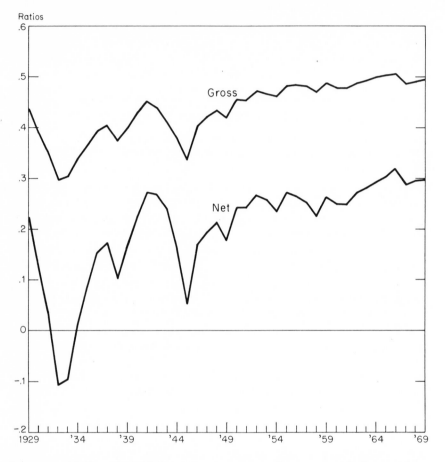

between 1929 and 1948, but this was more than counterbalanced by a rise in the ratio for tangibles, which subsequently stabilized.

The net increase in the ratio of saving (investment) to national product between 1929 and 1969 is considerably reduced when both variables are expressed in terms of constant 1958 dollars. The relative increase is almost as great, however, in constant as in current dollars from 1948 to 1969. This reflects a significantly greater increase in the implicit price deflator for total investment than in the deflator for national product, particularly between 1937 and 1948. The ratio of the former to the latter (on a gross basis) rose from 92.7 per cent in both 1929 and 1937 to 98.1 per cent in 1948, and after 1955 stayed within ±0.5 per cent of 100.0.

Reflecting the divergent movement of the deflators, the ratio of total real gross investment to real GNP dropped from 47.2 per cent in 1929 to 44.1 per cent in 1948, and thereafter climbed to 49.6 per cent in 1969. Although the net increase in the ratio to 1969 was about 5 per cent of the 1929 base, this was much less than in current prices. The ratio of total net investment to real NNP dropped from 24.8 per cent in 1929 to 21.1 per cent in 1948, and then rose sharply to 29.1 per cent in 1969. As in the case of current dollars, the increase in the real net ratio was considerably greater than in the real gross ratio between 1929 and 1969, but again relatively smaller in constant than in current dollars. From 1948 to 1969, however, the relative increases in both gross and net ratios were almost as great in constant as in current dollars because by 1948 the divergence between the investment and product deflators had narrowed greatly.

A word of caution is in order regarding the constant dollar results. As noted in the appendixes, the price deflators for investment are of uncertain quality.[1] Many of the component price indexes, particularly for intangible investment, are basically unit cost indexes which do not reflect productivity increases. Productivity may not have risen much in certain investment activities, such as education, but to the extent that it has, the deflators would tend to have an upward bias. This, in turn, would impart some downward bias to the trend in the real investment-to-product ratios. For this reason, more weight should be given to the current dollar estimates in evaluating the relative movements of total investment.

In summary, all the available measures point to a significant increase in the fraction of national income and product that was saved and invested between 1929 and 1969, particularly after 1948, when investment is defined broadly as including intangible as well as tangible investments in all sectors. The increase is most pronounced in what is probably the most significant measure—total net investment as a fraction of NNP, in current dollars—assuming reasonable depreciation estimates. The increase is smallest in what is, in our judgment, the least significant measure—total real gross investment as a fraction of real GNP. But even the latter measure shows a small net increase from 1929 to 1969, and a significant rise in the 1948–1969 period.

These estimates suggest that as per capita real income and wealth increase, the fraction of income saved and devoted to the total investment tends to rise. Keynes had theorized that the saving ratio might tend to rise in advanced countries, but the statistics did not show this in

---

1. This view is documented in a study now in progress by Robert J. Gordon for the National Bureau, tentatively entitled "The Measurement of Durable Goods Prices."

terms of his narrow definition of investment (consisting largely of business tangibles).[2] But the broadening of the investment definition produces estimates that seem to support his hunch. Certainly, as per capita income grows, individuals and the community can afford to save a larger fraction of additional income than the average proportion of income saved in the past, and apparently they have done so in the United States, at least since World War II.

Formulation of a general, dynamic "law" in respect to saving and investment behavior must, however, await further studies of the economy of the United States and other countries. With regard to the United States, it is probable that the ratio of total investment to income and product was rising for several decades prior to 1929, since available statistics show a marked rise in the intangible investment ratio and little change for the tangible investment ratio.[3] Also, the stability or decline of the total investment ratio between 1929 and the post-World War II period can be attributed to the effects of the Great Depression and the war, with the subsequent rise representing a "catching-up" and resumption of the longer-run trend. But further work is needed before confident generalizations can be made.

Trends in Total Investments, by Type

First we look at total gross investment in current dollars, by major type (see Table 3-3), and then indicate generally any difference in patterns of movement in net investment or in the constant dollar series. The major conclusion that emerges is that all of the relative increase in total investment over 1929–1969 has been due to a sharp increase in the proportion of GNP devoted to intangible investment, particularly after 1948 (see Chart 3-2). The tangible investment share sagged a bit, and the ratio of gross intangible to tangible investment rose from about 40 per cent in 1929 to over 75 per cent in 1969. In fact, total intangible investment in 1969, at $268 billion, was almost as large as tangible nonhuman investment, at $286 billion.

2. The narrow definition of investment is useful for business cycle analysis, of course; a much higher percentage of business tangible investment is financed through financial intermediaries than in the case of nonbusiness and intangible investments.

3. My earlier study presented figures showing that intangible investments (R&D, education, and health) tripled between 1909 and 1929 when GNP had less than doubled. See my *Productivity Trends in the United States*, Princeton, Princeton University Press for NBER, 1961, Table 21, p. 105; Table 24, p. 109; and Table A-IIb, pp. 296–297.

Table 3-3. Total Gross and Net Investment, by Type (Current Prices), as Percentages of National Product

Line No.		TOTAL GROSS INVESTMENT/GNP			TOTAL NET INVESTMENT/NNP		
		1929	1948	1969	1929	1948	1969
1.	Domestic investment	43.1	42.7	49.5	21.5	20.6	29.8
2.	Tangible	30.8	29.0	28.1	14.9	12.5	13.8
3.	Human	7.7	5.6	5.1	5.1	3.6	4.8
4.	Nonhuman	23.1	23.4	22.9	9.9	8.9	9.1
5.	Structures	9.0	8.5	7.6	4.8	5.0	3.8
6.	Equipment	12.1	13.4	14.3	2.3	1.8	3.9
7.	Inventory	2.0	1.5	1.0	2.7	2.1	1.3
8.	Intangible	12.3	13.7	21.5	6.6	8.1	16.0
9.	Human	12.1	13.0	19.4	6.5	7.6	15.2
10.	Education and training	8.6	9.4	15.4	6.2	6.4	13.6
11.	Health	1.5	1.6	2.2	.7	.9	1.1
12.	Mobility	2.0	2.0	1.7	-.5	.2	.5
13.	Nonhuman	.2	.7	2.1	.1	.5	.8
14.	Basic research	.03	.1	.3	0	.1	.4
15.	Applied R & D	.17	.7	1.8	.1	.4	.4
16.	Net foreign investment	.6	.6	-.1	.8	.8	-.1
17.	Total investment	43.7	43.3	49.4	22.3	21.4	29.7

Chart 3-2. *Gross Investment-Product Ratios, by Major Type, Based on Current Dollars, 1929, 1948, 1969*

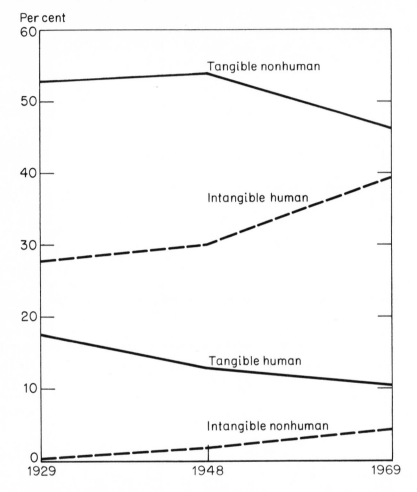

The relative decline in gross tangible investment from 30.8 per cent of GNP in 1929 to 28.1 per cent in 1969 was almost entirely due to a decline in the tangible human (rearing cost) proportion—from 7.7 to 5.1 per cent. Tangible nonhuman investment was close to 23 per cent in both years, after a slight relative increase in 1948. On a net basis, there was only a small relative decline in the rearing cost proportion, due to a smaller proportionate deduction for tangible human capital consumption at the end of the period than at the beginning. There was, however, a more pronounced decline in net tangible nonhuman investment than in the gross figure due to the increased proportion of depreciation noted earlier. In constant prices, the relative decline in tangible nonhuman investment is a bit larger than in current prices. But for real human investment, the relative drop becomes smaller on a gross basis and is transformed into an increase on a net basis. This is so because the deflator for rearing costs, which comprise the goods and services consumed by children, rises less than the deflators for other types of investment.

Within the tangible nonhuman category, investments in structures and inventories show a relative decline, particularly in constant prices, while equipment and other durable goods outlays show a relative increase.

Intangible investment shows a greater rise on a net than on a gross basis because of the declining depreciation ratio, as explained above. The relative increases in intangible investments on both gross and net bases are distinctly smaller in constant dollars than in current prices due to the significantly higher rate of increase in the intangible deflators than in the implicit price index for total national product. But even in constant dollars, the relative expansion in intangible investment is marked.

Among the various types of intangible investment, by far the most important category is education and training, which comprised over two-thirds of the total on a gross basis and over 90 per cent on a net basis in 1929 and a bit less in 1969. The net proportion is higher because the average life of educational investment is much longer than that of other types of intangibles except health. The ratio of educational and training investment to GNP increased by almost 80 per cent on a gross basis, and more than doubled on a net basis.

The largest proportionate increase (twentyfold on a gross basis from 1929 to 1969) occurred in R&D, although even in 1969 the R&D share of intangible investment was only 10 per cent on a gross basis and 5 per cent on a net basis. The ratio to GNP of investments in health and safety increased by about 50 per cent over the period, and by 1969 comprised about 10 per cent of total intangibles, too.

Mobility outlays, on a gross basis, were the only form of intangibles to show a decline in the ratio to GNP. This came about because mobility outlays are related to the size of the labor force, and the latter experienced significantly less growth than real GNP. It will be noted that in some years net mobility investment is negative due to the very short lives of some of the categories of mobility, such as job search, reflecting high rates of labor turnover. Thus, in some years gross mobility costs were less than the amortization of previous years' mobility investment.

Net foreign investment is a relatively minor category throughout. Its movements are erratic and exhibit no definite trend.

Changes in the percentage distributions of total investment result-

Table 3-4. *Percentage Distribution of Total Gross and Net Investment, by Type*

Line No.		Total Gross Investment		Total Net Investment	
		1929	1969	1929	1969
1.	Domestic investment	98.6	100.1	96.3	100.3
2.	Tangible	70.4	56.8	66.7	46.5
3.	Human	17.5	10.4	22.6	16.0
4.	Nonhuman	52.9	46.4	44.1	30.5
5.	Structures	20.6	15.5	21.5	12.9
6.	Equipment	27.8	29.0	10.4	13.1
7.	Inventory	4.5	1.9	12.3	4.5
8.	Intangible	28.2	43.4	29.5	53.9
9.	Human	27.7	39.2	29.0	51.1
10.	Education and training	19.8	31.2	27.8	45.8
11.	Health	3.4	4.5	3.3	3.8
12.	Mobility	4.5	3.5	-2.1	1.6
13.	Nonhuman	.5	4.2	.6	2.7
14.	Basic research	.1	.6	.2	1.4
15.	Applied R & D	.4	3.6	.4	1.3
16.	Net foreign investment	1.4	-.1	3.7	-.3
17.	Total investment	100.0	100.0	100.0	100.0

ing from the relative trends discussed above are summarized in Table 3-4. Here items whose share of national product remained relatively constant, such as tangible nonhuman investment, show a decline as a percentage of total investment, which rose in relation to product. Even in terms of per cent distributions of total investment, all the intangible categories, except mobility, rose significantly over the forty years.

Subperiod and Recession Behavior of Total Investment

SUBPERIODS

In Table 3-5, we divide the forty-year period 1929–1969 into six subperiods bounded by the seven business-cycle peak years (omitting 1954). Looking at the overall investment-to-product percentages (Part A of the table), we see that all measures show much the same patterns, but in varying degrees. The investment ratios all declined sharply between 1929 and 1937, which is not surprising in view of the fact that the economy was still substantially below full employment even at the peak of the 1933–1937 expansion.

Between 1937 and the full recovery of 1948, the current dollar ratios rose markedly, and in 1948 were less than one percentage point below the 1929 percentages. The recovery in the constant dollar ratios was much weaker, with the 1948 percentages still significantly below 1929. This reflected the relative increase in the investment deflator during the 1937–1948 subperiod, as noted earlier.

The largest proportionate increase in all the investment ratios came in the 1948–1953 subperiod. By 1953, all ratios significantly exceeded those of 1929 except total gross investment in constant dollars, which represented approximately the same percentage of real GNP as in 1929.

From 1953 to 1957, the gross investment ratios rose further, but the net ratios receded somewhat as capital consumption allowances grew faster than gross investment. Between 1957 and 1960, all the ratios receded. It will be remembered that the 1955–1960 period was one of relatively slow growth, reflected in the rising unemployment rates between peak years. The slower growth in investment than in product was a significant aspect of this period. Retardations in growth of gross investment are generally accentuated in the net investment measures.

In the subperiod of strong growth, 1960–1969, total investment

Table 3-5. *Total Investment as Percentage of National Product, in Peak Years*

Line No.		1929	1937	1948	1953	1957	1960	1969
	A. Total Gross and Net Investment in Current and Constant Dollars (billions)							
	Total gross investment/GNP							
1.	Current dollars	43.7	40.6	43.3	46.6	48.2	47.8	49.5
2.	Constant (1958) dollars	47.2	43.7	44.1	47.0	48.0	47.8	49.6
	Total net investment/NNP							
3.	Current dollars	22.3	17.4	21.4	25.8	25.4	24.9	29.7
4.	Constant (1958) dollars	24.8	19.2	21.1	26.1	25.3	24.9	29.1
	B. Total Gross Investment in Current Dollars, by Type							
1.	Gross domestic investment	43.1	40.5	42.7	47.1	47.6	47.5	49.5
2.	Tangible	30.8	27.6	29.0	32.4	31.3	30.0	28.1
3.	Human	7.7	6.0	5.6	5.7	6.1	6.2	5.1
4.	Nonhuman	23.1	21.6	23.4	26.7	25.3	23.8	22.9
5.	Structures	9.0	7.0	8.5	9.1	9.2	8.7	7.6
6.	Equipment	12.1	11.5	13.4	16.4	15.5	14.1	14.3
7.	Inventory	2.0	3.1	1.5	1.2	.5	1.0	1.0
8.	Intangible	12.3	12.9	13.7	14.6	16.2	17.5	21.5
9.	Human	12.1	12.6	13.0	13.5	14.4	15.4	19.4
10.	Education and training	8.6	8.7	9.4	10.0	10.7	11.5	15.4
11.	Health	1.5	1.6	1.6	1.7	1.9	2.0	2.2
12.	Mobility	2.0	2.2	2.0	1.9	1.8	1.9	1.7
13.	Nonhuman	.2	.3	.7	1.2	1.8	2.1	2.1
14.	Basic research	.03	.1	.1	.1	.2	.2	.3
15.	Applied R & D	.17	.3	.7	1.1	1.6	1.9	1.8
16.	Net foreign investment	.6	.1	.6	-.5	.6	.3	-.1

once again grew significantly faster than national product. The increase in the investment ratios was particularly marked on the net basis as capital consumption increased less rapidly than gross investment.

The overall subperiod movements just summarized reflect the net effect of divergent changes in the investment components. Part B of Table 3-5, showing the gross investment to GNP ratios for the peak years, is the focus of our discussion, which will touch upon significant divergences in the movements of the other measures.

Our most important conclusion is that the occasional downward movements in the total investment ratios during the subperiods were caused chiefly by declines in the tangible investment ratios. The total gross intangible investment ratio was in a steady uptrend across all the peak years, whether measured in current or constant prices. Both net intangible investment ratios did drop between 1929 and 1937, and the constant dollar net real intangible investment ratio eased slightly between 1948 and 1953. But the general picture is one of strong growth in the total intangible investment ratios, with most of the subperiod declines in the total investment ratios resulting from declines in the tangible investment ratio during subperiods of retarded growth.

The gross tangible human investment ratios dropped from 1929 through 1937 and 1948, reflecting the relatively low birth rates that prevailed until the early postwar period. By contrast, the relatively high birth rates that followed and characterized most of the 1950s were reflected in rising ratios from 1948 through 1960. The trend was reversed again: the 1969 ratio was below that of 1960 as a result of the declining birth rates of the late 1950s and the 1960s. The net ratios followed the same patterns, except that 1948 was already higher than 1937.

Tangible nonhuman investment fell proportionately more than national product from 1929 to 1937 according to all four measures. The gross current dollar ratio showed recovery between 1937 and 1948, but the constant dollar measure dropped a bit further, and both net measures showed more pronounced declines. Between 1948 and 1953 the ratios for all four measures rose markedly. Thereafter, the ratio of gross nonhuman investment to GNP in current dollars sagged in each succeeding peak year, although in real terms there was a mild reversal in the 1960–1969 period. The net ratios showed an even more pronounced decline than the gross ratio in 1953–1957 and 1957–1960. Finally, between 1960 and 1969 both showed a rise.

As to intangible investments, on a gross current dollar basis all types except mobility showed rising (or, occasionally, stable) ratios over all subperiods. On a constant dollar basis, the human intangible ratios to real GNP showed small decreases between 1948 and 1953—the subperiod during which the tangible ratios were rising sharply. There were also minor declines in the 1960–1969 period in medical and R&D outlays, while the real education ratio was still rising substantially.

The net intangible investment ratios were more sensitive. Thus, for most of the types, in both current and constant dollars, they dropped between 1929 and 1937. There were also declines in the constant dollar human intangible ratios from 1948 to 1953. And in both current and constant dollars, the net R&D ratio dropped between 1960 and 1969 (most of the decline occurring in the latter part of the subperiod).

RECESSIONS

Even on a total investment basis (including intangibles), investment declined more than product between the peak and trough years of the business cycles during the 1929–1969 period, with the exception of the 1960–1961 contraction, when the investment ratios were virtually unchanged. There was a marked contrast between the 1930s and the post-World War II years, as shown in Table 3-6. Total investment fell drastically relative to national product between 1929 and 1933, and substantially (though much more moderately) during 1937–1938. Since 1948, however, recession declines in the investment ratios have been small.

Downturns in the net investment ratios from peaks to troughs have been significantly greater than those in the gross investment ratios. This is to be expected, since capital consumption allowances in recessions continue to grow at rates near those of expansion periods while gross investment either drops or is much retarded in growth. The changes in the ratios are much the same in current and constant dollars, since the time periods involved are too short to permit much divergence between price deflators for investment and for national product.

From a look at the gross investment ratios by type (Part B of Table 3-6), it is apparent that the declines in the total investment ratio between peak and trough years have been entirely due to declines in tangible nonhuman investment relative to national product. Rearing cost ratios have risen in recessions (except from 1929 to 1933) concomitantly with the growing number of children. All of the intangible investment ratios have also gone up or remained stable in recessions, reflecting their strong secular growth or their countercyclical tendencies, as in the case of mobility costs. On a net basis, the intangible investment ratios generally dropped somewhat in the contractions of the 1930s and the first two postwar contractions, but proportionately much less than the net tangible nonhuman investment ratios. In the last

Table 3-6. *Percentage Point Changes in Investment/Product Percentages between Peak and Trough Years of Business Cycles, 1929–1933 to 1960–1961*

Line No.		1929–33	1937–38	1948–49	1953–54	1957–58	1960–61
	A. Aggregate Measures						
	Total gross investment/GNP						
1.	Current dollars	-13.6	-3.3	-1.5	-.7	-1.3	0
2.	Constant (1958) dollars	-13.9	-3.3	-1.5	-.6	-1.1	0
	Total net investment/GNP						
3.	Current dollars	-31.9	-7.3	-3.6	-1.4	-2.9	-.1
4.	Constant (1958) dollars	-35.4	-7.5	-3.3	-1.5	-2.8	-.2
	B. Changes in Percentages of Current Dollar Gross Investments to GNP, by Type						
1.	Gross domestic investment	-13.2	-4.2	-1.1	-1.1	-.6	-.2
2.	Tangible	-15.1	-4.7	-1.1	-1.0	-1.1	-.7
3.	Human	-.2	.2	.2	.3	.2	0
4.	Nonhuman	-14.9	-4.9	-1.3	-1.3	-1.4	-.7
5.	Structures	-4.5	.3	.2	.5	0	0
6.	Equipment	-4.5	-1.8	.3	-1.1	-1.4	-.4
7.	Inventory	-6.0	-3.3	-1.8	-.7	.1	-.3
8.	Intangible	1.8	.5	0	0	.6	.5
9.	Human	1.7	.4	0	-.2	.4	.4
10.	Education and training	.5	.1	-.1	-.3	.3	.3
11.	Health	.5	.2	.1	.1	.1	.1
12.	Mobility	.7	.1	0	0	0	0
13.	Nonhuman	.2	.1	0	.1	.2	.1
14.	Basic research	.1	0	0	0	0	.1
15.	Applied R & D	.1	.1	0	.1	.2	.1
16.	Net foreign investment	-.4	1.0	-.4	.4	-.6	.1

two recessions covered—1957–1958 and 1960–1961—the net intangible investment ratio and most if its components rose slightly.

One may conclude that intangible investments and tangible human investment outlays are much less cyclical than tangible nonhuman investment. They account for the much smaller recession declines in the ratio of total investment to product than in the tangible nonhuman investment ratios alone. In fact, the human and intangible investment outlays play a countercyclical role by helping to cushion recessions on a gross outlay basis, which is what is relevant in cycle analysis.

Trends in Total Investment, by Sector

An examination of the investment trends by sector over the long period and the subperiods reveals that it was the government sector that accounted for all of the growth relative to national product on a gross basis, and for most of it on a net basis. (See Table 3-7.) Looking at the total gross investment ratios of the end-years 1929 and 1969, one sees a slight rise in total gross investment of the personal sector, a slight drop in the business sector, and a jump in the government sector—from 4.6 to 11.3 per cent, in current dollars—that slightly exceeds the 6.5 percentage point increase in the total gross domestic investment ratio.

In constant dollars, the pattern is only moderately different. The real total gross personal investment ratio rises a bit more than in current dollars, chiefly because of the less than average increase in the deflator for rearing costs (which cover consumer products). Contrariwise, the total real gross business investment ratio falls more than in current dollars, and the government investment ratio rises less. Still, the rise in the government ratio exceeds the lesser increase in the real total gross domestic investment ratio by a wider margin than in the current dollar case.

The patterns of the total net domestic investment ratios in the table reveal an important difference. In constant dollars, and even more so in current prices, substantial increases in the total net personal investment ratio as well as in the government ratio contribute significantly to the rise in the total ratio—which is notably larger on a net basis than on a gross basis. In the government sector, the increases in the net investment ratios are about the same as those in the gross ratios, although the net ratios are larger relative to the gross ratios than in the private sectors. In the business sector, net investment ratios fall more than gross ratios, while in the personal sector they rise more than the

Table 3-7. *Total Investment, by Domestic Sector, as Percentage of National Product, Gross and Net, in Current and Constant Dollars*

Line No.		1929	1937	1948	1953	1957	1960	1969
	Gross domestic investment/GNP							
1.	Current dollars, total	43.1	40.5	42.7	47.1	47.5	47.5	49.6
2.	Personal	26.1	22.3	24.8	24.9	25.5	25.8	26.5
3.	Business	12.4	11.5	12.6	10.6	11.1	10.8	11.8
4.	Government	4.6	6.7	5.3	11.6	10.9	10.9	11.3
5.	Constant dollars, total	46.4	43.6	43.6	47.4	47.4	47.6	49.6
6.	Personal	26.0	23.0	24.5	24.3	25.5	25.9	27.1
7.	Business	14.5	12.3	13.3	11.0	11.0	10.8	12.1
8.	Government	5.9	8.3	5.8	12.1	10.9	10.9	10.4
	Total net investment/NNP							
9.	Current dollars, total	21.5	17.4	20.6	26.5	24.6	24.6	29.9
10.	Personal	9.7	4.0	11.3	10.1	9.7	10.1	12.8
11.	Business	7.3	6.6	9.2	5.5	5.3	4.8	5.8
12.	Government	4.5	6.8	.1	10.9	9.6	9.7	11.3
13.	Constant dollars, total	23.9	19.1	20.2	26.7	24.4	24.5	29.2
14.	Personal	9.4	3.7	10.9	9.5	9.6	10.2	13.2
15.	Business	8.5	6.6	9.5	5.7	5.2	4.8	5.9
16.	Government	6.0	8.8	-.2	11.5	9.6	9.5	10.1

corresponding gross ratios because of the relative decline in capital consumption allowances (due to the greater importance of intangibles in the personal sector). The similar relative movements of government investment, both gross and net, suggest that the proportions of tangible and intangible investments were similar to those in total domestic investment.

It is evident from the subperiod estimates shown in Table 3-7 that the trends in the ratio were not linear. Turning first to the gross investment sector of general government, note that there was already a significant increase in its investment ratio by 1937, reflecting expanded New Deal public works programs in the context of a slack overall economy. The ratio receded somewhat in 1948, when the economy was fully employed. Between 1948 and 1953, given the impetus of the Korean engagement, the government total gross investment ratio more than doubled, whether measured in current or constant dollars. The ratio was somewhat lower in both 1957 and 1960 than in 1953. By 1969 it rose a bit in current dollars, but dropped somewhat in constant dollars.

The general pattern for government is much the same in terms of the net investment-product ratios, except that the ratio fell almost to zero in 1948, reflecting high capital consumption allowances on the still large (but declining) stock of military capital goods coupled with reduced new gross investment. Also, in net terms both the current and constant dollar ratios rose between 1960 and 1969.

In the personal sector, the total gross investment ratio, based on both current and constant dollars, remained relatively stable over all the peak years, except for a drop in 1937, followed by recovery in the postwar period, and a noticeable increase between 1960 and 1969. The pattern was essentially the same on a net basis, except that the drop in the 1930s and the rise in the 1960s were much more marked.

Business sector gross investment in relation to GNP varied only a little between peak years, around a mild downward trend, which is more noticeable in the constant than in the current dollar estimates. On a net basis, the current and constant dollar estimates for 1948 were noticeably higher than in the previous peak years, particularly 1937. But the ratios for the peak years in the subsequent two decades varied moderately around a distinctly lower level.

SECTOR TOTAL INVESTMENT AND SAVING RELATIVE TO DISPOSABLE INCOME

The trends of total investment by sector relative to national product become more meaningful if we first examine the movement of each sector's disposable income relative to national product, and then look at the proportions of sector disposable incomes saved and invested (see Chart 3-3). The disposable income of each sector basically equals its income earned from current production plus transfers received from other sectors (and tax receipts, in the case of government) less transfer payments (including taxes paid by the private sectors). The computations are analogous to those prepared by the Council of Economic Advisers (see Appendix A). Total gross disposable income of the sectors equals GNP less statistical discrepancy. The saving of each sector (disposable income less current consumption) may exceed or fall short of its tangible plus intangible investment total, yielding a residual net financial investment (which, if negative, reflects net borrowing from other sectors).

Table 3-8 gives a quick picture of the sectoral distribution of total gross disposable income in peak years over 1929–1969. The outstanding trends are a drop in the share of disposable personal income from almost four-fifths in 1929 to two-thirds in 1969, and a counterbalancing increase in the share of disposable government income from little more than one-tenth in 1929 to over 23 per cent in 1969. Disposable business income (gross "cash flow" less dividends) held around 10 per cent throughout the period, while net transfers to the rest of the world were generally of only fractional magnitude, except during the early post-World War II period.

On a net basis, the relative trends in sector ratios of disposable income to total income were much the same. In the personal and governmental sectors the ratios were higher on a net than on a gross basis, however, reflecting the much lower ratio of business disposable income on the former basis (since depreciation comprises more than half of cash flow less dividends) and a somewhat rising fraction, as noted earlier. Net foreign transfers, unaffected by depreciation, are obviously higher in relation to NNP than to GNP, but still relatively unimportant.

PERSONAL SECTOR. As the ratio of gross disposable personal income gradually declined from almost 79 per cent of adjusted GNP in 1929 to 67 per cent in 1969, the proportion of DPI invested rose from about one-third in 1929 to almost 40 per cent in 1969. As a result, personal sector gross investment remained a relatively stable fraction of GNP at around one-fourth in good years (see Table 3-9). Thus, the average investment propensity was rising during these four decades not only in the total economy, as noted earlier, but also in the personal sector. This is also true of saving, for the personal sector generally showed a small excess of saving over total investment, with net lending amounting to about 2 per cent of DPI in 1929 and 1 per cent in 1960.

Chart 3-3. *Ratios of Gross Investment to GNP and Disposable Income, by Sector, with Ratios of Sector Disposable Incomes to GNP, Based on Current Dollars, 1929, 1948, 1969*

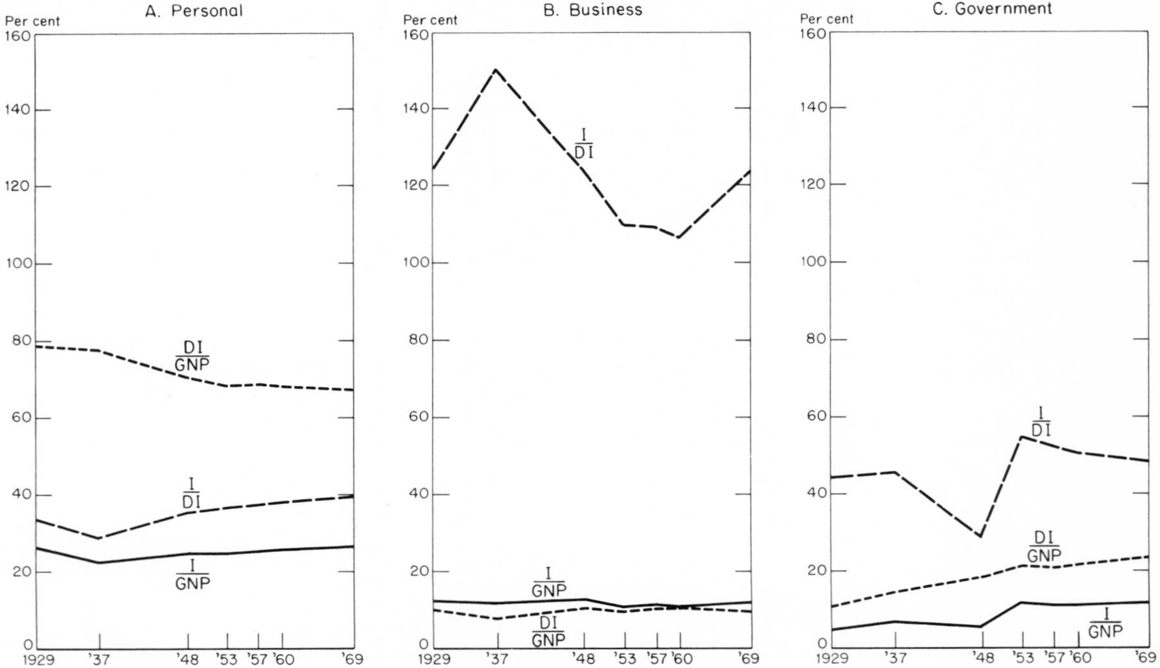

84

Table 3-8. *Total Gross Disposable Income, by Sector, Percentage Distribution*

Line No.		1929	1937	1948	1953	1957	1960	1969
1.	Total gross disposable income	100.0	100.0	100.0	100.0	100.0	100.0	100.0
2.	Persons	79.2	77.6	70.0	68.5	68.5	67.8	67.0
3.	Business	10.0	7.7	10.1	9.7	10.1	10.1	9.5
4.	Government	10.5	14.5	18.5	21.2	20.9	21.7	23.3
5.	Rest of world	.3	.2	1.4	.5	.4	.4	.2

Table 3-9. *Gross Investment and Saving, by Sector, Relative to Gross Product and Disposable Income*

Line No.		1929		1937	
		% of GNP	% of DI	% of GNP	% of DI
	Personal sector				
1.	Disposable income	78.8	100.0	77.6	100.0
2.	Total gross investment	26.1	33.2	22.3	28.8
3.	Net financial investment	1.7	2.2	3.5	4.5
4.	Total gross saving	27.8	35.8	25.8	33.2
	Business sector				
5.	Disposable income	10.0	100.0	7.7	100.0
6.	Total gross investment	12.4	124.4	11.5	150.1
7.	Net financial investment	−2.4	−24.5	−3.9	−50.2
8.	Total gross saving	10.0	100.0	7.7	99.9
	Government sector				
9.	Disposable income	10.4	100.0	14.5	100.0
10.	Total gross investment	4.6	44.3	6.7	45.9
11.	Net financial investment	.8	7.4	.4	3.0
12.	Total gross saving	5.4	51.7	7.1	48.9

(We lacked final estimates of current consumption and saving for 1969 at the time our estimates were completed in 1970.)

Note that by our broader definitions, personal saving is a much larger fraction of sector disposable personal income, near 40 per cent in 1969, than by the official definitions, which placed it at 6 per cent.

On a net basis (see Table 3-10), the personal saving and investment trends were similar, except that from 1929 to 1969 investment had risen proportionately more in relation to disposable income on the net than on the gross basis—from near 12 to over 18 per cent. So, despite the virtually identical proportionate drop of the disposable income-product ratio on a net and gross basis, the ratio of personal net investment to NNP rose from less than 10 per cent to almost 13 per cent in 1969. Almost all of this relative increase took place after 1960, however. Since net financial investment is the same in the net as in the gross calculations, the relative net saving trends parallel the relative net investment trends, although at a somewhat higher level.

BUSINESS SECTOR. Table 3-8 showed the remarkable stability of gross business disposable income in good years at around 10 per cent of GNP. Note that by definition (since consumption of intermediate goods and dividend payments are already out), gross disposable income is

1948		1953		1957		1960		1969	
% of GNP	% of DI	% of GNP	% of DI	% of GNP	% of DI	% of GNP	% of DI	% of GNP	% of DI
70.4	100.0	68.1	100.0	68.5	100.0	68.0	100.0	67.0	100.0
24.8	35.2	24.9	36.6	25.5	37.3	25.8	38.0	26.5	39.4
1.0	1.5	1.4	2.1	1.6	2.3	.6	.9	(.6)	(.9)
25.8	36.7	26.3	38.7	27.1	39.6	26.5	39.0	(27.4)	(40.3)
10.2	100.0	9.6	100.0	10.1	100.0	10.1	100.0	9.5	100.0
12.6	123.8	10.6	109.9	11.1	109.5	10.8	106.6	11.8	123.9
-2.4	-23.8	-1.0	-9.9	-1.0	-9.5	-.7	-6.6	-2.3	-23.9
10.2	100.0	9.6	100.0	10.1	100.0	10.1	100.0	9.5	100.0
18.7	100.0	21.1	100.0	20.9	100.0	21.7	100.0	23.4	100.0
5.3	28.6	11.6	55.0	10.9	52.2	10.9	50.3	11.3	48.1
2.6	13.7	-1.6	-7.5	0	-.1	.4	2.0	(.4)	(2.0)
7.9	42.3	10.0	47.5	10.9	52.1	11.4	52.3	(11.7)	(50.1)

equal to the gross saving of the sector. In good years, the business sector typically invests more than its internally generated disposable income (or saving). The resulting negative net financial investment (or net borrowing) was a bit above and below 24 per cent of disposable income in 1929 and 1969, respectively (see Table 3-9). Since disposable income relative to GNP was also fractionally lower in 1969 than in 1929, the business gross investment ratio to GNP fell slightly from 12.4 per cent to 11.8 per cent. In good years, the ratio varied between 10.5 and 12.5 per cent. There was no real trend in any of the three key ratios—disposable income to product, investment to income, and investment to product.

On a net basis, disposable business income represents a much smaller and shrinking proportion of national product. Although net business investment rose from 185 per cent of disposable income (net saving) in 1929 to 221 per cent in 1969 (see Table 3-10), the ratio of net investment to NNP still declined from over 7 per cent to under 6 per cent. Vis-à-vis the relative stability of the gross investment ratio, this reflects the growth of depreciation allowances as calculated in relation to retained earnings.

GOVERNMENT SECTOR.   Here the dramatic rise in the ratio of

Table 3-10. *Net Investment and Saving, by Domestic Sector, Relative to Net Product and Disposable Income*

Line No.		1929		1969[a]	
		% of NNP	% of Net DI	% of NNP	% of Net DI
	Personal Sector				
1.	Disposable income	82.3	100.0	69.3	100.0
2.	Total net investment	9.7	11.8	12.8	18.4
3.	Net financial investment	2.4	2.9	(.9)	(1.3)
4.	Total net saving	12.1	14.6	(13.7)	(19.7)
	Business Sector				
5.	Disposable income	4.0	100.0	2.6	100.0
6.	Total net investment	7.3	185.0	5.8	221.3
7.	Net financial investment	−3.3	−85.0	−3.2	−121.3
8.	Total net saving	4.0	100.0	2.6	100.0
	Government Sector				
9.	Disposable income	12.6	100.0	28.2	100.0
10.	Total net investment	4.5	36.0	11.3	40.1
11.	Net financial investment	1.1	8.5	(.6)	(2.5)
12.	Total net saving	5.6	44.4	(11.9)	(42.6)

[a]Because of the absence of net financial investment estimates for the government and personal sectors for 1969, we have entered the estimates for the previous peak year, 1960, in parentheses, and derived the net saving estimate, also shown in parentheses.

disposable income to GNP plus a moderate expansion in the share of income devoted to total investment accounted for the increase in total gross investment from 4.6 per cent in 1929 to 11.3 per cent in 1969 (see Table 3-9). Since the public sector has tended to generate positive net financial investment in peak cycle years, by our definition, the trend of the gross saving ratio has paralleled that of gross investment. The net investment picture exhibits much the same trends (see Table 3-10). Note that, while the fraction of gross disposable income invested by governments was below average in 1948, in the peak years 1953, 1957, and 1960 it exceeded 50 per cent, before declining to 48 per cent in 1969 (compared with 44 per cent in 1929). It is not commonly realized that governments devote around half of their disposable income to investment, counting intangibles along with tangibles—an even higher fraction than that allotted by persons. Thus, the relative shift of income from persons to government has contributed to the rise in the national investment ratio on top of the rising trend of the investment ratio in both sectors.

DIFFERENCES IN SECTORAL INVESTMENT MIX, 1929–1969

Differences in the composition of sectoral investment and changes from 1929 to 1969 are shown in Table 3-11. Note that rearing costs are ascribed solely to the personal sector, where its share of total gross investment dropped from 29 to 19 per cent between 1929 and 1969. Tangible nonhuman investment constituted a smaller proportion of total gross investment in the personal sector than in the others but declined only modestly between 1929 and 1969, while it dropped much more in the other two domestic sectors due, chiefly, to significant declines in the nonresidential construction ratios. Equipment outlay ratios rose in both business and government sectors, but not enough to offset relative declines in construction (and in inventory accumulation in the business sector). Note that, even after its relative downturn, nonhuman tangible investment still accounted for over three-fourths of business investment in 1969, while it comprised less than 40 per cent in the other sectors.

Intangible investment rose sharply in all sectors in relation to total gross investment. Its ratio was markedly higher in the public sector—at around 50 per cent in 1929 and 61 per cent in 1969—than in the private sectors. It was lowest in business, but showed the sharpest rise in that sector, from 14 to 24 per cent over the period under review.

Within the intangibles area, almost all of the relative increase in the public sector was due to R&D. In the private sectors there were

Table 3-11. *Gross Domestic Investment in Current Dollars, Percent Distribution by Type and Sector*

Line No.		Personal Sector		Business Sector		Government Sector	
		1929	1969	1929	1969	1929	1969
1.	Gross sector investment	100.0	100.0	100.0	100.0	100.0	100.0
2.	Tangible investment	68.3	55.5	86.1	76.0	49.6	39.1
3.	Human	29.4	19.4	0.0	0.0	0.0	0.0
4.	Nonhuman	38.9	36.2	86.1	76.0	49.6	39.1
5.	Structures	7.9	8.4	39.7	26.4	43.6	20.5
6.	Equipment	28.5	27.6	35.5	43.9	6.1	16.6
7.	Inventories	2.5	0.8	10.8	5.7	0.0	0.5
8.	Intangible investment	31.7	44.5	13.9	24.0	50.4	60.9
9.	Human	31.6	44.1	12.8	17.3	49.2	50.1
10.	Education and training	20.6	32.5	10.4	15.3	42.7	44.4
11.	Health	4.4	6.0	0.4	0.5	6.2	5.2
12.	Mobility	6.6	5.6	2.0	1.5	0.3	0.5
13.	Nonhuman	0.1	0.3	1.0	6.8	1.2	10.8
14.	Basic research	0.1	0.2	0.1	0.3	0.2	1.7
15.	Applied R & D	0.0	0.1	1.0	6.4	1.0	9.0

Chart 3-4. *Composition of Gross Domestic Investment, by Type of Sector, Percentage, Based on Current Dollars, 1929 and 1969*

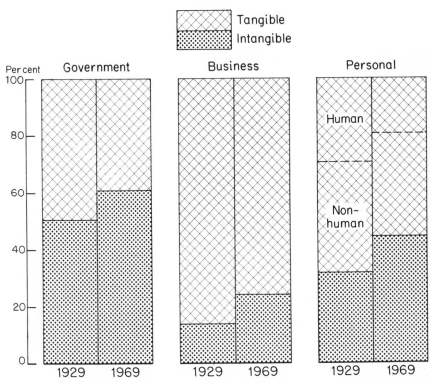

significant relative increases in human intangible investment (except mobility) as well. Yet, even in 1969 the public sector still devoted a substantially higher proportion of its total gross investment to human intangibles (particularly education) than did the personal sector. The business sector, understandably, brought up the rear in this department, but showed as high a relative increase as did the personal sector. (See Chart 3-4.)

SECTORAL INVESTMENT BEHAVIOR IN CONTRACTIONS

Declines in the ratio of total investment to product are typical in recessions, as noted earlier, although they have been moderate since the 1930s. When we study the sectoral picture in Table 3-12, we see that declining gross investment ratios occur invariably only in the

Table 3-12. Sector Changes in Gross Disposable Income, Investment, and Saving as Percentages of GNP between Cycle Peaks and Troughs (percentage points)

Line No.		1929–33	1937–38	1948–49	1953–54	1957–58	1960–61
	Personal Sector						
1.	Disposable income/GNP	2.2	−1.2	.7	.9	1.1	.5
2.	Investment/disposable income	−8.5	−.6	.7	.2	−.8	−.8
3.	Investment/GNP	−6.1	−.8	.7	.5	−.1	−.3
4.	Saving/GNP	−7.4	−3.6	−.2	−.2	0	.3
5.	Financial investment/GNP	−1.3	−2.9	−1.0	−.7	.1	.7
	Business Sector						
6.	Disposable income/GNP	−5.9	.7	.3	.2	−.4	0
7.	Investment/disposable income	−46.6	−69.0	−34.0	−12.2	−13.2	−7.0
8.	Investment/GNP	−9.2	−4.7	−3.2	−1.0	−1.7	−.8
9.	Financial investment/GNP	3.3	5.5	3.5	1.2	1.3	.8
	Government Sector						
10.	Disposable investment/GNP	3.3	0	−2.1	−1.0	−.9	−.6
11.	Investment/disposable income	4.6	8.8	11.5	−.3	8.7	5.5
12.	Investment/GNP	2.1	1.2	1.3	−.6	1.3	.9
13.	Saving/GNP	−.7	−.9	−2.3	−.6	−1.0	−.4
14.	Financial investment/GNP	−2.8	−2.1	−3.6	0	−2.3	−1.2

business sector. In the personal sector the picture is mixed, while in the public sector the ratio of total gross investment to GNP has risen in all contractions, with the minor exception of 1953–1954.

The related disposable income data help us to analyze cyclical investment behavior more fully. In the personal sector, DPI rose relative to GNP in all recessions except 1937–1938, reflecting the operation of built-in stabilizers. Investment was reduced as a proportion of DPI in all contractions except 1948–1949 and 1953–1954, which were affected by backlogs of durable goods demand. The net result was a shrinking investment-product ratio in all contractions except the two noted above. The declines in the investment ratios, particularly vis-à-vis GNP, were modest, however, except in the Great Depression of 1929–1933. It is interesting that in all recessions through 1954, net financial investment was reduced, so that the ratio of gross saving to GNP fell more than the investment ratio, or declined when the investment ratio rose. In the subsequent two recession years, however, net lending rose, so that the gross saving ratio did not drop, although the gross investment ratio did decline slightly in both years.

In the business sector, except for a marked drop in 1929–1933, the ratio of disposable income (gross saving) to GNP did not change much during contractions. However, the proportion of disposable income invested did drop significantly, although the declines have tended to become smaller in recessions since 1937–1938. This has meant significant declines in the business gross investment-GNP ratio during contractions, although these, too, have tended to become smaller. It is noteworthy that the investment cuts were used to strengthen financial structure. In every contraction net financial investment rose, going from minus to plus without exception.

Finally, the public sector exhibits a downtrend in the ratio of gross disposable income to GNP since the 1930s, reflecting an effect of built-in stabilizers which is the reverse of that operating in the personal sector. Further, the proportion of disposable income devoted to investment rose significantly in all contractions except that of 1953–1954, when there was a small decline due to the post-Korean cutbacks. The net result was a significant increase in the gross government investment-GNP ratio in all contractions (except 1953–1954). It is interesting that in the government sector, net financial investment was reduced in all contractions except 1953–1954, when there was no change: that is, general governments as a whole went from surpluses on current account in peak years to deficits in contraction years. As a result, the ratio of gross public saving to GNP declined in all cyclical contractions, which, together with the investment increases, exerted an important countercyclical influence.

4

Total Capital Stock, by Type and Sector, in Relation to Income and Product

The rates of growth in man-made capital stocks relative to income and product are directly related to the saving and investment functions covered in the preceding chapter. This is so statistically as well as theoretically, since our reproducible stock estimates are derived from the investment estimates by means of the perpetual inventory method explained in chapter 2.

Here we are concerned with the movements of stocks in relation to product, with particular reference to the gross versions of each. As we shall see, the ratios of gross to net capital and product have changed little over the four decades under review; also, the gross stock estimates are more relevant for an analysis of changes in productive capacity and productivity. Due to the probable upward biases of the capital deflators, which affect the various types and sectors differentially, the percentage distributions are calculated from the aggregates in current dollars as well as in constant dollars.

The sector distributions relate to the financing of investment and the resulting capital stocks. But since we are also interested in the stocks used, or "commanded," particularly in the private domestic business economy, where the capital and product estimates are independent of each other, we present capital estimates on a use basis for that sector in the following chapter. This means, in particular, that much of the human capital, which is largely financed by the personal sector, is allocated to the business sector on a basis of sector employment ratios.

Total National Wealth

The current value of total gross capital stock increased from about $1.2 trillion in 1929 to $10.9 trillion in 1969, or at an average annual rate of 5.7 per cent. The growth rate of adjusted GNP was 0.2 percentage point higher. This was associated with a modest drop in the total capital-output ratio from 9.4 in 1929 to 8.7 in 1969—most of it occurring after 1948, when the ratio was 9.2. Conversely, the ratio of product (income) to total capital increased from 0.106 to 0.115, an average growth rate of less than 0.2 per cent a year. With some adjustments to convert product to factor income, this relation can be used to calculate rates of return on capital (see the following chapter).

When the growth in current dollar total GNP is reduced by a 2.8 per cent average annual rate of increase in the implicit price deflator for total gross national wealth (GNW), real GNW is seen to have grown at a 2.8 per cent average annual rate over the period under review. The implicit price deflator for adjusted GNP rose at a significantly slower rate than that for total GNP—2.4 per cent—so the rate of increase in real adjusted GNP was 3.4 per cent a year. Thus, total capital productivity grew at an average rate of 0.6 per cent a year, although the upward bias in the GNW price deflator suggests that the true increase was probably less than that. Nevertheless, it does appear that the growth in real stock of total capital does not explain all the increase in real GNP, as hypothesized by Schultz. In terms of real total capital coefficients, the decline was from 10.5 in 1929 to 9.4 in 1948 and 8.4 in 1969—a more marked and more regular decline than that in the current dollar ratio. (See Chart 4-1 and Table 4-1.) We defer until the next chapter a more detailed analysis of the role increasing capital productivity plays in economic growth.

On a net basis, the real capital-output ratio is lower than on a gross basis and drops slightly more. This reflects the fact that the ratio of net to gross real total wealth was 65.8 per cent in 1929 and 63.4 per cent in 1969, whereas the ratio of real net to gross national product was on a higher level, and rose slightly from 70.2 per cent to 71.1 per cent over the period. In other words, total capital productivity increased a bit more on a net basis than on a gross basis. Different methods of computing depreciation could result in somewhat different results, of course.

Although over the entire 1929–1969 period the average growth rate of real total NNW was almost as high as that of real total GNW—2.7 versus 2.8 per cent—it was 0.4 percentage point lower during 1929–1948 and 0.2 higher during 1948–1969. This reflects the fact that there was a significant drop in the ratio of net to gross wealth between 1929

Chart 4-1. *Real Gross National Wealth and Product, United States, 1929–1969*

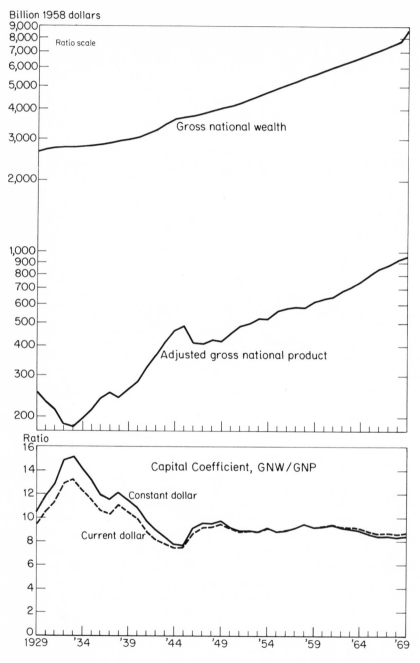

Table 4-1. *U.S. Total Gross National Wealth and Product*

	Current Dollars (billions)	Price Deflators (indexes, 1958 = 100)	Constant Dollars (billions)
A. Absolute Levels			
Adjusted GNP			
1929	127.3	50.5	252.4
1948	327.7	77.9	420.6
1969	1,247.9	130.4	957.2
Total GNW			
1929	1,202.7	45.4	2,647.6
1948	3,012.2	76.0	3,963.6
1969	10,906.6	135.2	8,069.9
Employed GNW			
1929	915.0	44.0	2,079.6
1948	2,373.1	75.8	3,132.5
1969	8,583.5	135.0	6,358.3
B. Average Annual Percentage Rates of Change			
Adjusted GNP			
1929–69	5.9	2.4	3.4
1929–48	5.1	2.3	2.7
1948–69	6.6	2.5	4.0
Total GNW			
1929–69	5.7	2.8	2.8
1929–48	4.9	2.7	2.1
1948–69	6.3	2.8	3.4
Employed GNW			
1929–69	5.8	2.8	2.8
1929–48	5.1	2.9	2.2
1948–69	6.3	2.8	3.4
C. Ratios, GNW/GNP			
Total GNW/GNP			
1929	9.4	.90	10.5
1948	9.2	.98	9.4
1969	8.7	1.04	8.4
Employed GNW/GNP			
1929	7.2	.87	8.2
1948	7.2	.97	7.4
1969	6.9	1.04	6.6

Table 4-2. *Ratios of Total Net to Gross Wealth and Product, Peak Years, 1929–1969*

Year	Wealth	Product	Year	Wealth	Product
1929	.658	.702	1957	.613	.695
1937	.631	.696	1960	.616	.695
1948	.609	.708	1969	.634	.711
1953	.616	.717			

and 1948, with a partial recovery thereafter (particularly between 1960 and 1969), as shown in the preceding table. By contrast, the ratios of net to gross real product fluctuated within a much narrower range.

When real total capital stocks *employed* are related to real national product, the ratios are lower, of course, but the trends are virtually the same as for the total capital coefficients, both gross and net. This is because the ratio of employed to total real stocks changed very little in peak years for the entire period (except 1937). It was 0.785 in 1929, 0.790 in 1948, and 0.788 in 1969 on the gross basis, resulting in the same growth rate for employed as for total real gross stocks 1929–1969. The ratio rose slightly more on a net basis. On both bases the ratios fell in recession years, of course. It will be realized that the employment adjustment was made only for the human capital, since it is assumed that nonhuman stocks are consistently "employed."[1] The price deflators for employed stocks rose slightly more than for total stocks, so that the growth rates of employed stocks in current prices were 0.1 percentage point higher than for total stocks in current prices, both gross and net.

If an adjustment were made for "utilization," the ratios would be lower yet. But it is not certain what the relative trend would have been, since some decline in the utilization rate of human stocks (reflecting a decline in average hours worked) may have been offset by a rising trend in utilization of nonhuman capital. The data on the latter are not firm enough to provide a basis for adjustment.

Looking at movements of real gross capital coefficients between cycle peaks (see Table 4-3), we see that the downward trend was reversed between 1929 and 1937, and again between 1953 and 1957 and 1957–1960, as incomplete recoveries failed to bring production back to optimum rates of capacity utilization. This is also true, though to

---

1. Robert Solow of the Directors' Reading Committee points out that the employed human capital estimates may be overstated to the extent that the average education of employed persons is greater than that of nonemployed persons of working age. It is not obvious, however, that the *movements* of employed human capital would be biased.

a lesser degree, when real human stocks are adjusted by the proportions embodied in the employed work force.

It is also evident that the capital coefficients have invariably increased between the peak and trough years of all cycles shown. This is to be expected, since real stocks generally continue to rise during contractions, while production drops or rises only very little. Significant increases in the capital coefficients occurred during the contractions of the 1930s. They were very small since World War II, reflecting the mildness of postwar contractions. The smallest rise in the real capital coefficient (little more than one per cent on a total basis) was in 1960–1961, when real product rose modestly.

Finally, it is of some interest to look at the movements in the average real gross capital coefficients in relation to the incremental coefficients. For this purpose we have computed the average coefficients for the average stocks and product over successive business cycles (measured from peak to peak) and the incremental coefficients as ratios of changes in the two variables between successive business cycle averages. This abstracts from cyclical and erratic movements,

Table 4-3. *Real Total Gross Capital Coefficients in Peak and Trough Years of Business Cycles, 1929–1969, U.S. National Economy*

	REAL TOTAL GNW/ REAL ADJ. GNP		REAL TOTAL GNW EMPLOYED/ REAL ADJ. GNP	
Year	Peaks	Troughs	Peaks	Troughs
1929	10.5		8.2	
1933		15.2		11.2
1937	11.5		8.7	
1938		12.2		9.3
1948	9.4		7.5	
1949		9.7		7.6
1953	8.8		7.0	
1954		9.2		7.2
1957	9.1		7.2	
1958		9.5		7.4
1960	9.3		7.2	
1961		9.4		7.3
1969	8.4		6.6	

Table 4-4. U.S. National Economy: Capital Coefficients, Average and Incremental, Business Cycle Averages, 1929–1969

Years	Total Capital Coefficients		Tangible Nonhuman Capital Coefficients		Tangible Human Capital Coefficients		Intangible Capital Coefficients	
	Average	Incremental	Average	Incremental	Average	Incremental	Average	Incremental
1929–37	12.6		6.8		2.6		3.2	
1937–48	9.3	4.3	4.9	1.9	1.8	.8	2.6	1.7
1948–53	9.0	8.1	4.6	3.6	1.7	1.3	2.8	3.2
1953–57	8.9	8.2	4.5	4.0	1.6	1.3	2.8	2.9
1957–60	9.2	12.4	4.6	5.8	1.7	2.1	2.9	4.5
1960–69	8.7	7.1	4.2	2.9	1.6	1.2	2.9	3.0

NOTE: The "incremental" coefficients were computed as the ratio of the changes from the previous cycle average in real gross capital and in real adjusted GNP.

which impart instability particularly to the incremental capital coefficients. Changes in the coefficients reflect changes in output and capital
mix, factor substitutions, and possible changes in underlying production functions.

The total real gross capital coefficient for the national economy
dropped in every subperiod except 1957–1960, reflecting the fact that
incremental coefficients were lower than average coefficients. (See
Table 4-4.) The lowest incremental coefficient was in 1937–1948 relative to 1929–1937, reflecting the substantial slack in the economy
during much of the earlier period that permitted a greater proportionate
expansion in output than in capital and capacity. The highest incremental coefficient in 1957–1960 relative to 1953–1957 reflected the continued rapid expansion of investment and capital despite a slow rise in
output and an increasing slowdown in the economy. Over the period
under review, the average of the incremental coefficients was about 8.0,
compared with an average coefficient of 8.7 in the final subperiod. This
suggests that further declines in the average capital coefficient will be
limited and gradual, unless there is a significant change in the incremental productivity of total capital in the future.

The same observations apply to the tangible components of total
capital shown in the table. In the case of real intangible capital, the
incremental coefficients have been quite close to the average coefficients (although more variable, of course), so that the average ratios
have essentially remained on a plateau, with a slight upward tilt. If this
continues, further declines in the total capital coefficients and corresponding increases in capital productivity will obviously depend on the
incremental tangible capital coefficients remaining below the average
coefficients.

Real Total Gross Stocks, by Sector

Our discussion of sectoral behavior is confined to total real gross stocks,
but the picture would not differ much for stocks in current dollars or on
a net basis. The overall capital price deflators show much the same
trends (with prices in the personal sector rising less and those in the
public sector rising more than business and average prices), and gross-
net capital ratios have not changed significantly by sector. Also, real
gross capital coefficients are generally considered to be more significant in capacity and productivity analysis.

Over the period 1929–1969 as a whole, growth in real capital stocks in the business and rest-of-world sectors was far slower than the 2.8 per cent average annual rate of the total. Personal sector capital grew somewhat faster, and public capital, much faster (see Table 4-5). Consequently, business capital, one-third of the national total at the beginning of the period, dropped below 22 per cent in 1969, and American capital located abroad fell from 1.2 to 0.7 per cent. At the same time, personal sector capital rose from about 53 to 56 per cent, and public capital, from about 13 to almost 22 per cent.

In terms of the two major subperiods, most of the relative decline in business capital was completed by 1948; the relative expansion in public capital had taken place before then, followed by a slight relative decline during 1948–1969, while most of the relative increase in personal sector capital took place after 1948. The relative downtrend in U.S. net capital holdings abroad was evident in both subperiods.

It is obvious from the foregoing that only public sector capital grew in relation to the 3.4 per cent average annual growth rate in real (adjusted) GNP. The capital coefficients of the other sectors declined, with total real GNP used as the denominator. It is more meaningful, however, to relate real gross stocks of total capital by sector to the real gross product originating in each. Then the changes in sectoral shares of capital can be explained statistically by changes in sector shares of real GNP and changes in the sector capital coefficients relative to that of the economy.

Looking first at the shares of GNP originating in each sector (Table 4-6), one sees that the government share rose markedly between 1929 and 1948 and then subsided, but was still well above the 1929 level in 1969. The personal sector share fell a bit in the first major subperiod, but then rose somewhat above the 1929 level by 1969. The business share fell throughout, whereas the drop in the foreign sector share was over by 1948. (See Chart 4-2.)

The capital coefficient of the public sector was almost the same in 1969 as in 1929, in contrast to the 20 per cent drop in the overall capital coefficient; this relative increase magnified the effect the expanded public share of real GNP had on the public share of capital stock. The capital coefficient of the personal sector dropped a bit more than the overall coefficient, but not enough to prevent the sector's increased GNP share from showing up in an increased share in total capital as well. On the other hand, a marked relative decline in the business sector capital coefficient accentuated the effect of the decline in the sector's share of GNP on its capital stock share, and the same was true of the foreign sector.

Table 4-5. *Total Gross Capital Stocks and Product by Sector, Average Annual Rates of Change and Percentage Distributions, U.S. National Economy, 1929, 1948, and 1969*

	Total	Business	Personal	Government	Rest of World
A. Average Annual Percentage Rates of Change					
Real total GNW					
1929–69	2.8	1.7	3.0	4.2	1.5
1929–48	2.1	0.2	2.2	5.2	1.4
1948–69	3.4	3.1	3.7	3.2	1.5
Real adj. GNP					
1929–69	3.4	3.2	3.6	4.2	2.7
1929–48	2.7	2.5	1.5	5.9	
1948–69	4.0	3.9	5.5	2.7	5.9
B. Percentage Distributions					
Real total GNW					
1929	100.0	33.2	52.8	12.9	1.2
1948	100.0	23.2	53.1	22.7	1.0
1969	100.0	21.7	56.0	21.7	0.7
Real adj. GNP					
1929	100.0	73.9	17.6	7.9	0.6
1948	100.0	71.3	14.3	14.2	0.3
1969	100.0	69.8	19.0	10.8	0.4

Table 4-6. *Total Gross Capital Stocks and Product, by Sector, Billions of 1958 Dollars, and Capital Coefficients*

	Total	Business	Personal	Government	Rest of World
A. Billions of 1958 Dollars					
Total real GNW					
1929	2,647.6	878.1	1,397.5	340.7	31.3
1948	3,963.6	918.8	2,104.9	898.8	41.1
1969	8,069.6	1,747.6	4,518.3	1,748.2	55.8
Real adj. GNP originating					
1929	253.5	187.4	44.6	20.1	1.4
1948	417.8	297.7	59.7	59.2	1.2
1969	960.6	670.7	182.2	103.7	4.0
B. Total Capital Coefficients					
Ratios, GNW/GNP					
1929	10.5	4.5	31.3	17.0	22.4
1948	9.5	3.1	35.2	15.2	34.2
1969	8.4	2.6	24.8	16.9	14.0

Chart 4-2. *Real Gross National Wealth, by Sector, Per Cent Distribution: 1929, 1948, 1969*

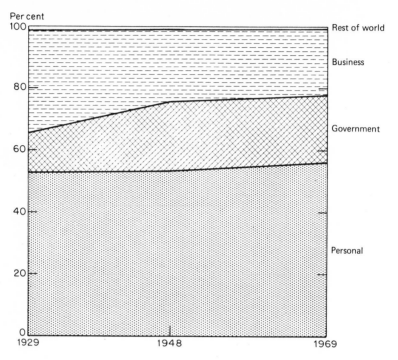

Real Total Stocks, by Type

Here our discussion relates only to the U.S. domestic economy, since net foreign assets cannot be broken down by type. The first thing that may strike the reader in looking at the distributions by type of capital presented in Table 4-7 is the substantially faster growth in intangible capital than in tangible capital. Over the 1929–1969 period, real total gross stocks of intangible capital grew at an average rate of 3.8 per cent, compared with a 2.4 per cent rate for tangible capital. The growth rates of each accelerated during 1948–1969 from the earlier subperiod, but the point differential remained about the same. Once capital is recombined into human and nonhuman categories, the former shows a 3.1 per cent annual growth rate, as against a 2.5 per cent rate for the latter, with human capital including most of the fast-growing intangibles.

If these rates are translated into partial factor productivity ratios, given the 3.4 per cent annual growth rate of real product, it follows that

Table 4-7. *Total Gross Capital Stocks, by Major Types, U.S. Domestic Economy*

Year	Total Gross Capital	INTANGIBLES			TANGIBLES		
		Total	Human	Nonhuman (R&D)	Total	Human	Nonhuman
		A. Total Gross Capital Stocks (billions of current dollars)					
1929	1186.2	275.0	272.5	2.6	911.1	290.4	620.7
1948	2974.6	803.4	784.2	19.2	2171.2	634.1	1537.1
1969	10837.4	4175.9	3889.9	286.0	6661.5	1650.9	5010.6
		B. Implicit Price Deflators (1958 = 100)					
1929	45.3	43.1	43.1	37.7	46.1	57.0	42.3
1948	75.8	68.9	69.1	60.8	78.8	85.3	76.3
1969	135.2	148.6	148.9	144.4	128.0	119.0	131.3
		C. Total Real Gross Capital Stocks (billions of 1958 dollars)					
1929	2616.3	638.7	631.9	6.9	1977.6	509.7	1467.9
1948	3922.6	1166.2	1134.6	31.6	2756.4	743.0	2013.4
1969	8014.1	2810.8	2612.7	198.1	5203.3	1387.3	3816.0
		D. Average Annual Percentage Rates of Change in Total Real Gross Stocks					
1929–69	2.8	3.8	3.6	8.7	2.4	2.5	2.4
1929–48	2.2	3.2	3.1	8.3	1.8	2.0	1.7
1948–69	3.5	4.3	4.1	9.1	3.1	3.0	3.1

the tangible capital productivity ratio rose at an average annual rate of 1.0 per cent, while the ratio of real product to real intangible capital fell by 0.4 per cent. The ratio of real product to real human capital grew 0.3 per cent a year, compared with 0.9 per cent for nonhuman capital productivity, on average.

Looking at the composition of the intangible category, we note that nonhuman capital resulting from research and development grew much faster than the human component, but that the latter had a much larger weight. Within the human intangibles, capital in the education and training and health areas grew at a much faster rate than that resulting from mobility outlays. (See Table 4-8.)

The human and nonhuman tangibles showed about the same rates of growth. Within the latter, equipment had the highest growth rate, followed, in descending order, by inventory stocks, structures, and land. The land factor reflected changes in the pattern of land use and the inclusion of the new states of Alaska and Hawaii in 1959 (which had little influence on other types of capital, however).

In line with the differential growth rates, real intangible stocks

Table 4-8. Total Gross Capital Stocks: Detail of Human Intangibles and Nonhuman Tangibles, U.S. Domestic Economy

Year	HUMAN INTANGIBLES				NONHUMAN TANGIBLES				
	Total	Education & Training	Health	Mobility	Total	Land	Structures	Equipment	Inventories
A. Total Gross Capital Stocks (billions of current dollars)									
1929	272.5	225.8	31.2	15.4	620.7	111.5	304.0	143.8	61.5
1948	784.2	674.0	83.1	27.1	1537.1	197.9	779.2	419.4	140.6
1969	3889.9	3331.4	460.0	98.5	5010.6	686.8	2520.6	1447.7	355.4
B. Implicit Price Deflators (1958 = 100)									
1929	43.1	42.7	47.2	42.3	42.3	41.7	37.8	50.6	54.5
1948	69.1	69.1	69.7	68.4	75.6	70.1	77.2	73.6	92.6
1969	148.9	148.6	153.1	138.3	131.3	169.1	141.9	110.6	109.7
C. Total Real Gross Capital Stocks (billions of 1958 dollars)									
1929	631.9	529.3	66.1	36.4	1467.9	267.2	803.6	284.2	112.8
1948	1134.6	975.7	119.3	39.6	2013.4	282.4	1009.3	570.0	151.8
1969	2612.7	2241.2	300.4	71.2	3816.0	406.2	1776.5	1309.4	323.9
D. Average Annual Percentage Rates of Change in Real Total Gross Stocks									
1929–69	3.6	3.7	3.9	1.7	2.4	1.1	2.0	3.9	2.7
1929–48	3.1	3.3	3.2	0.4	1.7	0.3	1.2	3.7	1.6
1948–69	4.1	4.0	4.5	2.8	3.1	1.7	2.7	4.0	3.7

Chart 4-3. *Real Gross Domestic Wealth by Major Type, Per Cent Distribution: 1929, 1948, 1969*

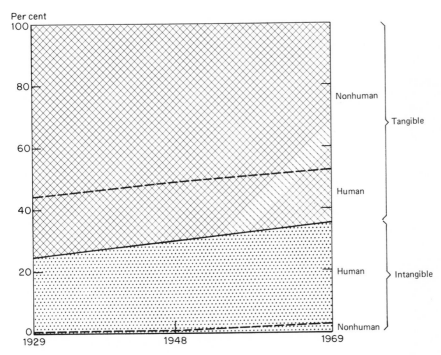

grew from under one-fourth of the total in 1929 to more than one-third in 1969. (See Chart 4-3.) In current dollars the growth is relatively greater, due to a faster increase in the price deflator for intangibles than in that for tangibles. Also, because of a faster rising price index, nonhuman tangibles show a smaller drop in current than in constant prices, while the converse is true of tangible human equipment. (See Table 4-9.)

Within the human intangible category (Table 4-10), education is by far the largest grouping, accounting for more than 85 per cent in 1969, compared with under 12 per cent for health and about 2.5 per cent for mobility. Both of the first two percentages were a bit higher than in 1929, whereas the mobility proportion dropped.

Within the nonhuman tangible category, the land proportion dropped drastically in both current and constant dollar distributions, particularly the latter. The stock of structures held at near 50 per cent of the current dollar total, but fell relatively in the constant dollar distribution. Equipment rose in both the current and constant dollar distributions, particularly the former. Inventory stocks rose as a percentage of

Table 4-9. *Total Gross Capital Stocks, by Major Types, U.S. Domestic Economy, Percentage Distributions*

Year	Total Gross Capital	INTANGIBLES			TANGIBLES		
		Total	Human	Nonhuman (R&D)	Total	Human	Nonhuman
A. Percentage Composition of Real Total Gross Stocks							
1929	100.0	24.4	24.2	0.3	75.6	19.5	56.1
1948	100.0	29.7	28.9	0.8	70.3	18.9	51.3
1969	100.0	35.1	32.6	2.5	64.9	17.3	47.6
B. Percentage Composition of Current Dollar Total Gross Stocks							
1929	100.0	23.2	23.0	0.2	76.8	24.5	52.3
1948	100.0	27.0	26.4	0.6	73.0	21.3	51.7
1969	100.0	38.5	35.9	2.6	61.5	15.2	46.2
C. Percentage Composition of Current Dollar Total Gross Stocks, by Sector							
1929							
Business	100.0	7.2	6.8	0.4	92.8	0.0	92.8
Personal	100.0	26.9	26.9	0.0	73.1	42.2	30.9
Government	100.0	47.3	46.6	0.7	52.7	0.0	52.7
1969							
Business	100.0	16.6	12.7	3.9	83.4	0.0	83.4
Personal	100.0	40.6	40.4	0.2	59.4	27.8	31.6
Government	100.0	53.8	46.7	7.2	46.2	0.0	46.2
D. Percentage Composition of Current Dollar Total Gross Employed Stocks							
1929	100.0	17.7	17.4	0.3	82.3	13.2	69.1
1948	100.0	21.6	20.7	0.8	78.4	12.6	65.8
1969	100.0	32.7	29.3	3.4	67.3	8.5	58.8

the constant dollar aggregate, but fell somewhat in the current dollar distribution.

In the percentage distributions of gross capital *stocks employed,* the human components are smaller, since it is for this component alone that total capital is adjusted downward to that actually available for productive activity. (Since nonhuman capital does not have an alternative use, it is considered available for productive employment all the time.)

Sections C of Tables 4-9 and 4-10 show the per cent distributions by type and by sector (of finance) for the years 1929 and 1969. It is striking that the intangible capital proportion was much higher in government than in the other sectors, and that it was lowest in business.

Table 4-10. *Total Gross Capital Stocks: Detail of Human Intangibles and Nonhuman Tangibles, U.S. Domestic Economy, Percentage Distributions*

Year	Human Intangibles				Nonhuman Tangibles				
	Total	Education & Training	Health	Mobility	Total	Land	Structures	Equipment	Inventories
A. Percentage Composition of Real Total Gross Stocks									
1929	100.0	83.8	10.5	5.8	100.0	18.2	54.7	19.4	7.7
1948	100.0	86.0	10.5	3.5	100.0	14.0	50.1	28.3	7.5
1969	100.0	85.8	11.5	2.7	100.0	10.6	46.6	34.3	8.5
B. Percentage Composition of Current Dollar Total Gross Stocks									
1929	100.0	82.9	11.4	5.7	100.0	18.0	49.0	23.2	9.9
1948	100.0	85.9	10.6	3.5	100.0	12.9	50.7	27.3	9.1
1969	100.0	85.6	11.8	2.5	100.0	13.7	50.3	28.9	7.1
C. Percentage Composition of Current Dollar Total Gross Stocks, by Sector									
1929									
Business	100.0	93.0	2.5	4.5	100.0	23.7	47.5	17.0	11.8
Personal	100.0	79.0	13.3	7.6	100.0	6.7	46.2	36.9	10.1
Government	100.0	90.2	9.5	0.3	100.0	24.0	64.4	11.5	0.1
1969									
Business	100.0	94.4	3.5	2.1	100.0	20.1	42.6	26.8	10.4
Personal	100.0	82.4	13.9	3.6	100.0	9.3	49.7	34.7	6.2
Government	100.0	89.9	9.7	0.4	100.0	10.1	64.0	23.0	2.9

But government intangible capital had the lowest relative growth rate over the period (despite a relatively rapid growth of government R&D capital), while business had the highest rate.

Conversely, the tangibles comprised the greatest proportion of business and the smallest of government capital. Although the personal sector was in the middle with respect to total tangibles, it was the only sector financing human tangibles, and its proportion of tangible nonhuman capital alone, at around 31 per cent, was the lowest of the sectors.

A further look at the nonhuman tangible breakdowns shows that only the personal sector increased its share of land and structures. As to equipment, both business and government increased their proportions, while the personal sector's percentage fell slightly. Inventory proportions declined in both the business and personal sectors, but rose in governments. Within the human intangibles category, sector proportions of education and training and health rose on the whole at the expense of the mobility percentage, except for the government sector, which shows a slight drop in the education-training proportion and a relative rise in that of mobility.

5

Total Capital and Economic Growth

An attempt is made via a growth accounting exercise to quantify the contributions of various factors to the growth of real product in the national economy and the business sector.[1] Following this discussion we analyze the implications of the increase in total capital productivity for rates of return on total capital when both income and capital are expressed in terms of current dollars. Rates of return on human and nonhuman capital are considered separately and in combination.

Contribution of Total and Intangible Capital to Economic Growth

The analysis in this section stems from the hypothesis suggested by Schultz and others, as recounted in chapter 1.[2] To state the analytical framework in its simplest form, income or product (Y) may be viewed as the product of the aggregate stock of total capital (K) and all the other

1. This section follows the general approach pioneered by Edward F. Denison, most recently elucidated in his *Accounting for United States Economic Growth, 1929–1969*, Washington, D. C., The Brookings Institution, 1974.
2. For further discussions of the concept of capital as income-producing capacity, see John W. Kendrick, "Theoretical Aspects of the Measurement of Capital," American Economic Association *Papers and Proceedings,* May 1961; and R. H. Parker and G. C. Harcourt, eds., *Readings in the Concept and Measurement of Income,* Cambridge at the University Press, 1969.

111

"residual" forces (R) which affect the productivity of aggregate capital. "R" can be computed as the quotient of Y and K to satisfy the identity

$$Y = R \cdot K. \tag{1}$$

When the income and stock variables are measured in current prices, R may be viewed as an average rate of return. When Y and K are measured in constant prices, R may be thought of as an average physical productivity variable reflecting the net effect of the noncapital forces that affect the movements of real product, discussed later. The identity may be further elaborated to highlight the separate contributions of tangible capital (K_1)—human and nonhuman (measured without allowance for quality change)—and the embodied intangible capital (K_2), as well as the net effect of the residual forces, as follows:

$$Y = K_1 \cdot (1 + K_2/K_1) \cdot R. \tag{2}$$

This formulation opens the way to estimating the contribution of intangible capital per unit of tangible capital to total tangible factor productivity, and thus testing the hypothesis I put forward in 1956 (see Preface). It would also provide a test of the Schultz hypothesis, although Schultz was referring to the growth of intangible human capital alone, whereas I include intangible nonhuman capital resulting from R&D as well, and place greater stress on the possible influence of residual, noncapital forces (see below). In this formulation, one divides both sides of equations (1) or (2) (with both Y and K expressed in constant prices) by the real stock of intangible capital:

$$Y/K_2 = K/K_2 \cdot R. \tag{3}$$

This formulation abstracts from changes in utilization rates of the real human and nonhuman stocks, although such adjustments could be added if wanted. A general limitation of all these formulations in terms of real stocks rather than services of the factors is the implicit assumption that the contribution to output (income) of each type of capital is proportionate to its value, i.e., that the productivity or net rates of return on the various types of capital are equal. We shall discuss this limitation further below. It should also be noted that, when product and capital are related on a gross basis, the relationship can be affected by changes in the capital mix with respect to durability.

Looking at 1929 and 1969 (Table 5-1), we note that real total gross capital stocks grew at an average annual rate of 2.4 per cent in the private domestic business economy, compared with a 3.4 per cent

Table 5-1. Major Components of U.S. Economic Growth: Average Annual Percentage Rates of Change, 1929–1969 and Subperiods

	Private Domestic Business Economy			National Economy		
	1929–69	1929–48	1948–69	1929–69	1929–48	1948–69
Real adjusted product	3.4	2.7	4.0	3.4	2.7	4.0
Real tangible capital	1.7	0.6	2.6	2.4	1.8	3.1
Real intangible capital	3.8	3.3	4.3	3.8	3.2	4.3
Real total capital	2.4	1.4	3.3	2.8	2.2	3.5
Ratio: Real total capital/ real tangible capital	0.7	0.8	0.6	0.4	0.4	0.4
Real tangible factor productivity	1.7	2.1	1.4	0.9	1.0	0.9
Total capital productivity (Residual factors)	1.0	1.3	0.7	0.5	0.6	0.5

NOTE: The capital estimates represent capital employed, but without adjustment for rates of utilization.

growth rate in real gross product. Thus, total capital accounted for about 70 per cent of the economic growth rate, while the 1.0 per cent a year rate of increase in the residual factors comprised by "total capital productivity" accounted for the other 30 per cent.

During the subperiod 1929–1948, real total capital accounted for a somewhat smaller proportion of the slower rate of economic growth than over the 40-year period as a whole. Between 1948 and 1969, on the other hand, it accounted for a higher proportion—over 80 per cent—of the faster growth rate.

In regard to the national economy portion of Table 5-1, it is evident that real total capital accounted for an even higher proportion of aggregate economic growth than in the private domestic business economy. This was true in both subperiods and the entire 40-year span. As observed earlier, the lesser importance of total capital productivity in the economy as a whole was due to the method of estimating real product originating in the nonbusiness sectors without allowance for productivity advance.

Although real intangible capital grew at a much higher rate than real tangible capital stocks, its relative size was much smaller (about one-third in 1929), so that the contribution of its growth was smaller than that of the tangible capital—0.7 and 1.7 percentage points, respectively, over 1929–1969, as shown in the table for the private domestic business economy. This statement, again, assumes that the marginal productivity of the two categories of capital was the same, an assumption that will be examined later.

It is also of interest to consider the contribution of real intangible capital stock expansion to the growth of total tangible capital productivity. The latter variable is obtained by dividing real gross product by the real stocks of tangible capital, human and nonhuman. As shown in Table 5-1 for the business economy, productivity (item 6) rose at an average annual rate of 1.7 per cent from 1929 to 1969. This rate is lower than the 2.3 per cent reported in *Postwar Productivity Trends in the United States, 1948–1969*, since there labor input was measured in terms of weighted man-hours worked, which both rose less than the real stock of tangible human capital used in the measure shown here and had a larger weight. The contribution of intangible capital is measured by the growth in the ratio of real total capital (including intangible) to real tangible capital, assuming equal marginal productivity in the two types of capital.

Via this approach, the relative growth of real intangible capital contributed 0.7 percentage point, or 41 per cent, to the 1.7 per cent growth rate of total tangible factor productivity over 1929–1969. The 0.8 per cent rate of growth represented a somewhat smaller proportion of a

Chart 5-1. *Components of Economic Growth, Average Annual Percentage Rates of Change*

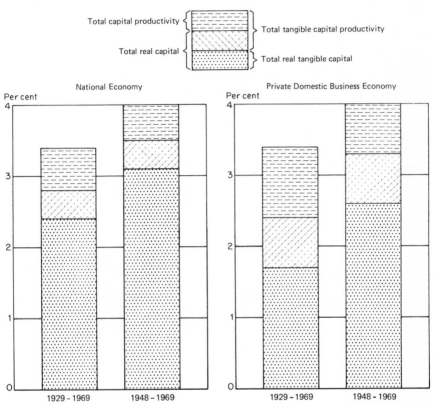

higher rate of productivity advance from 1929 to 1948, and the 0.6 per cent rate from 1948 to 1969, a somewhat greater proportion of a lower rate of productivity advance. (See Chart 5-1.)

From these calculations it would appear that other, noncapital factors accounted for more than half of the increase in total tangible factor productivity since 1929. Apart from the cyclical influence of changing rates of capacity utilization, which would have little or no influence on comparisons between the peak years 1929 and 1969, the chief noncapital factors may be listed as follows: (1) economies of scale; (2) improved economic efficiency, i.e., a pattern of production conforming more closely to the community's preferences due to institutional and other changes; (3) changing average inherent quality of natural and human resources, including the effect of a changing mix; (4) changing efficiency of labor relative to the potential of given technologies, including the effect of a downward trend in average hours worked per week and per year, and changing values and incentives; (5) in the case of the business economy, an increase in unmeasured governmental inputs relative to real private costs (inputs); and (6) possible errors in the estimates and limitations of methodology.

It is beyond the scope of this study to attempt quantifying the individual and net effects of these forces. As roughly estimated by Denison, however, some of them have had a significant positive effect. Yet, as specified in an earlier analysis by the author,[3] Denison attributed a greater relative effect on growth and on tangible factor productivity (as we measure it) than we have to increases in average education and advances in knowledge.

It is quite possible (and, I suspect, probable) that we have underestimated the contribution of intangible capital formation to productivity advance and thus to economic growth in the United States. In the first place, the magnitude and growth rate of real intangible capital may be understated by our estimates. The probability of some upward bias in the price deflators for intangible investments has already been alluded to, which imparts downward bias to the real investment and stock estimates. Some intangible investments and stock are not included in the estimates, such as informal R&D, and learning-by-doing. It must also be noted that our formal R&D stock represents the pool of knowledge which is drawn on for current production, but does not include the accumulated R&D embodied in the stock of tangible nonhuman capital used in current production. Inclusion of the latter would raise the amount of intangible capital, but it is not certain what it would do to the rate of growth.

Secondly, the growth of intangible stocks in relation to tangible stocks, in real terms, does not tell the whole story. Even if the two types of capital grew at the same rate, productivity would probably continue to rise. The annual R&D that replaces previous with new productive knowledge would increase the productivity of new capital goods and of retrained workers even if it merely replaced capital goods and workers retired during the year.

Further, the marginal productivity and rate of return for intangible capital may be higher than for tangible capital. If so, this would proportionately increase the estimated contribution of intangible capital to growth. For example, assuming that the rate of return on intangible capital was twice that on tangible capital in 1929 (instead of equal on a

3. See John W. Kendrick, "The Treatment of Intangible Resources as Capital," *Review of Income and Wealth*, March 1972, pp. 109–125 (especially pp. 123–124). Note that Denison did not estimate the contribution of investments in health, safety, and mobility separately.

stock one-third the size, but one with a 2.1 per cent higher average annual growth rate), then the relative growth of real intangible capital would have contributed 1.4 of the 1.7 percentage point growth rate in total tangible capital productivity, or 82 per cent. The computations in the following section of this chapter substantiate the view that the return on intangible capital has been higher than on tangible capital; they show rates of return on human capital consistently above those on nonhuman capital (in 1929 the gross rate was approximately 27 per cent higher), and a much higher ratio of intangible to total capital for human than for nonhuman capital. If we assume the same differential between rates of return on intangible and tangible capital, the relative growth of the former in real terms would have contributed 0.9 of the 1.7 percentage point growth rate in total tangible capital productivity, or more than half.

Also, as stressed by Nelson,[4] growth accounting assumes a high degree of substitutability among inputs, whereas there is actually a high degree of complementarity in the growth process. For example, technological progress resulting from R&D and its embodiment in tangible capital is indispensable in increasing demand for more highly educated workers and thus in sustaining the rate of return on an expanding volume of educational activity. And all of the intangible investments help to sustain the tangible investment demand curve, so that capital outlays can absorb the rising volume of saving generated by a growing economy without the decline in rates of return predicted by Keynes. It is the interaction of the various inputs in the growth process that are difficult to quantify and to partition among individual factors.

In addition to the growth accounting exercise described above, we also experimented with statistically fitting production functions of the Cobb-Douglas and other (nonhomogeneous) varieties. The dependent variable was real gross product (private domestic business economy), and the independent variables were real gross utilized stocks of nonhuman tangibles, nonhuman intangibles, human tangibles, and human intangibles—separately and combined into total tangibles and intangibles and, alternatively, into human and nonhuman stocks. The coefficients of correlation were generally very high, reflecting good predictive power of the equations. But the output elasticities indicated by the coefficients frequently were not plausible, and were unstable depending on the specification of the function. For that reason we do not report the results here. It should be noted, however, that the nonhomogeneous functions yielded better results than the homogeneous Cobb-Douglas function.

4. See Richard R. Nelson, "Recent Exercises in Growth Accounting: New Understanding or Dead End?," *American Economic Review*, June 1973.

Rates of Return on Capital

In order to obtain the measures of capital productivity discussed above, product is related to capital in real constant dollar terms. When product (income) is related to capital in current prices, however, the result can be viewed as the percentage rate of return on capital. The difference in movement between the productivity and rate of return measures is due significantly to the relative movements of the implicit price deflators for product and capital. Thus, in chapter 4 we saw that total capital productivity (the reciprocal of the capital coefficient) rose by an average 0.5 per cent a year in the domestic economy from 1929 to 1969, while the implicit price deflator for capital rose by 0.4 per cent a year more than the product price deflator. Consequently, the ratio of product to capital in current prices rose by only 0.1 per cent a year on the average. This is the chief reason why the rates of return on total capital discussed in this section show relatively little change between 1929 and 1969, in contrast to the significant increases in average capital productivity discussed above. There are, however, several other adjustments necessary in order to make explicit the rate of return implications of the capital productivity estimates, although their net effect is small compared with the movement in relative prices of capital and product.

First, from the gross product estimates in current prices, indirect business taxes (less subsidies) and the statistical discrepancy must be deducted in order to obtain gross factor income. Also, in order to obtain estimates of net as well as of gross rates of return, as presented below, capital consumption allowances must be deducted from gross factor income and divided by net rather than gross capital stocks. Actually, since capital consumption reserves and allowances have not changed much as percentages of gross stocks and gross product, respectively, gross and net rates of return show much the same movements, although the levels differ somewhat, particularly as to the human and nonhuman components.

Finally, to be consistent with property returns (which are calculated after allowance for maintenance expenses), we have also deducted estimates of the maintenance costs of human beings from labor compensation, gross and net of depreciation. As described in the appendix in detail, human maintenance cost calculations are based on minimum budget estimates for families of various sizes, farm and nonfarm, and for institutional populations, with allowance for increases in average planes of living over the period. Since personal consumption expenditures have increased less than national income and labor compensation, labor returns less maintenance costs have risen more than gross returns, although the levels and derived rates are much lower, of course.

Since the net property return on nonhuman capital in the nonbusiness sectors was imputed by applying interest rates to the stock estimates, we concentrate our analysis on the private business sector, where the compensation estimates are independent of the stock estimates. We shall also look further at returns in the total domestic economy, since there at least the labor returns are independent of the human stock estimates.

AVERAGE RATES OF RETURN

As shown in Table 5-2 for peak cycle years, the average rate of return on total gross capital employed in the private business sector was 10.2 per cent in 1929. The lower return in 1937 reflects the less than full recovery of that year: even though human capital is measured only for the employed work force, return is affected by hours of work, and the nonhuman capital stock is all counted as employed, so that average

Table 5-2. *Gross and Net Rates of Return on Capital Employed, by Major Type, U.S. Domestic Economy and Business Sector, Peak Years, 1929–1969* (percentage)

	Gross			Net		
Year	Total	Human	Nonhuman	Total	Human	Nonhuman
	Private Domestic Business Economy					
1929	10.2	11.7	9.2	10.0	10.1	10.0
1937	9.3	11.3	7.8	9.2	9.6	8.9
1948	12.1	12.2	12.0	13.4	12.6	14.2
1953	12.1	13.5	10.8	13.1	14.8	11.4
1957	11.4	12.7	10.1	11.6	13.4	9.9
1960	11.0	12.3	9.7	11.0	12.9	9.2
1969	10.8	11.7	9.9	10.6	12.2	8.9
	Total Domestic Economy					
1929	9.1	11.5	8.1	8.3	9.8	7.6
1937	8.2	11.2	6.8	7.5	9.4	6.5
1948	9.3	11.7	8.1	9.1	11.8	7.7
1953	9.5	12.7	7.9	9.2	13.3	6.9
1957	9.2	11.9	7.8	8.3	12.0	6.4
1960	9.1	11.6	7.7	8.1	11.6	6.2
1969	9.4	11.1	8.3	8.5	11.2	6.7

rates of utilization affect rates of return. The highest rates of return were realized in 1948 and 1953, at 12.1 per cent. Later the rate of return declined slowly over subsequent cycle peaks. The 10.8 per cent return in 1969 was only modestly above the rate reached forty years earlier.

The rate of return on human capital remained above that on nonhuman and total capital throughout the period, although the difference was minor when the latter peaked in 1948. The difference was smaller in 1969 than in 1929, since the rate of return on human capital was the same in both years (at 11.7 per cent), while the rate for nonhuman capital rose (from 9.2 per cent to 9.9 per cent).

Note also that the decline in the rate of return between 1929 and 1937 was sharper for nonhuman capital than for human capital, for reasons indicated above. Further, while the rate of return on nonhuman capital was at a high in 1948, the rate for human capital peaked in 1953. Finally, whereas the latter continued its gradual decline, the former was slightly higher in 1969 than in 1960, possibly due to higher rates of utilization of fixed plant capacity in the later year. In fact, adjustment for differences in utilization rates would probably make the rates of return on nonhuman capital at least as stable as those on human capital.

On a net basis, the average return on total capital was 0.2 percentage point below the gross rate of return in both 1929 and 1969. The close correspondence between the rates on gross and net bases indicates that the ratio of annual depreciation to accumulated depreciation reserves was not greatly different from the ratio of net factor income (excluding maintenance) to the value of net capital stock. (See Chart 5-2.)

The pattern of movement of the net rates of return is similar to that of the gross rate, despite possible changes in the average durability of capital. Net rates rose above gross rates in the early postwar period, however, peaking in 1948 at 13.4 per cent. The net rate then declined gradually over the successive cycle peaks to 10.6 per cent in 1969, modestly above 1929, like the gross rate.

Taking rates of return on human and nonhuman capital separately, we note that here the pattern of net rates deviated somewhat from the pattern of the gross rates. In the case of human capital, the net rate of return at 10.1 per cent was well below the gross rate of 11.7 per cent, and quite close to the 10.0 per cent rate of return on nonhuman capital in 1929. By 1948, the net rate at 12.6 per cent exceeded the gross rate and remained higher, although the net rate also declined gradually from its peak in 1953 in subsequent cycle peak years. It should be recalled that no imputation was made for the value of leisure time in calculating the returns on human capital. On the other hand, human

Chart 5-2.   *Net Rates of Return on Total Capital, by Type, Peak Years, 1929–1969, U.S. Private Domestic Business Economy*

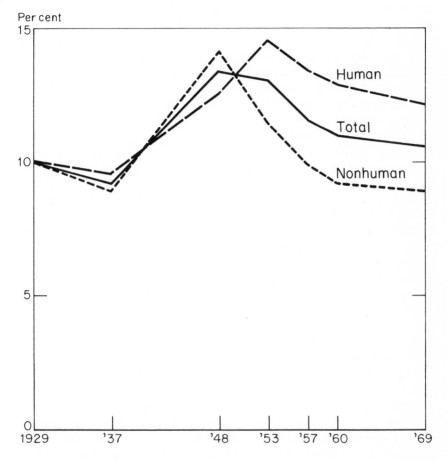

labor may involve disutilities which are not involved in the use of nonhuman capital.[5]

Conversely, the net rate of return on nonhuman capital was above the gross rate in 1929 and remained above it through 1953. After the peak of 1948, however, it fell more than the gross rate, and dropped below it in 1957 and succeeding peak years. The 1969 net rate of return on nonhuman capital, at 8.9 per cent, was below the 1929 rate, whereas the gross rate of return of 9.9 per cent was above the corresponding 1929 rate.

5. I am indebted to Robert Eisner, member of the staff reading committee, for these observations.

It is of interest to examine some variant return measures we do not deem significant enough to be featured in the text table. First, consider the gross rate of return on human capital *before* deduction of estimated maintenance costs. In 1929, the gross return, at 22.1 per cent, was almost twice as great as the return after adjustment for maintenance and remained at much the same level during the postwar period 1948 through 1957. Thereafter, however, it declined gradually to 19.7 per cent in 1969, while the adjusted rate that year was the same as in 1929. The relative rise in the adjusted rate, as noted earlier, is due to the smaller increase in consumption per capita—used to adjust maintenance estimates—than in income per capita. The fact that the adjusted rate is much closer to the rate of return on nonhuman capital helps support the theoretical arguments for adjusting human as well as property returns to exclude maintenance expenses.

Another variant is the rate of return on "utilized" human capital. Here, in addition to eliminating that portion embodied in persons not formally employed, we further adjusted the human capital denominator to the proportion of total available hours at work. This results in a much higher gross rate of return for 1929—26.9 per cent (after adjustment for maintenance). The rate of return was even higher in the postwar period—at 32.5 per cent in 1969—because of the decline in average hours worked per year after 1929. But since we did not adjust nonhuman capital for percentage of time utilized, it is not symmetrical to make that adjustment for human capital. Also, it can be argued theoretically that calculations should be, and are, made on the basis of returns to total capital embodied in the factors of production employed, rather than on that portion of useful capital actually utilized.

Finally, at the other extreme, one can estimate the rate of return on total human capital, including that embodied in persons who are not in the labor force at all or are unemployed. This, of course, produces a lower gross rate of return (excluding maintenance)—6.9 per cent in 1929, rising to 8.4 per cent in 1969. But this alternative does not seem appropriate, either, except from a very broad social viewpoint. Even then, an opportunity cost should be estimated for those not employed in market activities, which then produces circularity in estimating rates of return.

It was to minimize the influence of imputations that we concentrated on the private domestic business economy, since the estimates shown for the domestic economy in our table are influenced by the returns on nonbusiness property, which are imputed. The rates of return on human capital, unaffected by imputations, are a bit lower for the total domestic economy than for the business sector on both gross and net bases over the whole period. This means that rates of return in the nonbusiness sectors are lower. Further, between 1929 and 1969 there was a small relative decline in the nonbusiness sectors, suggesting that the increase in average labor compensation is smaller than in the business sector over the four decades as a whole. But the pattern of movement between peak years is quite similar.

The rates of return on nonhuman capital are at a distinctly lower level for the whole domestic economy than for the business sector, particularly on a net basis. This reflects the use of interest rates to impute returns in the nonbusiness sectors.

The rates of return on total capital in the domestic economy average about 3 percentage points less than the rates in the business sector. It is interesting to observe how stable the overall rates of return were during the period under review in the domestic economy as a whole— moving between 9.0 and 9.5 per cent in all peak years, except for the lower rate recorded in 1937.

All series, for both the domestic economy and business sector, show decreases in rates of return between peak years and the subsequent troughs, particularly on a net basis. The drops were drastic in the contractions of the 1930s, but mild since World War II. The mildest was the 1960–1961 contraction, when the net rate of return on total capital employed in the business sector fell only from 10.97 per cent to 10.73 per cent.

INCREMENTAL RATES OF RETURN

Additional information can be obtained by calculating and interpreting incremental rates of return. On a year-to-year basis, changes in income in relation to changes in capital stock are too erratic and too heavily influenced by cyclical forces to reveal underlying tendencies. These problems can be overcome to a significant degree by averaging factor compensation and the associated stock over successive cycles, and then calculating ratios of the increments, as shown in Table 5-3 for the private domestic business economy.

Average rates of return for the cycle averages are also shown in the table, since these are related to the incremental rates. That is, when the incremental rate is above the average rate in the preceding period, the average rate is pulled up, and vice versa. It will be noted that, except for the cycle average 1929–1937, which included the Great Depression, the average rates of return for the cycle averages showed even less variation than those for the peak years. Like the peak year rates, the cycle average rates show a declining tendency since the end of World War II.

With regard to incremental *net* rates of return, which are more

Table 5-3. *Average Incremental Gross and Net Rates of Return on Capital Employed, by Major Type, U.S. Private Domestic Business Economy, Cycle Averages, 1929–1969*

Cycle	NET			GROSS		
	Total	Human	Nonhuman	Total	Human	Nonhuman
A. Average Percentage Rates of Return						
1929–37	6.9	7.9	6.3	8.1	10.7	6.4
1937–48	14.1	14.7	14.0	12.3	13.6	11.2
1948–53	12.9	13.3	12.6	12.0	12.6	11.3
1953–60[a]	11.8	13.4	10.3	11.4	12.6	10.2
1960–69	11.2	12.5	10.0	11.2	12.0	10.3
B. Incremental Percentage Rates of Return (over Previous Cycle)						
1937–48	26.1	23.0	33.3	19.4	17.1	22.6
1948–53	11.7	12.0	10.9	11.6	11.6	11.6
1953–60	8.8	13.4	4.5	10.2	12.4	7.7
1960–69	10.4	11.3	9.6	10.7	11.0	10.6

[a]The cycles 1953–57 and 1957–60 have been combined for these computations.

relevant to investment decisions than the gross rates, we first look at the rates for total capital. Between the depressed 1929–1937 period and the years between 1937 and 1948, dominated by the war and postwar boom, the incremental rate of return was, of course, abnormally high. In 1948–1953 it was 11.7 per cent, dropped to 8.8 per cent in the slightly depressed 1953–1960 period, and recovered to 10.4 per cent during 1960–1969.

Except for the initial high rate of 1937–1948, the incremental rates of total capital reflected above-average rates for human capital and below-average rates for nonhuman capital. The incremental rate of return on human capital was slightly over 12 per cent in both 1948–1953 and 1953–1960, receding a bit to 11.3 per cent during 1960–1969. For nonhuman capital, the rate was 10.9 per cent in 1948–1953, plummeting to 4.5 per cent during 1953–1960 as capacity utilization rates fell significantly, and recovering to 9.6 per cent in the 1960–1969 period. The latter rate was still 1.7 percentage points below the corresponding rate of return on human capital, however,

The incremental gross rates of return showed much the same patterns, as indicated in Table 5-3.

Thus, not only have the average rates of return been higher for human than nonhuman capital, but, since World War II, the incremental rates have been significantly higher as well. This suggests that there has been pronounced underinvestment in human capital in recent decades—a conclusion that supports the findings of other students of human capital, notably Schultz, with regard to particular types of human investment. It is all the more significant when the nonpecuniary returns to human investment are taken into account, together with the consideration that the maintenance outlays deducted from our compensation estimates also yield current satisfactions.

6

Summary and Research Agenda

The foregoing chapters have been replete with detail. To help the reader see the forest from the trees, here we summarize the chief points made in the study, particularly the findings of the substantive chapters 3, 4, and 5.

Further, since every research project—good, bad, or indifferent—implies an agenda for future research, the concluding section of this chapter explicitly points out some of the further work the author believes important for increasing our understanding of economic growth. Improvements of the data and methodology underlying the estimates of total investment and capital are suggested, as well as further analyses of their role in the growth process.

Summary

CONCEPTUAL FOUNDATIONS AND METHODOLOGY

This study rests squarely on the concept of capital as output- and income-producing capacity, and of investments as outlays that maintain or enhance productive capacity. On the basis of this definition, it is argued that total investment and the associated stocks of capital should include not only the tangible nonhuman capital outlays of all sectors, but also rearing costs (tangible human investment) and intangible

126

investments that are embodied in, and improve the quality or productive efficiency of, tangible factors. The intangibles are viewed as including outlays for research and development, education and training, health and safety, and mobility.

It is hypothesized that (1) comprehensive estimates of total real capital stocks should largely (if not completely, as conjectured by Schultz) explain the growth of real product, and (2) the growth of real intangible relative to that of tangible capital stocks should significantly narrow the tangible factor productivity residual.

The estimates of total gross and net investment and the associated capital stocks, by type, are presented within a compatible economic accounting framework, ensuring consistent and presumably more accurate estimates of income, saving, investment, and capital, by sector. The description of estimating methodologies and data sources, detailed in the appendixes and summarized in chapter 2, enable the reader to evaluate the reliability of the estimates for himself. It is our judgment that the quality of the estimates is comparable to that of the official Commerce Department national income accounts, from which much of our material is drawn.

THE RISING TOTAL INVESTMENT AND SAVING RATIO

In contrast to the declining secular trend shown by the conventional series, all of our measures of total capital formation indicate a significant rise in the proportion of income and product saved and invested between 1929 and 1969. By 1969 virtually half of adjusted GNP was devoted to the forward-looking outlays we term total gross investment, up from around 43 per cent in 1929. The ratio of net investment to NNP rose even more, proportionately—from near 21 per cent to almost 30 per cent over the forty-year period. In constant dollars the net increases were smaller, reflecting a faster increase in the investment price index than in the product price index, especially before 1948.

All of the growth in gross investment relative to GNP was due to a sharp increase in the proportion of GNP devoted to intangible investment, particularly after 1948, as the ratio of intangible to tangible investment almost doubled. The tangible nonhuman investment proportion of GNP remained virtually constant, while the rearing cost ratio declined (although more moderately in real terms). Within the former category, new construction and inventory investment declined and equipment and other durable goods expenditures rose relatively.

The relative increase in intangible investments, both gross and net, was smaller in constant than in current prices due to a faster increase in the price deflators for intangibles than in the implicit price deflator for national product. Among intangibles, by far the largest proportionate increase came in R&D outlays. The share of GNP devoted to education and training, the largest of the intangibles category, rose by 80 per cent, while the health and safety investment ratio increased by half. Mobility cost was the only type of intangible investment to rise proportionately less than GNP.

Looking at movements of total gross investment ratios across sub-periods bounded by peak years of the business cycle, we see occasional declines—between 1929 and 1937, for example, and in the latter 1950s—reflecting incomplete economic recoveries. These occasional declines were due entirely to downturns in tangible investment ratios, however, since the gross intangible investment ratio increased across all subperiods. The movements appear less regular when the estimates are taken net of depreciation and in constant prices.

The investment ratios also declined in all cyclical contractions, with a greater amplitude in the net than the gross measures. Here again the declines were entirely due to the tangible nonhuman components. The gross intangible investment ratios rose, reflecting their strong uptrends and a countercyclical tendency of mobility and certain educational outlays.

On a sector basis, virtually all the rise in the several investment ratios vis-à-vis national product was accounted for by government, although on a somewhat irregular pattern by subperiod. The ratio of personal investment to product tilted up (especially on a net basis), while that for business tilted down. Net foreign investment shows an irregular pattern, with no particular trend.

Next we assess the proportions of GNP accounted for by sectoral investment via changes in the sectoral distribution of income and in the proportions of sector disposable incomes devoted to investment. Thus, a major rise in the public sector share of GNP plus a modest rise in the ratio of investment to sector income were responsible for the dramatic rise in the ratio of gross government investment to GNP. Despite a drop in the ratio of gross personal income to adjusted GNP from 79 per cent in 1929 to 67 per cent in 1969, the proportion of DPI invested rose from one-third to almost 40 per cent, maintaining the personal sector ratio of gross investment to GNP. The business sector ratio of gross disposable income (saving, for this sector) remained quite stable in good years at around 10 per cent, although it was a bit lower in 1969 than in 1929. With gross investment at 124 per cent of gross disposable income in both of these years, the business sector ratio of gross investment to GNP was likewise modestly lower. On a net basis the decline was more pronounced.

The movements of the saving ratios of the various sectors were similar to those of the investment ratios, but at different levels. Thus, persons and governments were net savers (by our definitions), whereas business was a net borrower.

During economic contractions, investment ratios declined consistently in the business sector, while behavior in the personal sector was mixed. But in the government sector ratios of investment to product invariably rose while the saving ratio fell, providing a strong countercyclical effect.

With regard to changes in the investment mix by type and sector, the rise in the intangible investment proportion stands out in all sectors. Although the proportion was highest in the public sector and lowest in business, it was in the business sector that the ratio of intangible to total investment showed the greatest relative increase between 1929 and 1969.

TOTAL CAPITAL STOCK MOVEMENTS

By 1969, net investment and price movements had resulted in a current dollar value of total gross national wealth (GNW) of almost $11 trillion. This was 8.7 times adjusted GNP, compared with a $1.2 trillion stock in 1929, which was 9.4 times adjusted GNP. This implies a 0.2 per cent annual rate of increase in the product-capital ratio in current prices.

In constant dollars real total GNW increased at an average rate of 2.8 per cent a year, compared with a 3.4 per cent rate of growth in real GNP. Thus, total capital productivity rose at an average annual rate of about 0.5 per cent a year. This result does not support the hypothesis that the growth of real total capital explains the entire growth of real income; there must be further residual factors of significance, as discussed later. The relation of NNW to NNP is much the same as the relationship based on the gross estimates. The downward trend of the real capital coefficient was interrupted only in those subperiods in which output grew less than productive capacity. In business cycle contractions capital coefficients obviously rose, since capital stocks continued to grow during downturns, even during the Great Depression. Incremental capital coefficients, measured between business cycle averages, were generally lower than average coefficients for total and for tangible capital, but not for intangible capital; there they were slightly higher, giving an upward tilt to the average intangible capital coefficients.

With regard to the distribution of total capital by financing sector, only the public sector showed a marked increase, which occurred before 1948. The business and foreign sector shares fell significantly, while the personal sector proportion was in a modest uptrend.

The growth in the governmental share of capital can be traced to the major increase in the proportion of GNP originating in government, combined with a relatively stable sectoral capital coefficient. The modest expansion in the personal sector was caused by an increase in the sectoral share of adjusted GNP which was not entirely offset by a relative decline in the sector's capital coefficient. In the business and foreign sectors, the decline in the shares of total capital was due both to declining percentages of GNP and declining sectoral capital coefficients.

Consistent with the marked increase in intangible investment relative to the tangible variety, real stocks of intangible capital increased at a 3.8 per cent average annual rate, compared with 2.4 per cent for tangibles. Slicing real capital in terms of embodiment, human capital, which includes the bulk of the intangibles, grew at a 3.1 per cent annual rate, and nonhuman capital, at a 2.5 per cent rate. These rates of capital growth compare with a 3.4 per cent rate of increase in real GNP.

Reflecting the differential growth rates, real intangible stocks grew from less than one-fourth to more than one-third of the total between 1929 and 1969. Within the intangible category, R&D stocks showed the most rapid growth, followed by education and training, health, and mobility, in that order. Within the tangible category, human and nonhuman tangibles showed about the same rate of growth, around 3 per cent per annum. Within the latter group, equipment showed the highest rate, followed by inventories, structures, and land.

The government-financed portion of intangible capital was much higher than that of the other sectors. Business, on the other hand, financed the smallest portion of intangibles but accounted for the highest proportion of tangible capital stocks. The personal sector, sole financier of human tangibles, accounted for the smallest share of the nonhuman tangibles.

The largest employer of capital is, of course, private business. Looking at the total capital used in the private domestic business sector, we note that its productivity rose at an average rate of 1 per cent a year. In relation to tangible capital alone, real private domestic business product rose at a 1.7 per cent annual rate; in relation to real intangible capital, it fell at a 0.4 per cent rate, reflecting the growth of intangible capital relative to tangibles of over 2 per cent a year.

THE CONTRIBUTION OF CAPITAL TO ECONOMIC GROWTH

The 2.4 per cent yearly growth rate in real total capital represents 70 per cent of the 3.4 per cent average annual growth of real product in the private domestic business economy over 1929–1969. Thus, the 1 per cent annual growth rate in "total capital productivity," reflecting the net impact of various residual forces, accounted for 30 per cent of the economic growth rate. The proportion attributable to residual productivity was somewhat smaller in the period prior to 1948 and larger thereafter. In the national economy as a whole, the proportion of economic growth attributable to expansion of total capital was larger than in the business sector, but the calculations for the business sector are more meaningful.

Assuming the same marginal productivity of tangible and intangible capital in the business sector, the contribution of the former was 1.7 percentage points, compared with 0.7 percentage point for the latter. Although the growth of real intangible stock was significantly faster, its relative magnitude was much smaller, about one-third in 1929. It follows that of the 1.7 per cent annual increase in tangible capital productivity (exactly half of the overall economic growth rate in the business economy), the relative growth of real intangible capital accounted for more than 40 per cent. The proportion was a bit larger in the 1948–1969 subperiod.

The chief residual forces accounting for the remainder of growth are: (1) scale economies; (2) changes in economic efficiency; (3) changes in the inherent quality of natural and human resources; (4) changing labor efficiency with given technologies; and (5) for the business sector, changes in unmeasured governmental inputs relative to real private costs.

We suspect, however, that our estimates tend to overstate the net contribution of the residual, noncapital-related forces. Among the reasons for this qualification is a probable understatement of the growth of the real intangible capital stocks and of their marginal productivity.

Nevertheless, it does appear that the growth of real total capital cannot account for all of the growth of real product in recent decades, and so the hypothesis of Schultz and others is not confirmed by the present estimates. Even in current dollars there was some increase in the factor income-capital ratio.

Due largely to the significant increase in the implicit price deflator for capital stocks relative to that for adjusted national product, the ratio of factor income to total capital increased significantly less than total real capital productivity over 1929–1969 in both the national and business economies. The average gross rate of return was 10.2 per cent in

1929 and 10.8 per cent in 1969 (having peaked in the 1948–1953 subperiod).

The gross rate of return on total human capital was above that on nonhuman capital throughout the period. It stood at 11.7 per cent in both 1929 and 1969, compared with 9.2 and 9.9 per cent for nonhuman capital at the beginning and end of the forty-year span. The net rates of return were very similar to the gross rates.

In the total domestic economy rates of return were somewhat lower than those in the business sector. While this reflected slightly lower labor compensation in the nonbusiness sectors, it was chiefly due to significantly lower returns on capital as a result of the imputations adopted in estimating nonbusiness property income. Over the whole period there was less variation in rates of return between peak cycle years than in the business sector, as well as less of an upward tilt.

The reader is warned that the calculated rates of return, even for the business sector, are affected by methods of estimation, particularly with regard to deductions for maintenance of human capital. Returns before deduction of maintenance are much higher, of course, and show a downward trend. On the other hand, when factor income is related to *utilized* capital stocks the upward trend is more pronounced than that shown by the rates cited above.

When incremental rates of return between cycle averages are calculated, the rates on human capital remain consistently above the rates on nonhuman capital since World War II. It is hard to escape the conclusion that society has been underinvesting in human beings relative to nonhuman capital, at least in recent decades. This is particularly true when weight is given to the psychic satisfactions from much of the human investment over and above the pecuniary returns.

Research Agenda

The chief contribution of this study, in the author's view, is the development of a consistent and comprehensive body of estimates of total gross and net investment and the associated stock estimates in current and constant prices within a systematic economic accounting framework for the national economy and its major sectors. This embraces the movements of the key variables and their interrelationships, with some attempt at interpretation.

But even on the basis of the present body of estimates there is much room for further analysis. In particular, statistical analyses of the saving and investment functions for the national economy and its major sectors are called for in order to explain the upward trend of the total saving and investment ratios, which contrast strikingly with the conventional saving and investment functions. Beyond the overall functions, the behavior of the various types of tangible and intangible investments should be analyzed. In addition to the income variables, national and sectoral, other variables should be brought into the regression analyses, such as asset holdings, interest rates, and relative output and input price movements.

The other main direction in which further analysis would be fruitful is in statistically fitting production functions and otherwise analyzing the growth process. The close relationship between the growth of real total capital stocks and real product is clear; less clear is the role of the various types of capital, the elasticity of output with respect to each major type, and the relative importance of the several residual, noncapital-related forces. Perhaps new types of production functions and new analytical techniques should be developed. Also, elasticities and rates of return on the various types of capital might be estimated by alternative approaches to the methods developed here for estimating average and incremental rates of return on human and nonhuman capital, separately and in combination.

Granted the usefulness of the total investment and capital estimates, improvements in the underlying data and in the estimating methodology should come with time. The data base is particularly weak with regard to outlays for training and mobility among the intangibles, nonbusiness inventory accumulation, and the stocks of land and other natural resources.

The methodology used to estimate rearing costs and human maintenance contains original elements, as does the methodology employed in estimating the stocks of intangible and tangible human capital. These could undoubtedly be refined through constructive criticism, and alternative methodologies developed. The price deflators also leave something to be desired, particularly those based largely on input prices, as well as the price indexes for land and other natural resources.

Finally, it is to be hoped that an increasing proportion of the total investment and associated stock categories will be included or identified in the regularly published official U.S. national income and product estimates. The separate identification of forward-looking developmental outlays would be helpful, even if these are not classed as investment. As this writer has urged elsewhere, a fundamental restructuring of the economic accounts along the lines suggested here would facilitate economic growth analysis. The structure of the present U.S. national income accounts was based largely on the concepts of Keynes, who was concerned with diagnosing cyclical fluctuations of income and employment and therefore accorded a central role to business tangible investment. But for purposes of growth analysis the broader concepts and measures of total investment and capital are needed. The upsurge of interest in social accounts and indicators in recent years adds urgency to the case for including estimates of intangible and human investments and capital alongside the tangible nonhuman investment and capital estimates for all sectors. Perhaps this study, by demonstrating the feasibility and relevance of such estimates, will accelerate work on their development and analysis.

Appendixes

A

Adjusted National Income and Product, Sector Current and Capital Accounts, and Related Tables: Sources and Methods

The summary descriptions of the sources and methods of estimation in this appendix are related to the twelve basic tables, seven of which (Tables 2-1 through 2-7) are presented in chapter 2, with the remaining five (Tables A-1 through A-5) at the end of these notes. The first seven tables are the basic national income and product accounts, by sector, adjusted to our concepts as described in chapters 1 and 2. The other five which are derived from, or related to, the basic accounts, present estimates that have been used in the analyses of investment and capital.

In general, the accounts and related tables show estimates for only the three key years 1929, 1948, and 1966 (or 1969). Time series covering all the years from 1929 to 1969 are presented for the variables used in the analyses (such as total adjusted GNP), in current and constant dollars, and the disposable income of each sector in Appendix B.

An economic accounting framework was used for the estimating procedures. It (a) ensures consistency of the product, income, saving, investment, and stock estimates and (b) facilitates analysis of saving and investment with reference to income, and of capital stocks in relation to income and product, at the national and sectoral levels. We follow the precedent of the Commerce Department in presenting the detailed interlocking national and sectoral accounts to show precisely the composition and interrelationships of the various flows. But it is the major time series employed in the analyses that are important rather than the detailed accounts, so the latter are presented only for selected years. The last year for which the full detail in the accounts was worked out was 1966, although all the chief variables were extended through 1969.

Table 2-1 shows the adjusted national income and product accounts. It will be recalled that our GNP contains a much larger investment component than the official estimates, including some investments charged to current expense. Since our national income and product figures also include the imputed rental values of the nonbusiness tangible capital goods, they are considerably larger than the official estimates. The precise reconciliations between our adjusted GNP estimates and the official Commerce Department estimates in current and constant dollars are shown in Tables A-1 and A-2.

Tables 2-2 through 2-5 contain the current and capital accounts for the personal, business, government, and foreign sectors. In addition to the broadened investment concepts and measures for each of the domestic sectors accommodated in separate sector capital accounts, current incomes and outlays differ because of the expanded imputations and other items shown in the reconciliation tables. Note that the capital accounts provide for capital transfers, as does the United Nations standard system of national accounts, except that our transfers are from the financing sectors to the sectors benefiting from use, or "control," of the capital. The capital transfer estimates are described in the final part of Appendix B.

The consolidated capital formation account (Table 2-6) contains the contra-entries to the investment transactions and capital transfers of the various sectors, thus summarizing adjusted national investment, by sector and major type. Note that the capital transfers among the domestic sectors plus net capital transfers from abroad (chiefly human capital transferred by net immigration) sum to zero. So do net financial investments of the domestic sectors plus net foreign investment, when allowance is made for the statistical discrepancy.

Table 2-7 shows the derivation of gross disposable income in each sector, and its disposition in terms of consumption, investment, and the residual "net financial investment." Unlike the total economy, sectors do not show an equality of real investment and saving. Saving, defined as income less consumption, equals real (tangible plus intangible) investment plus net financial investment, positive or negative. As shown in the table, the gross disposable income of each sector plus statistical discrepancy equals adjusted GNP.

We have already referred to the reconciliations in Tables A-1 and A-2. Table A-3 presents adjusted GNP by sector of origin. The constant dollar estimates in Table A-4 are confined to the gross business product, since this is the only sector in which the income and product estimates are independent of the capital estimates and thus relevant to production function analysis.

Table A-5 contains estimates of gross and net factor compensation (labor and nonlabor) and human maintenance costs, which make possible net labor compensation estimates comparable to net property compensation, already excluding maintenance costs.

To save space, methodology for entries on our accounts will be given only once and for the most detailed breakdown. Sources will not be shown for lines that represent totals of documented detail. Nor will sources be repeated for counterentries. The second place where an entry appears on the accounts is shown in parentheses. If documentation is desired for a line and is not shown for that line or its detail, it normally can be found for the counterentry given in parentheses. Note, however, that no methodology is given in Appendix A for investment, depreciation, and capital transfer entries, or for underlying capital stock series. Such technical notes are provided by type of capital in the relevant portions of subsequent appendixes.

In the interest of further condensing our technical notes, frequent sources will be referred to by an abbreviated citation. For example, "OBE, Table 1.1, line 1" means that the source of the 1929–1963 figures is the U.S. Department of Commerce, Office of Business Economics,[1] *The National Income and Product Accounts of the United States, 1929–1965, Statistical Tables,* a Supplement to the *Survey of Current Business,* Washington, D.C., U.S. Government Printing Office (1966), Table 1.1, line 1. The sources for the 1964–1966 figures are the comparable tables and lines in the national income issues of the *Survey of Current Business* in which the last revision of each year's figures appears (July 1967 for 1964 figures, July 1968 for 1965 figures, and July 1969 for 1966 figures). Another abbreviated citation used is *Business Statistics* for U.S. Department of Commerce, Office of Business Economics, *1967 Business Statistics,* 16th Biennial Edition, a Supplement to the *Survey of Current Business,* Washington, D.C., U.S. Government Printing Office (1967).

To form some of our continuous time series we have had to draw on two or more independent, but closely related, series for different portions of the chronology. Unless otherwise specified, linkage of two contiguous portions of such a series is accomplished essentially by

---

1. Under a reorganization effective January 1, 1972, the OBE is redesignated the Bureau of Economic Analysis (BEA) in a new Social and Economic Statistics Administration, and is referred to as such in the text of this volume. However, in the appendixes the old designation is used for the sake of statistical continuity.

applying an adjustment ratio (of an estimate from the later series to an estimate for the same year from the earlier series) to each figure in the earlier series. Where it was necessary to convert basic data from a fiscal year to a calendar year basis, we employed the usual convention of building a calendar year estimate from half of the estimate for the coincident fiscal year plus half of the estimate for the following fiscal year.

Notes to Table 2-1:   *National Income and Product Account*

Line No.

2.	OBE, Table 2.1, line 2.
3.	OBE, Table 1.9, line 11.
4.	OBE, Table 1.10, line 8.
5.	OBE, Table 1.10, line 9.

Proprietors' compensation, by industry group, is estimated by multiplying the number of proprietors by average annual earnings per full-time employee (OBE, Table 6.5). The number of proprietors in each industry grouping are persons engaged in production (OBE, Table 6.6) less full-time equivalent employees (OBE, Table 6.4).

9. Net rental income from auxiliary business activities represents the net return to persons from business-type activities which are not full-time business activity or are not imputed for self-rental of housing. This item is derived by subtracting from OBE's rental income of persons (Table 1.10, line 17) OBE's net rent for owner-occupied nonfarm residences (from unpublished detail supporting OBE, Table 7.3, line 55) and then adding our estimates of net rent for tenant-occupied, farmer-owned farm residences. In OBE's framework this last category is part of proprietors' income. Our estimates of the category are OBE's (unpublished detail with a data gap from 1930–1945 interpolated by the per cent deviation from a linear trend of owner-occupied residential net rents), plus a depreciation valuation adjustment (DVA). This DVA represents the deviation of OBE's depreciation on tenant-occupied farm residences over ours.

12. Net rental income of government represents the excess of imputed interest on government tangible capital over gross interest paid by government. (The latter are unpublished OBE figures.) The calculations are made separately for the federal government and for state and local governments. For a discussion of imputed interest on government capital, see the notes for Table 2-4, lines 3 through 5.

Line No.

14.   OBE, Table 2.1, line 14.

15.   Interest paid by persons on brokers' loans; unpublished OBE figures.

16.   Interest received by federal, state, and local governments; unpublished OBE figures.

17.   Unproductive interest paid by federal government is taken as any interest paid in excess of imputed interest on federal government capital. (See line 12 above.)

25.   OBE, Table 1.9, line 15.

26.   OBE, Table 1.9, line 4, plus those parts of personal tax and nontax payments that we have classified as taxes on durable goods (i.e., motor vehicle license fees, property taxes, and automobile use taxes—OBE, Table 3.1, footnote 1, and Table 3.3, lines 5 and 6).

27.   OBE, Table 1.9, line 7, plus our estimates of depreciation on government enterprise structures and equipment. (This addition results, in effect, in a subtraction from current surplus of government enterprises.)

28.   OBE, Table 1.9, line 6.

44.   OBE, Table 1.1, line 18.

45.   OBE, Table 1.1, line 19.

Notes to Table 2-2: *Personal Sector Accounts*

Line No.

1.   OBE, Table 2.1, line 21, less the taxes reallocated to indirect tax and nontax charges (see Table 2-1, line 26, above).

4.   OBE, Table 2.5, line 22, plus unpublished detail for OBE, Table 7.3, line 59.

5.   The gross rental value of institutional plant consists of our estimates for imputed interest, depreciation, and repair and maintenance on institutional structures and for imputed interest on institutional site land. Imputed interest is estimated by applying the Federal Reserve series on bank rates for short-term business loans in nineteen cities (*Business Statistics*, 1967 edition, p. 89; for years prior to 1939, extrapolated by our household lending rate) to net annual average stocks of capital.

        Repair and maintenance of institutional structures is estimated by applying to gross stocks of institutional structures the ratio of repair and maintenance of civilian government structures to gross annual average stocks.

Line No.

6.   Gross rentals for the services of consumer durables and household inventories consist of imputed interest (net return), depreciation, taxes on durables, reclassified from personal tax and nontax payments (see notes for Table 2-1, line 26), repair and maintenance expenses, and fire and theft insurance premiums.

Imputed interest consists of interest paid by consumers on the part of the net stock financed by credit plus an imputed interest on the residual net stock they own outright. The interest rate applied to this latter portion of the net stock is the opportunity cost of owning the stock, or household lending rate, calculated as the weighted yield on personal holdings of bank time deposits, U.S. government securities, and common stocks (with underlying data drawn from various FRB sources).

The cost of repair and maintenance of consumer durables are OBE figures (OBE, Table 2.5, lines 64, 83, and unpublished consumption expenditure detail on watch, clock, and jewelry repair; electrical repairs, upholstery and furniture repairs; and rug, drapery, and mattress cleaning and repair). Figures on fire and theft insurance premiums are from OBE, with an old OBE series linked in 1946 to their revised series for 1946 and subsequent years.

7.   Institutional equipment gross rentals are made up of imputed interest, depreciation, and repair and maintenance. As with institutional structures, the FRB series on bank rates for short-term business loans in nineteen cities is used to impute interest returns on institutional equipment. Repair and maintenance is estimated by applying to institutional equipment gross stock the ratio of repair and maintenance to gross stock of consumer durables.

8.   Imputed rentals allocated to rearing costs are either directly allocated to this type of investment or estimated via ratios of rearing cost expenditures to total expenditures, by category. Rentals allocated to intangible investment are estimated as 5.8 per cent of the investment outlay, the 1958 proportion. (Detailed figures for other years indicate that the proportion has not varied substantially from year to year.)

9.   This line represents the remainder of OBE consumption expenditures (OBE, Table 2.5) not allocated to gross rentals or to personal sector investment.

10.   OBE, Table 2.1, line 26.

Line No.

12. The current account residual after subtracting lines 1, 2, 10, and 11 from Net Personal Income.

17. This is the same as the comparable investment series discussed under personal sector investment in education.

18. This corresponds to personal sector mobility investment in the frictionally unemployed, except that a deduction is made for the amount of frictional unemployment compensation subsidized through unemployment compensation. This adjustment is calculated by applying to unemployment compensation payments (OBE, Table 3.9, lines 5 plus 7) the ratio of frictional unemployment to average unemployment. Frictional unemployment is assumed to be 3.0 per cent of the civilian labor force, or actual unemployment for years when the unemployment rate falls below 3.0 per cent. In the average unemployment series, persons engaged in work relief are classed as employed. (In official government employment rates, persons on work relief are classed as unemployed. For further details on our employment and unemployment rates, see the technical notes for employed stocks.)

19. Withdrawal of proprietors' profits consists of OBE's proprietors' income before inventory valuation adjustment (OBE, Table 1.10, lines 14 plus 16) less the sum of our estimates of proprietors' compensation (see Table 2-1, line 6) and OBE's estimates of farmers' net tenant rent (see Table 2-1, line 9) and of net rent for owner-occupied farm residences (see Table 2-2, line 23). Undoubtedly some of these profits are retained in unincorporated businesses rather than withdrawn, but we found it impossible from the available data to estimate retained unincorporated business profits.

21. Same as Table 2-1, line 9.

23. Net rental on owner-occupied residences consists of OBE's estimates for farm and nonfarm categories (unpublished detail supporting OBE, Table 7.3, lines 55 and 66) plus an adjustment for the amount by which OBE's depreciation included in these net rent figures exceeds ours.

24. Net rent imputed for the value of institutional plant and site land is estimated as the imputed interest on the net capital stock (see notes for Table 2-2, line 5) minus OBE's figures on interest paid by institutions (unpublished detail for OBE, Table 7.3, line 58).

25. The part of the net rent on consumer durables and

Line No.

household inventories that accrues to persons is taken as the imputed interest on that portion of the capital stock which is not financed on credit (the "lending rate stock," see notes for Table 2-2, line 6). The net rent (imputed interest) on stock financed on credit is assumed to accrue to the creditors and is thus not included as part of personal income.

26.   Net rental income on institutional equipment is the interest imputed on the net stock. (See notes to Table 2-2, line 7.)

27.   OBE, Table 2.1, line 13.

31.   OBE, Table 3.1, line 26, plus Table 3.3, line 30.

32.   OBE, Table 2.1, line 20.

55.   Net financial investment of the personal sector is the residual after subtracting lines 34 and 48 from Finance of Gross Accumulation.

73.   OBE, Table 1.9, line 11.

Notes to Table 2-3:   *Business Sector Accounts*

Line No.

3.   OBE, Table 1.10, line 20.

6.   Not available. See notes to Table 2-2, line 19.

7.   OBE, Table 1.10, line 23.

8.   Same as Table 2-3, line 14; the total of lines 15 and 16.

9.   OBE, Table 1.10, line 15 plus line 24.

12.   Same as Table 2-3, line 6.

13.   OBE, Table 1.10, line 19.

15.   The tangible capital amortization adjustment to profits represents the amount by which OBE's capital consumption allowances on capital allocated by us to the business sector exceeds our capital consumption allowances. This adjustment series includes the difference between expenditures on producers' durable equipment conventionally charged to current account and our depreciation on these series. (With these expenditures no longer charged to current account, profits are increased by the difference.)

16.   The intangible capital amortization adjustment is found by subtracting intangible capital depreciation charged to the business sector from intangible capital investment financed by the business sector. Reallocating intangible capital expenditures to investment increases current profits by the amount of the transferred expenditures, less current depre-

Line No.

ciation. The depreciation charged to the business sector is on that capital we assume to be "controlled" by the business sector, not necessarily on capital financed by the business sector. (See the technical notes on capital transfers for this distinction.)

17.   Same as Table 2-3, line 9.

36.   Net financial investment of the business sector is calculated by subtracting lines 18 and 30 from Finance of Gross Accumulation.

Notes to Table 2-4:   *Government Sector Accounts*

Line No.

3.   The imputed rental for the services of public land equals imputed interest, calculated by applying an interest (or yield) rate to the annual average stock. The calculations are made separately for federal land and for state and local government land. Rentals are not imputed to government enterprise site land, since enterprises are treated as business entities for accounting purposes, and only their profit (i.e., surplus or deficit) conceptually enters into government income. (Ideally, the current surplus of government enterprises should appear as a credit item in government income, but statistical inadequacies dictated that we follow OBE's practice of netting these surpluses against government subsidies on the debit side of the current account.)

The yield rate applied to federal stocks is taken as the interest rate paid on the annual average net debt outstanding of the federal government. These calculations are based on OBE's unpublished interest paid series and unpublished OBE and U.S. Treasury Department figures on debt outstanding.

The yield rates used for state and local government capital are comparably derived from unpublished OBE figures on state and local government interest paid and debt outstanding.

4.   Gross imputed rental for the services of structures consists of imputed interest, depreciation, and repair and maintenance expenditures. Again, rentals are not imputed for government enterprise capital.

Imputed interest is calculated by applying the yield rates discussed under line 3 above to net capital stocks.

Line No.

Government repair and maintenance from 1929 to 1957 is derived from statistics of the U.S. Department of Commerce, Building Materials and Construction Industries Division. It includes repair and maintenance for military construction, Corps of Engineers construction, highways, 85 per cent of sewage and water supply works, and 75 per cent of an "all other" category (which excludes also residential; farm service building; nonresidential, nonfarm business structures; and public utility categories). The 1958–1966 figures are rough estimates based on the 1957 level and the gross stock trend.

5.   Gross imputed rental for government equipment and inventories is comprised of imputed interest on inventories and of imputed interest, depreciation, and repair and maintenance on equipment. No rental is included for government enterprise capital.

Imputed interest is calculated by applying the yield rates discussed under Table 2-4, line 3, to net capital stocks. Repair and maintenance on equipment is estimated by applying to gross stocks the ratio of consumer durables repair and maintenance to gross stocks.

6.   Imputed rentals allocated to intangible investment are estimated as 18.5 per cent of intangible investment expenditures, the 1958 proportion.

7.   Other consumption expenditures represent that part of OBE's government purchases of goods and services (OBE, Table 1.1, line 20) that has not been allocated to investment or capital service rentals.

10.   OBE, Table 3.1, line 27.

13.   The current account balancing item; equal to Government Income less the sum of lines 1, 8, 11, and 12.

39.   The capital account balancing entry; equal to Finance of Gross Accumulation less lines 22 and 33.

Notes to Table 2-5:   *Foreign Sector Accounts*

Line No.

5.   Surplus of the nation on current foreign account is the residual after subtracting the sum of lines 2, 3, and 4 from Receipts from Foreigners.

12.   Net foreign investment is calculated by subtracting line 11 from Source of Accumulation. Our net foreign investment series is the same as OBE's (OBE, Table 4.1, line 8).

Notes to Table 2-6: *Consolidated Capital Formation Account*

All of the entries in Table 2-6 are contra-entries to variables contained in preceding tables, as indicated in the references on each line. The investment time series are contained in Appendix B.

Notes to Table 2-7: *Current-Dollar Disposable Receipts and Expenditures, by Sector*

The entries for the composition and disposal of each sector's income are cross-referenced on the table vis-à-vis the corresponding items in our modified national income accounts.

Notes to Table A-1: *Current-Dollar Reconciliation of Adjusted GNP and Commerce Department GNP*

Line No.

1.   OBE, Table 1.1, line 1.

2.   Same as Table 2-2, line 17; enters GNP as investment.

3.   Same as Table 2-2, line 18; enters GNP as investment. That part of the corresponding investment item which is subsidized by unemployment compensation is assumed to have already been in GNP through personal consumption expenditures.

4.   Imputed rentals on consumer durables and household inventories that are added to GNP consist of imputed interest, depreciation, and reclassified taxes. (See notes to Table 2-2, line 6.) The other components of gross imputed rentals of repair and maintenance expenditures and fire and theft insurance premiums are already in OBE's GNP figure as part of purchases of goods and services.

5.   Institutional imputed rentals added to GNP consist of imputed interest on the net stock, less OBE's institutional interest paid, and of our depreciation, less OBE's depreciation, on institutional stocks. These deductions and repair and maintenance expenses are already in OBE's GNP figure as part of personal consumption expenditures. (See notes to Table 2-2, lines 5 and 7.)

6.   Tangible investment conventionally charged to current account enters GNP in our framework reclassified as investment. In OBE's framework these expenditures are written off against business profits.

Line No.

7.   Intangible business investment is added to adjusted GNP due to its reclassification from current expense to capital investment.

8.   All of government gross imputed rentals except repair and maintenance expenditures are additions to GNP. (See notes to Table 2-4, lines 3 through 5.) Repair and maintenance outlays are already part of OBE's GNP as part of government purchases of goods and services.

Notes to Table A-2:   *Constant-Dollar Reconciliation of Adjusted GNP and Commerce Department GNP*

Line No.

1.   OBE, Table 1.2, line 1.

2.   Unpublished detail supporting OBE, Table 5.3.

3.   Unpublished OBE series.

5.   See notes for the corresponding constant-dollar investment item.

6.   See notes for the corresponding constant-dollar investment item (personal sector frictional unemployment cost). The same deflator series as the one used to deflate total frictional unemployment compensation is used to deflate this imputed compensation excluding unemployment compensation subsidies.

7.   See notes for Table 2-2, line 6, and Table A-1, line 4. Constant-dollar imputed interest is calculated by applying the 1958 yield rate to 1958-dollar net stocks. See the technical notes re investment and capital for the deflators used for investment entering stock and for depreciation. Indirect taxes are converted to 1958 dollars by applying the overall consumer durables implicit deflator series.

8.   See notes for Table 2-2, lines 5 and 7, and for Table A-1, line 5. Constant-dollar imputed interest is calculated by multiplying 1958-dollar net stocks by the 1958 yield rate. OBE's institutional interest paid (which is deducted) is converted to constant dollars by applying a deflator series obtained through multiplying OBE's implicit deflator for nonresidential fixed investment (OBE, Table 8.1, line 8) by a 1958 = 100 index of the FRB series on bank rates for business short-term loans.

OBE's institutional depreciation, which is deducted from our institutional depreciation, is converted to 1958

Line No.

dollars by OBE's implicit deflator for nonresidential fixed investment (OBE, Table 8.1, line 8).

9.   For the deflators used, see the technical notes for this category under business investment.

10.   See the business intangible investment notes for the deflators used.

11.   Constant-dollar imputed interest is calculated by applying the 1958 yield rates to constant-dollar net stocks. See the investment and capital notes for the derivation of 1958-dollar depreciation.

Notes to Table A-3:   *Current-Dollar Adjusted Gross National Product by Sector of Origin*

Line No.

1.   OBE, Table 1.13, line 34; corresponds to unpublished detail for OBE, Table 1.7, line 6.

2.   Same as Table 2-2, lines 17 plus 18.

3.   Same as Table A-1, line 4.

4.   Corresponds to Table A-1, line 5, but without the deductions of OBE's institutional interest paid and OBE's depreciation on institutional stocks.

5.   Unpublished detail supporting OBE, Table 7.3, line 51, and the components of line 62 pertaining to dwellings. Our entry represents the space rental value of owner-occupied dwellings exclusive of associated purchases of goods and services. These associated purchases are considered value added by the businesses from whom the purchases are made and are thus part of business product.

7.   Unpublished detail supporting OBE, Table 1.7, line 2.

8.   Same as Table A-1, line 6.

9.   Same as Table A-1, line 7.

10.   Same as line 5 above.

11.   Unpublished detail supporting OBE, Table 7.3, lines 57 plus 58.

12.   Annual figures of GNP originating in government enterprise back to 1947 are unpublished OBE detail. Estimates for 1929 through 1946 are derived from extrapolating the 1947 total via OBE's figures on compensation of government enterprise employees (OBE, Table 1.13, line 27).

14.   OBE, Table 1.13, line 30; corresponds to unpublished detail for OBE, Table 1.7, line 8.

Line No.

15. Same as Table A-1, line 8.

16. Same as line 12 above.

18. OBE, Table 1.13, line 38; corresponds to unpublished detail for OBE, Table 1.7, line 7.

Notes to Table A-4: *Constant-Dollar Adjusted Gross Business Product*

Line No.

1. Unpublished detail supporting OBE, Table 1.8, line 3.

2. Same as Table A-2, line 2.

3. Same as Table A-2, line 3.

5. Same as Table A-2, line 9.

6. Same as Table A-2, line 10.

7. See notes for Table A-3, line 5. The imputations for nonfarm owner-occupied dwellings are deflated by OBE's implicit deflator for the space rental value of owner-occupied nonfarm dwellings (OBE, Table 8.6, line 36). The imputations for owner-occupied farm dwellings are deflated by OBE's implicit deflator for the rental value of farmhouses (OBE, Table 8.6, line 38).

8. See notes for Table A-2, line 8 for the explanation of how OBE's current-dollar figures are converted to 1958-dollar estimates.

9. GNP originating in government enterprises back to 1947 is from unpublished OBE detail. Our current-dollar estimates for 1929 through 1946 (Table A-3, line 12) are converted to constant dollars by a deflator obtained by linking to the implicit 1947 deflator OBE's implicit deflator for GNP originating in general government (OBE, Table 8.4, line 8).

Notes to Table A-5: *Factor Compensation, Gross and Net*

A. *U.S. Domestic Economy*

Line No.

1. Gross domestic factor compensation equals adjusted domestic income plus capital consumption (lines 3 + 2).

2. Capital consumption, nonhuman: See Appendix B1.

3. Adjusted domestic income (factor compensation) equals adjusted national income (Table 2-1) minus rest-of-the-world property compensation (OBE, *S.C.B.*, Table 1.13, lines 40 + 41).

Line No.

4.   Human maintenance: See Annex on p. 152 below.

5.   Adjusted gross domestic income less maintenance equals lines 3 minus 4.

6.   Human depreciation: See Appendix B4.

7.   Adjusted net domestic income less maintenance: lines 5 minus 6.

8.   Employee compensation: OBE, *S.C.B.*, Table 6.1, line 1.

9.   Imputed proprietors' labor compensation equals the number of proprietors times annual average earnings. The number of proprietors is from the *Survey of Current Business*, "persons engaged in production" (Table 6.6) minus "full-time equivalent employed by industry" (Table 6.4). Average annual earnings are from the *S.C.B.*, Table 6.5.

10.   Imputed compensation of students and frictionally unemployed: Table A-1, lines 2 + 3.

11.   Total gross labor compensation equals 8 + 9 + 10.

12.   Total gross labor compensation excluding maintenance equals lines 11 − 4.

13.   Total net labor compensation equals lines 12 − 6.

14.   Gross capital compensation equals lines 1 − 11.

15.   Net capital compensation equals lines 3 − 11.

B. *Private Domestic Business Economy*

1.   Gross factor income equals (a) private domestic business gross employee compensation plus (b) private domestic business gross property compensation.

(a) equals: labor compensation of total economy minus student and frictional unemployment compensation (Table A-1, lines 2 + 3), minus employee compensation for the personal sector (*S.C.B.*, Table 1.13, line 35); government sector (*S.C.B.*, Table 6.1, line 73); and rest-of-the-world (*S.C.B.*, Table 6.1, line 86).

(b) equals: private domestic business net property compensation plus private domestic business capital consumption.

2.   Human maintenance equals total human maintenance (see Annex on p. 152) times the ratio of persons engaged in the private domestic business sector to the number of persons engaged in the total economy.

3.   Gross income less maintenance equals lines 1 − 2.

4.   Capital consumption, nonhuman: See Appendix B1.

Line No.

5.   Human depreciation: See Appendix B4.

6.   Net compensation equals (a) private domestic business economy net labor compensation plus (b) private domestic business net property compensation.

(a) equals private domestic business economy gross labor compensation minus maintenance, minus private domestic business depreciation (human).

(b) equals sum of business profits (Table 2-1, line 11), net income from auxiliary business activities (Table 2-1, line 9), and private domestic business economy net interest (S.C.B., Table 1.13, lines 10 + 18 + 25); minus corporate profits for the rest of the world (S.C.B., Table 1.13, line 40), and interest paid on owner-occupied dwellings and institutional plant (see Appendix B1).

7.   Gross labor compensation, see B1 above.

8.   Gross labor compensation excluding maintenance equals lines 7 − 2.

9.   Net labor compensation excluding maintenance equals lines 8 − 5.

10.   Gross property compensation equals 11 + 4.

11.   Net property compensation, see B above.

Annex to Table A-5: *Human Maintenance, Sources and Methods*

Estimates of human maintenance were obtained by multiplying budgets for various sizes of farm and nonfarm households by the number of households in these categories and summing the results. Persons living in institutions were multiplied by a corresponding maintenance estimate, and the total was added to household maintenance.

Budgets

An attempt was made to work with actual household budgets set up over the years by governmental or private agencies, but these budgets, when available, were generally not comparable over time. The idea of interpolating between budgets was therefore discarded. Instead, the 1960 Social Security Administration poverty budget was used as a base and extrapolated forward and backward.[2]

The SSA assumed that a farm family would need 40 per cent less net cash than a nonfarm family of the same size. The basic budgets are as follows:

2. Mollie Orshansky, "Counting the Poor: Another Look at the Poverty Profile," *Social Security Bulletin,* January 1965, p. 28.

Family Size	Nonfarm	Farm
1 person	$1580	$ 960
2 persons	2050	1240
3 persons	2440	1410
4 persons	3130	1925
5 persons	3685	2210
6 persons	4135	2500
7 persons or more	5090	3055

Growth Rate

Oscar Ornati[3] derived maintenance estimates from some sixty budgets for workers' families prepared over the years by governmental and private agencies. The budgets used to derive "minimum subsistence" levels were set up for relief purposes. His series shows an average annual increase between 1925 and 1960 of 1.06 per cent (see below).

Year	Minimum Subsistence (1960 dollars)	Index (1960 = 100)
1925	1,844	69.3
1926	1,901	71.4
1927	1,936	72.7
1928	1,958	73.6
1929	1,960	73.6
1930	2,015	75.7
1931	1,963	73.7
1932	1,998	75.1
1933	2,003	75.2
1934	1,750	65.7
1935	1,682	63.2
1936	1,783	67.0
1937	1,722	64.7
1938	1,754	65.9
1939	1,780	66.9
1940	1,765	66.3
1941	1,682	63.2
1942	1,803	67.7
1943	2,087	78.4

(cont.)

3. Oscar Ornati, "The Poverty Band" and "The Count of the Poor," in *Poverty amid Affluence*, New York, The Twentieth Century Fund, 1966, Appendix 2, Table A, p. 147.

Year	Minimum Subsistence (1960 dollars)	Index (1960 = 100)
1944	2,318	87.1
1945	2,463	92.5
1946	2,468	92.7
1947	2,556	96.0
1948	2,594	97.4
1949	2,474	92.9
1950	2,378	89.3
1951	2,473	92.9
1952	2,418	90.8
1953	2,703	101.5
1954	2,691	101.1
1955	2,701	101.5
1956	2,659	99.9
1957	2,571	96.6
1958	2,726	102.4
1959	2,702	101.5
1960	2,662	100.0

We used his series with rising subsistence levels because we consider the minimum basket of goods and services used for estimating the annual money budget as constituting material and psychological requisites in that year. If one accounts only for changes in the prices of the specified basket over time, the resulting subsistence level is pertinent to a particular time and place only.

Budgets were then derived for family sizes of one through seven or more, for farm and nonfarm locations, according to the proportions derived from Social Security estimates. The basic two-person nonfarm budget was set equal to 100 and all other household sizes were derived as percentages of this basic budget.

Family Size	Nonfarm Budget	Farm Budget
1 person	77.1	46.8
2 persons	100.0	60.5
3 persons	119.0	68.8
4 persons	152.7	93.9
5 persons	179.8	107.8
6 persons	201.7	122.0
7 persons or more	248.0	149.0

The per capita institutional budget was set equal to the difference between the budgets of the two highest closed categories, namely those for five and six persons, respectively.

Number of Households

The sources are as follows. Nonfarm: *Historical Statistics,* Series A 243. Farm: *Historical Statistics,* Series A 244. Persons not living in households: *Historical Statistics,* Series A 254.

Size of Households

Households are distributed according to their size. Data are from the 1940 and 1950 population censuses.

	Households	
Family Size	1940	1950
1 person	7.7	9.3
2 persons	24.8	28.1
3 persons	22.4	22.8
4 persons	18.1	18.4
5 persons	11.5	10.4
6 persons	6.8	5.3
7 persons or more	8.7	5.8

For 1930 only a family breakdown is available.[4]

Family Size	Families, 1930
1 person	—
2 persons	26.1
3 persons	22.5
4 persons	18.8
5 persons	12.8
6 persons	8.1
7 persons or more	11.6

The difference between the total number of households in 1930 and the total number of families in 1930 was added in as one-person households, and the percentages adjusted accordingly.

4. See Paul Glick, *American Families,* New York, John Wiley, 1957, p. 24.

The most recent household data at the time of writing were the Social Security Administration data for 1963, which have a farm-nonfarm breakdown,[5] as follows:

Family Size	Farm	Nonfarm
1 person	10.6	19.6
2 persons	30.6	25.8
3 persons	15.7	16.8
4 persons	14.3	16.2
5 persons	10.8	10.7
6 persons	7.4	5.6
7 persons or more	10.6	5.3

Farm-Nonfarm Breakdown

While a breakdown by farm and nonfarm exists for 1963, only total farm and nonfarm data are available for the years 1930, 1940, and 1950. Farm and nonfarm percentages for other years are based on the 1963 distributions, on the assumption that the relation between farm and nonfarm in each subcategory remained constant during the period under review.

Since the overall percentage is a weighted average of the nonfarm and the farm percentage (the weights being the proportion of nonfarm households to total households in a given year and the proportion of farm households to total households, respectively), the nonfarm and farm percentages are derived as follows:

$$Z = X \ Xwt + Y \ Ywt$$
$$Z = \frac{X}{Y} Yst = Y \ Ywt$$
$$Y = \frac{Z}{\frac{X}{Y} Xwt + Ywt}$$

where Z is the overall per cent in the subgroup, X is the nonfarm per cent in the subgroup, and Y is the farm per cent in the subgroup. Between the 1930, 1940, 1950, and 1963 data, all percentages were interpolated.

5. Mollie Orshansky, op. cit., p. 29.

Tables A-1 through A-5

Table A-1. *Reconciliation of Adjusted GNP and Commerce Department GNP, 1929, 1948, and 1969* (billions of current dollars)

Line		1929	1948	1969
1.	GNP, Commerce concept	103.095	257.562	929.095
	Plus			
	Households and institutions:			
2.	Imputed student compensation (less unemployment adjustment)	5.141	15.660	92.265
3.	Imputed compensation of frictionally unemployed (less subsidies)	2.072	4.506	16.048
4.	Imputed rentals (excl. maintenance and insurance) on HH durables and inventories	10.405	20.499	100.057
5.	Imputed rentals (excl. maintenance) on institutional plant and equipment and land, over OBE depreciation and interest paid	0.337	0.544	5.711
	Business:			
6.	Tangible investment conventionally charged to current account	0.282	0.899	2.340
7.	Intangible investment conventionally charged to current account	2.187	6.953	35.387
	General government:			
8.	Imputed rentals (excl. maintenance) on land, durables, and inventories	3.825	21.048	66.967
	Equals			
9.	GNP, adjusted	127.344	327.671	1,247.870
10.	Ratio: Adjusted to Commerce GNP	1.235	1.272	1.343

Table A-2. *Reconciliation of Adjusted GNP and Commerce Department GNP, 1929, 1948, and 1969* (billions of 1958 dollars)

Line		1929	1948	1969
1.	GNP, Commerce concept, constant cost 1	203.6	323.7	724.7
	Less			
2.	Constant cost 1 purchases of nonresidential, nonfarm structures	13.535	11.341	23.800
	Plus			
3.	Constant cost 2 purchases of nonresidential, nonfarm structures	12.416	10.785	20.403
	Equals			
4.	GNP, Commerce concept, constant cost 2	202.481	323.144	721.303
	Plus			
	Households and institutions:			
5.	Imputed student compensation (less unemployment adjustment)	12.407	22.760	62.539
6.	Imputed compensation of frictionally unemployed (less subsidies)	5.029	6.549	11.222
7.	Imputed rentals on HH durables (excl. maintenance and insurance) and inventories	18.571	24.858	88.615
8.	Imputed rentals (excl. maintenance) on institutional plant, equipment, and land over Commerce depreciation and interest	1.216	1.056	3.276
	Business:			
9.	Tangible investment conventionally charged to current account	0.673	1.403	2.01
10.	Intangible investment conventionally charged to current account	4.629	10.298	25.222
	General government:			
11.	Imputed rentals on land, durables (excl. maintenance) and inventories	7.366	30.478	43.006
	Equals			
12.	GNP, adjusted	252.372	420.546	957.193
13.	Ratio: Adjusted to Commerce GNP, constant cost 2	1.246	1.301	1.327
14.	Ratio: Adjusted to Commerce GNP, constant cost 1	1.240	1.299	1.327

160

Table A-3. *Adjusted Gross National Product by Sector of Origin* (billions of current dollars)

Line		1929	1948	1966
	Gross National Product originating in households and institutions			
1.	Commerce concept	2.863	5.599	20.206
	Plus			
2.	Additional labor compensation imputations	7.213	20.166	73.223
3.	Imputations on household durables and inventories	10.405	20.499	76.468
4.	Imputations on institutional plant, equipment, and land	0.518	0.768	57.16
5.	Imputations on owner-occupied dwellings	5.624	7.662	40.882
	Equals			
6.	Adjusted gross household and institutional product	26.623	54.694	216.495
	Gross National Product originating in business			
7.	Commerce concept	95.087	233.534	648.940
	Plus			
8.	Tangible investment conventionally charged to current account	0.282	0.899	1.845
9.	Intangible investment conventionally charged to current account	2.187	6.953	27.045

Less				
10.	Imputations on owner-occupied dwellings	5.624	7.662	40.882
11.	Commerce institutional imputation	0.181	0.224	1.454
12.	GNP originating in government enterprises	0.968	2.743	9.374
	Equals			
13.	Adjusted gross business product	90.783	230.757	626.120
	Gross National Product originating in government			
14.	Commerce concept	4.335	17.438	76.607
	Plus			
15.	Imputations on land, durables, and inventories	3.825	21.048	49.866
16.	GNP originating in government enterprises	0.968	2.743	9.374
	Equals			
17.	Adjusted gross government product	9.128	41.229	135.847
	Gross National Product originating in rest of the world			
18.	Commerce concept	0.810	0.991	4.104
19.	Adjusted Gross National Product	127.344	327.671	982.566

Table A-4. *Adjusted Gross Business Product* (billions of 1958 dollars)

Line		1929	1948	1966
1.	Gross Business Product, Commerce concept, constant cost 1	182.100	285.961	584.918
	Less			
2.	Constant cost 1 purchases of nonresidential, nonfarm structures	13.535	11.341	23.300
	Plus			
3.	Constant cost 2 purchases of nonresidential, nonfarm structures	12.416	10.785	24.902
	Equals			
4.	GBP, Commerce concept, constant cost 2	180.981	285.405	586.520
	Plus			
5.	Tangible investment conventionally charged to current account	0.673	1.403	1.690
6.	Intangible investment conventionally charged to current account	4.629	10.298	21.750
	Less			
7.	Imputations on owner-occupied dwellings	6.828	10.164	36.865
8.	Commerce institutional imputations	0.454	0.316	1.228
9.	GNP originating in government enterprises	2.534	4.529	7.196
	Equals			
10.	Adjusted Gross Business Product	176.467	282.097	564.671

Table A-5. *Factor Compensation, Gross and Net* (billions of current dollars)

Line		1929	1948	1969
	A. U.S. Domestic Economy			
1.	Gross domestic factor compensation	117.764	308.332	1161.365
2.	Capital consumption (nonhuman)	20.503	56.727	223.874
3.	Adjusted domestic income (factor compensation)	97.261	251.605	937.491
4.	Human maintenance	33.974	83.425	216.145
5.	Adjusted gross domestic income less maintenance	63.287	168.180	721.346
6.	Human depreciation	14.566	34.568	126.376
7.	Adjusted net domestic income less maintenance	48.722	133.608	594.952
8.	Employee compensation	51.098	141.131	565.548
9.	Imputed proprietors' labor compensation	9.110	21.509	47.081
10.	Imputed compensation of students and frictionally unemployed	7.213	20.166	108.313
11.	Total gross labor compensation	67.421	182.806	720.942
12.	Total gross labor compensation excluding maintenance	33.447	99.381	504.797
13.	Total net labor compensation	18.881	64.813	378.421
14.	Gross capital compensation	50.344	125.522	440.405
15.	Net capital compensation	29.841	68.795	216.531
	B. Private Domestic Business Economy			
1.	Gross factor income	83.476	213.532	694.338
2.	Human maintenance	29.291	69.275	162.057
3.	Gross income less maintenance	54.185	144.257	532.281
4.	Capital consumption, nonhuman	9.016	19.446	95.557
5.	Human depreciation	12.558	28.705	94.752
6.	Net compensation excluding maintenance	32.611	96.106	341.972
7.	Gross labor compensation	52.251	137.253	469.772
8.	Gross labor compensation excluding maintenance	22.960	67.978	307.715
9.	Net labor compensation excluding maintenance	10.402	39.273	212.963
10.	Gross property compensation	31.225	76.279	224.566
11.	Net property compensation	22.209	56.833	129.009

B

Total Investment and Stock Estimates, by Type and Sector: Sources and Methods

The methodology and sources underlying the estimates of the formation and stocks of total capital are already summarized in chapter 2. Appendix B contains a more detailed description of this material, as well as summary tables of our estimates for each year of the 1929–1969 period. Since the detailed notes on sources and methods are of interest mainly to technicians, they have been set on microfiche, and may be found in the back cover of this volume, together with the detailed basic sector tables. (See Table of Contents for material on microfiche.)

The thirty-two main summary tables—Tables B-1 through B-32—appear at the end of this introductory section. The first twelve comprise the investment estimates, and the remainder, the capital stock estimates. The gross estimates are always presented first, followed by the net estimates, each in terms of current and constant dollars. They cover the national economy totals, by sector, the domestic economy totals, by type, and breakdowns for tangible nonhuman investment and stock. (The comparable breakdowns within each of the sectors are on microfiche, as indicated in the List of Tables on pp. xvi–xix. Note that in these sector tables, investment estimates are shown in terms of the sectors financing the outlays, while the stock estimates are shown in terms of the sectors that "command," or use, the capital.)

The last eight summary tables contain the variant capital estimates for the total private business economy. Since no adjustment is made to obtain the employed portion of tangible nonhuman capital, detailed tables for this item are unnecessary here.

Our notes on the sources and methods used in estimating the formation and stocks of total capital—gross and net, in current and constant dollars, by sector and major type—are divided into the following five major sections:

1. Tangible nonhuman investment and capital (B1).
2. Tangible human investment and capital (B2).
3. Intangible nonhuman investment and capital (B3).
4. Intangible human investment and capital (B4).
5. Stock variations and capital transfers (B5).

Note that Appendix B4, after some general remarks on the common methodology used in estimating the various types of human capital stock, is subdivided in turn into three sections: (a) education and training (B4a); (b) health and safety (B4b); and (c) human mobility (B4c).

Table B-1. *Total Gross Investment in Current Dollars, by Sector, U.S. National Economy* (billions of dollars)

YEAR	National Total	DOMESTIC INVESTMENT BY SECTOR				Net Foreign Investment
		Total	Personal	Business	Government	
1929	55.70	54.93	33.26	15.78	5.89	0.77
1930	44.07	43.38	26.71	10.31	6.36	0.69
1931	33.84	33.65	21.99	5.49	6.17	0.20
1932	22.01	21.84	15.27	1.36	5.20	0.17
1933	21.16	21.01	14.05	2.24	4.71	0.15
1934	27.18	26.76	17.08	4.15	5.52	0.43
1935	32.35	32.40	19.29	7.42	5.68	−0.05
1936	39.41	39.50	22.48	9.62	7.40	−0.09
1937	44.84	44.78	24.67	12.73	7.38	0.06
1938	38.83	37.72	22.40	7.11	8.22	1.11
1939	44.26	43.37	24.96	9.74	8.67	0.89
1940	52.36	50.85	28.40	12.74	9.71	1.51
1941	68.15	67.02	35.73	16.38	14.92	1.12
1942	84.17	84.37	36.18	10.67	37.53	−0.21
1943	95.00	97.24	39.23	7.49	50.52	−2.24
1944	100.16	102.26	40.45	8.42	53.39	−2.10
1945	93.36	94.80	45.35	11.71	37.74	−1.44
1946	106.34	101.77	61.53	30.24	10.00	4.57
1947	124.66	115.76	71.35	31.87	12.53	8.90
1948	141.80	139.89	81.20	41.22	17.47	1.92
1949	136.24	135.73	83.33	30.72	21.67	0.51

Table B-1. (Completed)

YEAR	National Total	DOMESTIC INVESTMENT BY SECTOR				Net Foreign Investment
		Total	Personal	Business	Government	
1950	163.57	165.81	97.79	46.27	21.74	−2.24
1951	186.55	186.39	101.68	54.38	30.34	0.16
1952	204.14	204.44	105.87	47.95	50.62	−0.31
1953	215.06	217.15	114.84	48.78	53.53	−2.10
1954	212.86	213.31	117.99	44.34	50.99	−0.45
1955	243.48	243.97	135.29	58.57	50.10	−0.49
1956	260.68	259.13	139.77	63.85	55.52	1.54
1957	275.36	271.97	146.07	63.51	62.40	3.38
1958	272.77	272.93	147.61	54.59	70.73	−0.16
1959	306.66	308.96	166.06	68.25	74.65	−2.30
1960	313.74	312.06	169.65	70.70	71.71	1.68
1961	322.70	319.67	172.43	67.63	79.61	3.04
1962	355.03	352.58	189.82	78.58	84.17	2.45
1963	378.84	375.73	203.24	82.20	90.28	3.11
1964	412.02	406.34	221.30	90.98	94.06	5.68
1965	449.79	445.73	240.97	107.92	96.84	4.07
1966	498.26	495.81	259.75	126.08	109.98	2.45
1967	511.09	508.85	265.34	122.18	121.33	2.24
1968	565.39	565.78	302.97	131.21	131.60	−0.39
1969	617.10	618.00	330.29	147.32	140.39	−0.90

Table B-2. Total Gross Investment in Current Dollars, by Type, U.S. Domestic Economy (billions of dollars)

YEAR	Grand Total	Intangible Total	HUMAN INTANGIBLES				NONHUMAN INTANGIBLES			TANGIBLES		
			Total	Education and Training	Medical and Health	Mobility	Total	Basic Research	AR&D	Total	Human	Nonhuman
1929	54.93	15.69	15.44	11.00	1.90	2.53	0.25+	0.04	0.21	39.24	9.77	29.47
1930	43.38	14.28	14.01	9.87	1.86	2.29	0.26	0.04	0.23	29.11	8.85+	20.26
1931	33.65−	12.76	12.46	8.60	1.72	2.14	0.30	0.05−	0.25+	20.87	7.46	13.42
1932	21.84	10.60	10.30	6.88	1.52	1.90	0.30	0.05−	0.25−	11.24	5.89	5.36
1933	21.01	9.95+	9.69	6.40	1.41	1.89	0.26	0.04	0.22	11.06	5.31	5.75+
1934	26.76	10.74	10.47	7.00	1.48	2.00	0.27	0.04	0.23	16.02	5.60	10.42
1935	32.40	11.54	11.24	7.57	1.57	2.10	0.30	0.04	0.25+	20.86	5.92	14.95−
1936	39.50	12.92	12.58	8.63	1.70	2.25+	0.34	0.05−	0.29	26.58	6.34	20.24
1937	44.78	14.26	13.89	9.67	1.82	2.40	0.38	0.06	0.32	30.52	6.69	23.83
1938	37.72	13.90	13.47	9.20	1.92	2.36	0.43	0.06	0.37	23.82	6.41	17.41
1939	43.37	14.95−	14.46	10.02	1.94	2.49	0.49	0.07	0.42	28.42	6.58	21.84
1940	50.85	16.41	15.83	11.14	2.04	2.65+	0.58	0.08	0.50	34.44	6.74	27.69
1941	67.02	20.11	19.06	13.75+	2.18	3.13	1.04	0.12	0.93	46.92	7.59	39.32
1942	84.37	27.09	25.92	19.38	2.43	4.11	1.18	0.12	1.06	57.28	8.89	48.39
1943	97.24	32.16	30.89	24.71	2.70	3.48	1.28	0.14	1.14	65.08	10.38	54.70
1944	102.26	33.20	31.82	26.17	3.00	2.65+	1.39	0.14	1.24	69.06	11.54	57.52
1945	94.80	34.50	33.03	26.28	3.26	3.50	1.47	0.15	1.32	60.31	12.74	47.56
1946	101.77	35.22	33.65−	24.26	3.89	5.50	1.57	0.13	1.44	66.55−	14.24	52.31

1947	115.76	40.66	38.67	28.03	4.52	6.13	1.99	0.17	1.82	75.10	16.40	58.70
1948	139.89	44.98	42.61	30.78	5.22	6.61	2.37	0.21	2.17	94.91	18.28	76.63
1949	135.73	44.82	42.45+	30.44	5.54	6.47	2.37	.021	.2.15+	90.91	18.80	72.10
1950	165.81	49.60	46.93	33.60	6.06	7.27	2.67	0.25−	2.42	116.21	19.87	96.34
1951	186.39	56.50	53.33	38.83	6.53	7.98	3.17	0.30	2.87	129.89	23.17	106.72
1952	204.44	62.29	58.09	42.57	7.14	8.38	4.20	0.41	3.79	142.15	24.97	117.18
1953	217.15+	67.58	62.16	45.93	7.64	8.59	5.42	0.52	4.91	149.57	26.48	123.09
1954	213.31	67.70	61.76	44.93	8.24	8.60	5.94	0.57	5.37	145.61	27.80	117.81
1955	243.97	76.15	69.17	50.89	8.82	9.45+	6.98	0.66	6.33	167.82	29.98	137.84
1956	259.13	85.13	75.99	56.23	9.67	10.10	9.15−	0.80	8.34	174.00	32.39	141.61
1957	271.97	92.74	82.45+	61.36	10.61	10.49	10.29	0.92	9.37	179.23	34.81	144.42
1958	272.93	97.47	85.92	63.74	11.45+	10.72	11.55−	1.09	10.46	175.46	36.64	138.82
1959	308.96	108.53	95.60	71.44	12.45+	11.70	12.93	1.24	11.69	200.43	38.58	161.85−
1960	312.06	114.82	100.78	75.27	13.34	12.17	14.03	1.45+	12.58	197.24	40.73	156.51
1961	319.67	121.62	106.70	79.88	14.17	12.66	14.92	1.73	13.19	198.05−	41.84	156.20
1962	352.58	133.44	117.07	88.29	15.31	13.47	16.37	2.06	14.31	219.14	43.76	175.38
1963	375.73	144.38	126.27	95.86	16.41	14.00	18.11	2.42	15.69	231.34	45.62	185.72
1964	406.34	158.74	139.16	106.19	18.01	14.97	19.57	2.78	16.79	247.60	48.34	199.26
1965	445.73	175.14	154.05+	118.40	19.60	16.05−	21.09	3.13	17.96	270.59	51.31	219.28
1966	495.81	198.08	175.82	137.42	21.42	16.98	22.27	3.13	19.14	297.72	54.62	243.10
1967	508.85	212.40	188.75	148.69	22.18	17.89	23.64	3.36	20.28	296.45	56.44	240.01
1968	565.78	240.03	214.94	170.40	25.07	19.47	25.08	3.64	21.44	325.75	59.74	266.01
1969	618.00	267.77	241.60	192.38	27.89	21.32	26.18	3.74	22.44	350.23	63.96	286.28

Table B-3. *Tangible Nonhuman Gross Investment in Current Dollars, by Type,* *U.S. Domestic Economy* (billions of dollars)

YEAR	Total	Land	Structures	Equipment	Inventories	Addendum: Military Reproducibles
1929	29.47	0.0	11.48	15.46	2.53	.21
1930	20.26		9.28	12.04	−1.06	.23
1931	13.42		6.79	8.73	−2.09	.24
1932	5.36		3.86	5.62	−4.12	.24
1933	5.75		3.19	5.38	−2.81	.24
1934	10.42		4.16	6.87	−.62	.27
1935	14.95		4.71	8.67	1.56	.35
1936	20.24		6.96	11.09	2.19	.39
1937	23.83		7.69	12.77	3.38	.44
1938	17.41		7.55	10.12	−.25	.54
1939	21.84		8.74	11.76	1.34	.76
1940	27.69		9.30	15.12	3.27	1.92
1941	39.32		12.63	20.81	5.88	5.46
1942	48.39		14.63	29.71	4.06	22.65
1943	54.70		8.92	44.35	1.42	35.38
1944	57.52		6.14	49.12	2.26	37.41
1945	47.56		6.67	40.74	.15	25.16
1946	52.31		15.65	29.39	7.27	2.82
1947	58.70		21.51	39.16	−1.98	2.13
1948	76.63		27.80	43.80	5.03	2.29
1949	72.10		28.43	44.60	−.92	3.29

Table B-3. (Completed)

YEAR	Total	Land	Structures	Equipment	Inventories	Addendum: Military Reproducibles
1950	96.34		35.58	53.36	7.39	4.54
1951	106.72		37.79	58.67	10.26	8.56
1952	117.18		39.49	70.45	7.23	23.72
1953	123.09		42.06	75.45	5.59	22.13
1954	117.81		44.60	70.85	2.37	19.00
1955	137.84		49.37	78.65	9.82	16.43
1956	141.61		51.95	81.89	7.77	17.84
1957	144.42		52.71	88.82	2.90	20.58
1958	138.82		53.60	81.89	3.32	20.41
1959	161.85		58.78	92.44	10.63	20.70
1960	156.51		57.35	92.81	6.35	17.82
1961	156.20		58.88	92.41	4.91	20.17
1962	175.38		63.14	102.19	10.05	20.48
1963	185.72		66.34	109.35	10.04	20.44
1964	199.26		69.44	118.34	11.48	18.29
1965	219.28		75.46	129.14	14.68	15.65
1966	243.10		78.97	142.06	22.07	17.94
1967	240.01		80.08	150.08	9.85	20.97
1968	266.01		88.93	165.57	11.51	22.15
1969	286.28		95.39	179.00	11.89	22.50

Table B-4. *Total Gross Investment in Constant Dollars, by Sector, U.S. National Economy* (billions of 1958 dollars)

YEAR	National Total	DOMESTIC INVESTMENT BY SECTOR				Net Foreign Investment
		Total	Personal	Business	Government	
1929	119.04	117.52	65.55	36.97	15.00	1.52
1930	98.39	96.99	54.43	25.67	16.89	1.40
1931	83.33	82.89	50.15	14.69	18.05	0.44
1932	61.39	60.97	39.69	4.44	16.84	0.42
1933	60.69	60.31	38.34	6.73	15.24	0.38
1934	73.62	72.60	44.05	10.66	17.89	1.02
1935	85.59	85.72	48.40	19.73	17.59	−.013
1936	104.78	104.99	55.41	25.80	23.78	−.022
1937	110.49	110.35	58.16	31.13	21.07	0.14
1938	97.51	94.99	53.56	17.63	23.80	2.53
1939	111.86	109.80	60.23	24.76	24.81	2.06
1940	128.72	125.28	68.02	30.75	26.51	3.44
1941	156.39	154.01	79.57	36.64	37.80	2.38
1942	176.23	176.62	71.68	21.93	83.01	−0.39
1943	189.28	193.23	71.04	15.10	107.08	−3.95
1944	191.85	195.46	69.29	15.55	110.62	−3.61
1945	171.32	173.73	74.54	21.06	78.14	−2.41
1946	170.46	163.60	93.28	51.03	19.30	6.86
1947	177.71	165.78	97.01	48.87	19.90	11.94
1948	185.61	183.21	103.14	55.78	24.28	2.41
1949	177.68	177.03	105.43	42.15	29.45	0.65

Table B-4. (Completed)

YEAR	National Total	Total	Personal	Business	Government	Net Foreign Investment
		DOMESTIC INVESTMENT BY SECTOR				
1950	208.18	210.97	120.02	60.62	30.33	−2.79
1951	220.83	220.65	116.98	65.22	38.45	0.18
1952	236.28	236.63	118.51	56.83	61.29	−0.35
1953	245.86	248.23	127.10	57.60	63.53	−2.37
1954	241.30	241.80	130.71	51.28	59.81	−0.50
1955	270.49	271.02	147.78	66.25	57.00	−0.54
1956	277.20	275.56	147.94	68.13	59.50	1.64
1957	281.15	277.68	149.36	64.53	63.79	3.47
1958	272.77	272.93	147.61	54.59	70.73	−0.16
1959	300.44	302.44	162.33	66.94	73.17	−2.00
1960	302.87	301.24	163.82	68.66	68.76	1.63
1961	308.37	305.47	164.94	65.35	75.18	2.90
1962	334.18	331.87	178.84	75.18	77.85	2.32
1963	351.19	348.29	188.33	78.05	81.91	2.90
1964	374.69	369.47	201.58	85.12	82.77	5.22
1965	402.49	398.82	217.12	99.24	82.46	3.67
1966	433.36	431.21	229.24	111.81	90.16	2.15
1967	430.25	428.34	227.18	104.79	96.37	1.91
1968	456.40	456.72	248.93	108.47	99.32	−0.32
1969	474.70	475.40	259.83	116.25	99.31	−0.70

Table B-5. *Total Gross Investment in Constant Dollars, by Type, U.S. Domestic Economy* (billions of 1958 dollars)

| YEAR | Grand Total | Intangible Total | HUMAN INTANGIBLES | | | | NONHUMAN INTANGIBLES | | | | TANGIBLES | |
			Total	Education and Training	Medical and Health	Mobility	Total	Basic Research	AR&D	Total	Human	Nonhuman
1929	117.52	36.28	35.61	25.53	4.03	6.05+	0.67	0.10	0.58	81.24	17.15−	64.09
1930	96.99	33.92	33.18	23.59	3.94	5.66	0.74	0.10	0.64	63.07	16.27	46.80
1931	82.89	32.33	31.43	21.98	3.76	5.70	0.90	0.13	0.77	50.56	15.76	34.80
1932	60.97	29.51	28.53	19.25−	3.48	5.80	0.98	0.14	0.84	31.46	14.40	17.06
1933	60.31	29.19	28.32	18.84	3.26	6.22	0.88	0.13	0.75−	31.11	13.50	17.61
1934	72.60	30.67	29.80	20.08	3.33	6.38	0.87	0.12	0.75−	41.94	13.23	28.71
1935	85.72	32.32	31.37	21.35−	3.54	6.49	0.95−	0.13	0.82	53.40	13.47	39.92
1936	104.99	35.72	34.69	24.16	3.77	6.75−	1.03	0.14	0.89	69.27	14.32	54.96
1937	110.35−	37.34	36.25−	25.58	3.97	6.70	1.10	0.15	0.94	73.01	14.52	58.49
1938	94.99	36.40	35.14	24.60	3.81	6.74	1.26	0.18	1.08	58.58	14.53	44.06
1939	109.80	39.34	37.97	26.74	4.24	6.99	1.38	0.20	1.18	70.46	15.19	55.28
1940	125.28	42.66	41.08	29.33	4.40	7.36	1.58	0.21	1.37	82.62	15.35+	67.27
1941	154.01	48.85−	46.33	33.86	4.52	7.95	2.52	0.29	2.23	105.16	15.97	89.19
1942	176.62	58.22	55.68	41.93	4.75−	9.01	2.54	0.27	2.27	118.40	16.16	102.24
1943	193.23	62.73	60.20	48.40	5.01	6.79	2.53	0.27	2.26	130.50	17.07	113.43
1944	195.46	62.51	59.89	49.57	5.42	4.90	2.62	0.27	2.35+	132.94	18.09	114.85+
1945	173.73	63.51	60.75−	48.70	5.80	6.26	2.76	0.29	2.48	110.23	19.25	90.97
1946	163.60	60.22	57.27	41.56	6.52	9.18	2.95−	0.26	2.69	103.38	19.89	83.49

Year												
1947	165.78	63.20	59.80	43.42	6.93	9.45–	3.40	0.29	3.11	102.58	20.40	82.18
1948	183.21	65.52	61.63	44.50	7.49	9.63	3.89	0.34	3.55+	117.69	21.42	96.27
1949	177.03	63.79	59.96	43.00	7.70	9.26	3.83	0.35	3.48	113.24	22.59	90.65+
1950	210.97	68.34	64.24	45.96	8.29	9.99	4.11	0.39	3.71	142.63	23.47	119.16
1951	220.65+	73.20	68.67	49.97	8.42	10.27	4.53	0.45–	4.09	147.46	25.18	122.28
1952	236.63	77.05	71.35–	52.23	8.79	10.33	5.71	0.51	5.20	159.58	26.81	132.77
1953	248.23	81.03	73.92	54.61	9.13	10.18	7.12	0.68	6.43	167.20	28.39	138.81
1954	241.80	79.52	71.98	52.40	9.58	10.00	7.54	0.73	6.81	162.28	29.74	132.54
1955	271.02	86.41	78.04	57.47	10.00	10.57	8.36	0.79	7.57	184.62	32.10	152.52
1956	275.56	91.77	81.85–	60.55–	10.50	10.80	9.93	0.88	9.05–	183.79	34.30	149.49
1957	277.68	95.69	85.13	63.27	11.06	10.80	10.56	0.95–	9.61	181.99	35.73	146.26
1958	272.93	97.47	85.92	63.74	11.45	10.72	11.55–	1.09	10.46	175.46	36.64	138.82
1959	302.44	104.36	92.06	68.87	11.99	11.20	12.31	1.18	11.13	198.08	38.55+	159.52
1960	301.24	107.41	94.38	70.63	12.41	11.34	13.03	1.34	11.69	193.83	40.19	153.63
1961	305.47	111.13	97.64	73.27	12.84	11.52	13.50	1.54	11.95	194.34	41.04	153.30
1962	331.87	118.63	104.23	78.78	13.55+	11.90	14.40	1.78	12.62	213.23	42.51	170.73
1963	348.29	124.98	109.41	83.20	14.19	12.03	15.56	2.03	13.53	223.31	43.80	179.51
1964	369.47	132.72	116.69	89.11	15.21	12.37	16.04	2.25–	13.79	236.75–	46.12	190.63
1965	398.82	142.47	125.46	96.46	16.14	12.86	17.01	2.45–	14.56	256.35+	48.09	208.26
1966	431.21	155.01	137.59	107.62	16.87	13.10	17.42	2.36	15.06	276.20	49.83	226.37
1967	428.34	160.17	142.25	112.05	16.46	13.74	17.92	2.46	15.46	268.17	50.82	217.35
1968	456.72	172.24	153.96	121.88	17.64	14.44	18.28	2.56	15.72	284.48	52.18	232.30
1969	475.40	181.32	163.12	129.96	18.22	14.94	18.21	2.51	15.70	294.07	53.73	240.34

Table B-6. *Tangible Nonhuman Gross Investment in Constant Dollars, by Type, U.S. Domestic Economy* (billions of 1958 dollars)

YEAR	Total	Land	Structures	Equipment	Inventories	Addendum: Military Reproducibles
1929	64.09	0.0	29.85	29.27	4.96	0.46
1930	46.80		25.30	23.49	−1.98	0.56
1931	34.80		20.58	18.58	−4.37	0.65
1932	17.06		13.66	13.29	−9.90	0.72
1933	17.61		11.27	13.57	−7.23	0.68
1934	28.71		14.85	16.12	−2.27	0.69
1935	39.92		15.78	20.72	3.42	0.90
1936	54.96		23.37	26.50	5.08	0.98
1937	58.49		22.69	28.62	7.18	0.98
1938	44.06		22.68	22.18	−.80	1.26
1939	55.28		25.82	26.23	3.23	1.81
1940	67.27		26.65	33.27	7.35	4.57
1941	89.19		33.69	43.09	12.41	12.57
1942	102.24		35.75	58.67	7.82	48.34
1943	113.43		20.28	90.09	3.06	74.76
1944	114.85		12.94	99.18	2.73	79.12
1945	90.97		12.94	79.17	−1.14	52.67
1946	83.49		26.39	45.72	11.38	5.13
1947	82.18		30.22	53.78	−1.83	3.32
1948	96.27		35.50	56.07	4.69	3.21
1949	90.65		37.11	55.15	−1.61	4.43

Table B-6.   (Completed)

YEAR	Total	Land	Structures	Equipment	Inventories	Addendum: Military Reproducibles
1950	119.16		44.95	65.05	9.16	5.99
1951	122.28		44.17	67.19	10.91	10.63
1952	132.77		44.56	80.88	7.32	28.64
1953	138.81		46.73	86.06	6.02	26.60
1954	132.54		49.86	80.76	1.91	22.51
1955	152.52		53.83	88.36	10.33	18.85
1956	149.49		53.97	87.74	7.78	19.07
1957	146.26		52.89	90.66	2.72	21.00
1958	138.82		53.60	81.89	3.32	20.41
1959	159.52		57.85	90.82	10.85	20.31
1960	153.63		56.06	91.41	6.17	17.45
1961	153.30		57.16	91.31	4.83	19.74
1962	170.73		60.04	100.77	9.91	20.00
1963	179.51		61.85	107.71	9.94	19.97
1964	190.63		63.28	116.08	11.27	17.74
1965	208.26		67.33	127.17	13.76	15.00
1966	226.37		66.31	139.38	20.68	17.13
1967	217.35		64.40	143.72	9.22	19.56
1968	232.30		67.64	154.40	10.26	19.86
1969	240.34		67.66	162.59	10.10	19.85

Table B-7.   *Total Net Investment in Current Dollars, by Sector, U.S. National Economy* (billions of dollars)

| YEAR | National Total | DOMESTIC INVESTMENT BY SECTOR | | | | Net Foreign Investment |
		Total	Personal	Business	Government	
1929	20.63	19.86	8.93	6.77	4.17	0.77
1930	10.04	9.35	3.03	1.54	4.77	0.69
1931	2.51	2.32	0.13	−2.46	4.64	0.20
1932	−5.04	−5.20	−3.77	−5.33	3.90	0.17
1933	−4.32	−4.47	−3.73	−4.06	3.31	0.15
1934	0.72	0.29	−1.46	−2.25	4.00	0.43
1935	5.41	5.46	0.34	0.99	4.12	−0.05
1936	10.98	11.07	2.44	2.89	5.74	−0.09
1937	13.88	13.81	3.17	5.23	5.41	0.06
1938	7.29	6.18	0.53	−0.53	6.18	1.11
1939	12.97	12.09	3.38	2.19	6.51	0.89
1940	20.31	18.80	6.72	4.74	7.33	1.51
1941	30.98	29.86	10.75	7.35	11.76	1.12
1942	39.56	39.77	6.75	0.62	32.39	−0.21
1943	42.79	45.04	6.78	−2.34	40.60	−2.24
1944	31.46	33.56	5.68	−1.49	29.37	−2.10
1945	10.00	11.44	7.29	1.44	2.70	−1.44
1946	32.34	27.77	18.55	18.07	−8.85	4.57
1947	41.18	32.28	22.52	15.85	−6.09	8.90
1948	50.51	48.59	26.67	21.77	0.15	1.92
1949	41.07	40.56	25.17	9.19	6.20	0.51

Table B-7. (Completed)

YEAR	National Total	DOMESTIC INVESTMENT BY SECTOR				Net Foreign Investment
		Total	Personal	Business	Government	
1950	62.71	64.95	34.71	22.49	7.75	−2.24
1951	72.44	72.28	29.77	27.06	15.45	0.16
1952	83.32	83.62	28.40	18.84	36.38	−0.30
1953	85.81	87.91	33.40	18.18	36.33	−2.10
1954	76.68	77.14	33.21	12.46	31.47	−0.45
1955	98.45	98.94	45.75	24.25	28.94	−0.49
1956	100.43	98.88	40.71	25.35	32.82	1.54
1957	101.05	97.66	38.46	21.16	38.05	3.38
1958	89.70	89.86	34.68	10.29	44.88	−0.16
1959	114.46	116.76	47.14	21.77	47.85	−2.30
1960	113.80	112.11	46.12	21.87	44.12	1.68
1961	116.21	113.17	44.34	16.84	51.99	3.04
1962	138.97	136.52	55.43	25.33	55.76	2.45
1963	151.86	148.74	61.49	26.06 .	61.20	3.11
1964	170.40	164.72	70.00	30.82	63.91	5.68
1965	192.81	188.74	79.80	43.04	65.90	4.07
1966	227.02	224.58	93.65	52.56	78.36	2.45
1967	217.64	215.39	86.32	41.01	88.06	2.24
1968	246.93	247.33	108.28	43.56	94.58	−0.39
1969	266.85	267.76	114.47	51.77	101.52	−0.90

Table B-8. *Total Net Investment in Current Dollars, by Type, U.S. Domestic Economy* (billions of dollars)

YEAR	Grand Total	Intangible Total	HUMAN INTANGIBLES				NONHUMAN INTANGIBLES				TANGIBLES	
			Total	Education and Training	Medical and Health	Mobility	Total	Basic Research	AR&D	Total	Human	Nonhuman
1929	19.86	6.09	5.98	5.73	0.69	-0.44	0.12	0.04	0.08	13.77	4.67	9.10
1930	9.35-	4.87	4.75-	4.70	0.60	-0.56	0.13	0.04	0.09	4.47	3.75-	0.73
1931	2.32	3.67	3.51	3.39	0.44	-0.33	0.16	0.05-	0.12	-1.35-	2.71	-4.06
1932	-5.20	2.31	2.15-	2.11	0.25+	-0.21	0.16	0.05-	0.12	-7.51	1.77	-9.28
1933	-4.47	2.06	1.94	1.85-	0.16	-0.07	0.12	0.04	0.08	-6.53	1.35+	-7.88
1934	0.29	2.54	2.44	2.24	0.21	-0.01	0.11	0.04	0.07	-2.25-	1.31	-3.56
1935	5.46	3.11	2.99	2.54	0.27	0.18	0.12	0.04	0.08	2.36	1.34	1.02
1936	11.07	3.88	3.74	3.29	0.34	0.11	0.14	0.05	0.09	7.19	1.57	5.62
1937	13.81	4.65+	4.49	3.86	0.41	0.22	0.16	0.06	0.10	9.16	1.70	7.47
1938	6.18	3.86	3.66	3.38	0.36	-0.08	0.20	0.06	0.14	2.32	1.65-	0.68
1939	12.09	5.00	4.77	4.28	0.49	0.01	0.24	0.07	0.16	7.08	2.03	5.05-
1940	18.80	6.75-	6.45-	5.16	0.53	0.76	0.30	0.08	0.22	12.05+	2.13	9.92
1941	29.86	8.85+	8.16	6.70	0.56	0.90	0.69	0.12	0.58	21.01	2.41	18.59
1942	39.77	13.39	12.65-	11.15+	0.65-	0.85-	0.74	0.12	0.62	26.38	2.98	23.40
1943	45.04	15.97	15.23	14.93	0.79	-0.48	0.74	0.14	0.60	29.06	3.80	25.26
1944	33.56	15.69	14.93	14.73	0.94	-0.74	0.76	0.14	0.62	17.87	4.19	13.68
1945	11.44	14.71	13.93	12.87	1.04	0.02	0.77	0.15	0.62	-3.27	4.71	-7.98
1946	27.77	12.61	11.85-	9.38	1.43	1.04	0.77	0.13	0.64	15.16	5.90	9.25+

1947	32.28	16.71	15.74	13.27	1.70	0.76	0.98	0.17	0.81	15.57	7.24	8.33
1948	48.59	19.13	17.88	15.23	2.06	0.59	1.26	0.21	1.05+	29.46	8.44	21.00
1949	40.56	17.42	16.27	13.98	2.08	0.21	1.14	0.21	0.93	23.14	8.95−	14.19
1950	64.95−	20.34	19.13	16.14	2.33	0.66	1.21	0.25−	0.96	44.61	9.56	35.05+
1951	72.29	23.90	22.48	19.53	2.40	0.56	1.41	0.30	1.11	48.39	11.79	36.60
1952	83.62	25.80	23.64	20.85+	2.59	0.20	2.16	0.41	1.75+	57.83	13.10	44.72
1953	87.91	28.39	25.29	22.50	2.83	−0.04	3.10	0.52	2.59	59.52	14.47	45.06
1954	77.14	26.29	23.00	20.34	3.05+	−0.38	3.29	0.57	2.72	50.84	15.56	35.29
1955	98.94	32.35−	28.50	25.52	3.22	−0.24	3.85+	0.66	3.20	66.59	17.40	49.19
1956	98.88	35.88	30.62	27.36	3.55−	−0.29	5.26	0.80	4.46	63.00	19.31	43.69
1957	97.66	38.47	32.80	29.46	3.83	−0.49	5.67	0.92	4.75−	59.20	20.93	38.26
1958	89.86	39.86	33.64	29.86	4.06	−0.29	6.22	1.09	5.13	50.00	22.02	27.98
1959	116.76	46.71	40.07	35.18	4.42	0.47	6.64	1.24	5.40	70.06	23.46	46.60
1960	112.11	49.78	42.94	37.96	4.66	0.32	6.84	1.45	5.38	62.33	25.29	37.05−
1961	113.17	52.23	45.48	40.30	4.87	0.32	6.76	1.73	5.03	60.94	26.46	34.48
1962	136.52	59.44	52.27	45.90	5.34	1.03	7.17	2.06	5.12	77.07	27.62	49.45
1963	148.74	65.89	58.02	50.82	5.75+	1.45−	7.87	2.42	5.45−	82.85+	28.75+	54.10
1964	164.72	73.76	65.77	57.68	6.58	1.51	7.99	2.78	5.22	90.96	30.56	60.41
1965	188.74	84.37	75.86	66.65	7.26	1.95−	8.51	3.13	5.38	104.38	32.33	72.05−
1966	224.58	102.14	94.91	82.78	8.39	3.73	7.23	3.13	4.10	122.44	37.20	85.24
1967	215.39	109.59	102.43	91.57	7.68	3.18	7.17	3.36	3.81	105.80	38.10	67.70
1968	247.33	128.74	121.09	107.16	9.17	4.76	7.65	3.64	4.01	118.59	40.08	78.51
1969	267.76	143.78	136.47	122.30	10.03	4.14	7.31	3.74	3.58	123.97	42.71	81.26

Table B-9. *Tangible Nonhuman Net Investment in Current Dollars, by Type, U.S. Domestic Economy* (billions of dollars)

YEAR	Total	Land	Structures	Equipment	Inventories	Addendum: Military Reproducibles
1929	9.10	0.0	4.44	2.14	2.53	−0.37
1930	0.73		2.39	−0.60	−1.06	−0.23
1931	−4.06		0.43	−2.40	−2.09	−0.20
1932	−9.28		−1.46	−3.70	−4.12	−0.09
1933	−7.88		−2.19	−2.87	−2.81	−0.07
1934	−3.56		−1.50	−1.44	−0.62	−0.09
1935	1.02		−0.92	0.37	1.56	−0.18
1936	5.62		1.16	2.28	2.19	0.09
1937	7.47		1.35	2.75	3.38	0.04
1938	0.68		1.21	−0.28	−0.25	0.14
1939	5.05		2.33	1.38	1.34	0.36
1940	9.92		2.66	3.99	3.27	1.39
1941	18.59		4.99	7.73	5.88	4.37
1942	23.40		4.74	14.61	4.06	20.06
1943	25.26		−1.93	25.77	1.42	28.41
1944	13.68		−4.79	16.21	2.26	16.57
1945	−7.98		−3.67	−4.46	0.15	−6.69
1946	9.25		4.39	−2.41	7.27	−12.40
1947	8.33		7.45	2.85	−1.98	−11.96
1948	21.02		11.80	4.19	5.03	−10.04
1949	14.19		12.18	2.94	−0.92	−7.37

Table B-9.   (Completed)

YEAR	Total	Land	Structures	Equipment	Inventories	Addendum: Military Reproducibles
1950	35.05		18.19	9.46	7.39	−4.79
1951	36.60		17.98	8.36	10.26	−1.00
1952	44.72		18.16	19.33	7.23	15.10
1953	45.06		19.58	19.89	5.59	10.90
1954	35.29		21.38	11.53	2.37	5.70
1955	49.19		24.52	14.85	9.82	1.94
1956	43.69		24.71	11.21	7.77	2.32
1957	38.26		23.21	12.16	2.90	4.09
1958	27.98		22.78	1.88	3.32	3.05
1959	46.60		26.43	9.54	10.63	2.77
1960	37.05		23.56	7.13	6.35	−0.37
1961	34.48		23.80	5.77	4.91	2.44
1962	49.45		26.36	13.04	10.05	2.53
1963	54.10		27.96	16.10	10.04	2.27
1964	60.41		29.04	19.89	11.48	−0.24
1965	72.04		32.82	24.54	14.68	−2.81
1966	85.24		32.17	31.00	22.07	0.14
1967	67.70		29.39	28.46	9.85	2.74
1968	78.51		33.69	33.31	11.51	2.65
1969	81.26		34.49	34.88	11.89	2.19

Table B-10. *Total Net Investment in Constant Dollars, by Sector, U.S. National Economy* (billions of 1958 dollars)

| YEAR | National Total | DOMESTIC INVESTMENT BY SECTOR | | | | Net Foreign Investment |
		Total	Personal	Business	Government	
1929	43.88	42.36	16.58	15.13	10.65	1.52
1930	22.21	20.81	4.82	3.48	12.51	1.40
1931	7.08	6.64	−0.16	−6.77	13.57	0.44
1932	−12.87	−13.29	−9.85	−15.73	12.29	0.42
1933	−11.66	−12.05	−10.33	−12.29	10.58	0.38
1934	2.10	1.08	−4.36	−7.68	13.12	1.02
1935	13.68	13.80	−0.35	1.46	12.69	−0.13
1936	30.03	30.25	4.61	6.99	18.65	−0.22
1937	33.79	33.65	6.54	11.57	15.54	0.14
1938	19.03	16.51	0.64	−2.10	17.97	2.53
1939	33.39	31.33	7.59	5.16	18.58	2.06
1940	49.98	46.54	16.19	10.48	19.86	3.44
1941	71.43	69.05	23.82	15.52	29.72	2.38
1942	85.50	85.89	13.48	1.15	71.26	−0.39
1943	88.89	92.84	11.41	−4.43	85.86	−3.95
1944	61.09	64.69	8.43	−3.40	59.66	−3.61
1945	13.98	16.39	9.98	1.80	4.62	−2.41
1946	46.47	39.61	25.65	29.89	−15.93	6.86
1947	55.86	43.92	29.15	24.46	−9.69	11.94
1948	62.67	60.26	32.49	28.35	−0.58	2.41
1949	51.94	51.30	30.79	12.42	8.08	0.65

Table B-10. (Completed)

YEAR	National Total	DOMESTIC INVESTMENT BY SECTOR				Net Foreign Investment
		Total	Personal	Business	Government	
1950	78.13	80.92	40.83	28.86	11.23	−2.79
1951	84.83	84.65	33.08	31.58	19.99	0.18
1952	96.11	96.46	30.40	21.93	44.13	−0.35
1953	97.88	100.25	35.75	21.45	43.06	−2.37
1954	85.97	86.47	35.92	13.81	36.74	−0.50
1955	108.38	108.92	49.18	26.97	32.77	−0.54
1956	106.05	104.40	42.54	26.81	35.05	1.64
1957	102.92	99.45	39.16	21.36	38.93	3.47
1958	89.70	89.86	34.68	10.29	44.89	−0.16
1959	112.69	114.69	46.40	21.48	46.81	−2.00
1960	109.53	107.90	44.90	21.25	41.75	1.63
1961	110.39	107.49	42.96	16.27	48.26	2.90
1962	129.87	127.55	52.84	24.25	50.47	2.32
1963	139.39	136.49	57.62	24.72	54.14	2.90
1964	153.28	148.05	64.77	28.95	54.34	5.22
1965	169.96	166.29	73.11	39.37	53.81	3.67
1966	193.47	191.32	83.03	46.54	61.74	2.15
1967	179.57	177.66	75.06	35.12	67.48	1.91
1968	193.86	194.18	89.11	35.67	69.40	−0.32
1969	198.11	198.81	90.12	40.16	68.52	−0.70

Table B-11. Total Net Investment in Constant Dollars, by Type, U.S. Domestic Economy (billions of 1958 dollars)

YEAR	Grand Total	Intangible Total	HUMAN INTANGIBLES				NONHUMAN INTANGIBLES			TANGIBLES		
			Total	Education and Training	Medical and Health	Mobility	Total	Basic Research	AR&D	Total	Human	Nonhuman
1929	42.36	13.94	13.64	13.28	1.46	-1.10	0.30	0.10	0.20	28.42	8.19	20.23
1930	20.81	11.44	11.09	11.21	1.29	-1.41	0.35	0.10	0.24	9.38	6.89	2.49
1931	6.64	9.26	8.78	8.66	1.00	-0.88	0.48	0.13	0.35	-2.62	5.73	-8.34
1932	-13.29	6.50	5.97	5.97	0.67	-0.67	0.53	0.14	0.39	-19.79	4.34	-24.12
1933	-12.05	6.05	5.67	5.45	0.45	-0.23	0.38	0.13	0.25	-18.10	3.44	-21.54
1934	1.08	7.18	6.85	6.39	0.50	-0.04	0.33	0.12	0.21	-6.10	3.10	-9.21
1935	13.80	8.68	8.31	7.12	0.64	0.55	0.37	0.13	0.24	5.12	3.05	2.07
1936	30.25	10.73	10.31	9.22	0.78	0.31	0.42	0.14	0.28	19.51	3.55	15.97
1937	33.65	12.21	11.76	10.23	0.91	0.61	0.45	0.15	0.29	21.45	3.68	17.77
1938	16.51	10.13	9.55	9.10	0.71	-0.25	0.57	0.18	0.40	6.38	3.74	2.65
1939	31.33	13.25	12.61	11.50	1.09	0.01	0.65	0.20	0.45	18.08	4.69	13.39
1940	46.54	17.79	16.99	13.68	1.16	2.15	0.80	0.21	0.59	28.75	4.84	23.91
1941	69.05	21.63	19.96	16.49	1.15	2.31	1.67	0.29	1.39	47.42	5.07	42.35
1942	85.89	28.60	27.01	23.89	1.26	1.86	1.59	0.27	1.32	57.29	5.43	51.86
1943	92.84	30.93	29.47	28.96	1.46	-0.94	1.46	0.27	1.19	61.91	6.25	55.66
1944	64.69	29.57	28.13	27.78	1.69	-1.34	1.44	0.27	1.17	35.13	6.57	28.56
1945	16.39	27.17	25.72	23.82	1.85	0.05	1.45	0.29	1.17	-10.79	7.12	-17.91
1946	39.61	21.50	20.06	15.93	2.39	1.74	1.44	0.26	1.19	18.11	8.25	9.87

1947	43.92	26.04	24.37	20.58	2.61	1.18	1.67	0.29	1.38	17.88	9.01	8.88
1948	60.26	27.93	25.87	22.05	2.96	0.86	2.06	0.34	1.72	32.33	9.89	22.44
1949	51.30	24.85	23.00	19.83	2.87	0.30	1.85	0.35	1.50	26.45	10.75	15.70
1950	80.92	28.04	26.19	22.09	3.18	0.91	1.85	0.39	1.46	52.88	11.29	41.59
1951	84.65	31.01	28.99	25.17	3.09	0.73	2.02	0.45	1.57	53.64	12.81	40.84
1952	96.46	31.96	29.03	25.60	3.19	0.24	2.93	0.51	2.43	64.50	14.06	50.44
1953	100.25	34.17	30.10	26.78	3.38	-0.05	4.07	0.68	3.38	66.09	15.50	50.58
1954	86.47	30.98	26.81	23.71	3.55	-0.45	4.17	0.73	3.44	55.49	16.64	38.84
1955	108.92	36.81	32.21	28.82	3.65	-0.26	4.61	0.79	3.82	72.11	18.63	53.47
1956	104.40	38.73	33.01	29.47	3.86	-0.31	5.71	0.88	4.83	65.68	20.45	45.23
1957	99.45	39.69	33.87	30.37	3.99	-0.50	5.82	0.95	4.87	59.76	21.49	38.27
1958	89.86	39.86	33.64	29.86	4.06	-0.29	6.22	1.09	5.13	50.00	22.02	27.98
1959	114.69	44.93	38.61	33.91	4.25	0.45	6.32	1.18	5.14	69.76	23.44	46.31
1960	107.90	46.57	40.22	35.58	4.34	0.30	6.35	1.34	5.01	61.33	24.95	36.38
1961	107.49	47.70	41.59	36.88	4.42	0.29	6.11	1.54	4.57	59.79	25.95	33.84
1962	127.55	52.77	46.47	40.83	4.73	0.91	6.30	1.78	4.52	74.78	26.83	47.96
1963	136.49	56.90	50.15	43.93	4.98	1.24	6.75	2.03	4.72	79.59	27.60	51.99
1964	148.05	61.57	55.03	48.23	5.56	1.24	6.54	2.25	4.30	86.48	29.15	57.33
1965	166.29	68.46	61.61	54.07	5.98	1.56	6.85	2.45	4.40	97.84	30.31	67.53
1966	191.32	79.52	73.93	64.46	6.61	2.85	5.59	2.36	3.23	111.80	33.94	77.86
1967	177.66	83.52	78.15	69.37	5.70	3.07	5.37	2.46	2.91	94.14	34.29	59.85
1968	194.18	92.20	86.70	76.94	6.45	3.31	5.50	2.56	2.94	101.98	35.00	66.98
1969	198.81	96.80	91.79	82.52	6.55	2.71	5.00	2.51	2.50	102.01	35.89	66.12

Table B-12. *Tangible Nonhuman Net Investment in Constant Dollars, by Type, U.S. Domestic Economy* (billions of 1958 dollars)

YEAR	Total	Land	Structures	Equipment	Inventories	Addendum: Military Reproducible
1929	20.23	0.0	11.52	3.74	4.96	−0.92
1930	2.49		6.51	−2.04	−1.98	−0.69
1931	−8.34		1.63	−5.61	−4.37	−0.47
1932	−24.12		−5.15	−9.08	−9.90	−0.27
1933	−21.54		−7.20	−7.10	−7.23	−0.29
1934	−9.21		−3.31	−3.63	−2.27	−0.25
1935	2.07		−2.15	.80	3.42	−0.02
1936	15.97		5.47	5.41	5.08	0.08
1937	17.77		4.61	5.98	7.18	0.0
1938	2.65		4.42	−0.97	−0.80	0.29
1939	13.39		7.36	2.80	3.23	0.73
1940	23.91		7.85	8.71	7.35	3.31
1941	42.35		13.88	16.06	12.41	10.07
1942	51.86		13.06	30.98	7.82	42.52
1943	55.66		−2.68	55.28	3.06	59.96
1944	28.56		−9.34	35.17	2.73	35.03
1945	−17.91		−7.26	−9.51	−1.14	−14.00
1946	9.87		6.68	−8.19	11.38	−23.27
1947	8.88		9.97	.74	−1.83	−19.42
1948	22.44		14.69	3.06	4.69	−14.97
1949	15.70		15.60	1.70	−1.61	−10.50

Table B-12.   (Completed)

YEAR	Total	Land	Structures	Equipment	Inventories	Addendum: Military Reproducible
1950	41.59		22.61	9.82	9.16	−6.82
1951	40.84		20.85	9.07	10.91	−1.36
1952	50.44		20.38	22.74	7.32	18.07
1953	50.58		21.65	22.90	6.02	12.98
1954	38.84		23.76	13.17	1.91	6.56
1955	53.47		26.62	16.52	10.33	1.98
1956	45.23		25.59	11.86	7.78	2.23
1957	38.27		23.24	12.31	2.72	4.11
1958	27.98		22.78	1.88	3.32	3.05
1959	46.31		26.01	9.45	10.85	2.74
1960	36.38		23.08	7.13	6.17	−0.33
1961	33.84		23.14	5.87	4.83	2.40
1962	47.95		25.05	12.99	9.91	2.49
1963	51.98		25.99	16.05	9.94	2.26
1964	57.33		26.30	19.77	11.27	−0.20
1965	67.53		29.10	24.66	13.76	−2.67
1966	77.86		26.73	30.45	20.68	.21
1967	59.85		23.42	27.21	9.22	2.68
1968	66.98		25.47	31.25	10.26	2.49
1969	66.12		24.25	31.78	10.10	2.12

Table B-13. *Total Gross Stocks in Current Dollars, by Sector, U.S. National Economy* (billions of dollars)

| YEAR | National Total | DOMESTIC CAPITAL STOCKS BY SECTOR | | | | Net Foreign Assets and Monetary Metals |
		Total	Personal	Business	Government	
1929	1202.7	1186.2	687.5	363.4	135.3	16.5
1930	1182.7	1165.6	677.5	355.3	132.7	17.2
1931	1083.2	1066.9	618.5	324.3	124.0	16.3
1932	960.6	946.2	544.5	286.8	114.8	14.5
1933	931.2	918.2	522.1	275.3	120.8	13.0
1934	995.1	979.2	559.5	287.9	131.7	15.9
1935	1024.6	1007.5	577.0	292.8	137.7	17.1
1936	1062.2	1045.4	597.0	304.2	144.2	16.8
1937	1140.9	1123.8	640.1	324.8	158.8	17.2
1938	1151.2	1133.0	642.0	329.0	162.0	18.1
1939	1161.8	1142.2	644.1	328.7	169.4	19.6
1940	1204.9	1182.8	668.4	334.6	179.8	22.1
1941	1345.0	1320.3	743.9	371.6	204.8	24.7
1942	1571.1	1545.1	871.4	406.3	267.5	25.9
1943	1792.6	1766.8	983.0	430.7	353.1	25.8
1944	1957.1	1932.6	1071.0	444.6	417.0	24.5
1945	2070.9	2047.7	1149.9	459.1	438.6	23.2
1946	2302.7	2276.6	1283.9	507.0	485.6	26.1
1947	2710.0	2677.8	1503.2	594.1	580.4	32.3
1948	3012.2	2974.6	1673.2	665.2	636.2	37.6
1949	3082.9	3043.3	1717.0	686.9	639.3	39.6

Table B-13.   (Completed)

YEAR	National Total	DOMESTIC CAPITAL STOCKS BY SECTOR				Net Foreign Assets and Monetary Metals
		Total	Personal	Business	Government	
1950	3249.2	3210.4	1832.1	736.6	641.7	38.8
1951	3617.2	3578.7	2042.9	829.4	706.3	38.5
1952	3853.5	3814.3	2168.0	887.3	759.0	39.1
1953	4055.3	4015.7	2279.8	920.8	815.1	39.5
1954	4219.0	4179.7	2371.5	947.7	860.5	39.3
1955	4467.0	4428.0	2507.2	1004.1	916.7	38.9
1956	4834.0	4793.5	2693.6	1090.6	1009.3	40.5
1957	5214.3	5169.5	2892.2	1170.4	1106.8	44.8
1958	5502.2	5455.0	3056.0	1227.2	1171.8	47.2
1959	5809.5	5763.5	3232.5	1286.3	1244.7	46.0
1960	6113.6	6067.3	3401.2	1337.3	1328.8	46.3
1961	6382.8	6334.4	3558.3	1382.5	1393.6	48.4
1962	6716.8	6665.1	3744.7	1441.6	1478.8	51.7
1963	7081.0	7025.7	3950.7	1507.1	1567.9	55.3
1964	7582.8	7523.8	4179.5	1675.1	1669.2	59.0
1965	7944.9	7881.5	4421.7	1684.6	1775.2	63.4
1966	8517.7	8451.0	4686.4	1848.5	1915.6	66.7
1967	9161.6	9091.4	5030.9	1990.2	2070.4	70.2
1968	9945.9	9877.8	5447.0	2149.0	2281.8	68.1
1969	10906.6	10837.4	5947.2	2348.8	2541.3	69.2

Table B-14. *Total Gross Capital Stocks in Current Dollars, by Type, U.S. Domestic Economy (billions of dollars)*

| YEAR | Grand Total | Intangible Total | HUMAN INTANGIBLES | | | | NONHUMAN INTANGIBLES | | | | TANGIBLES | |
			Total	Education and Training	Medical and Health	Mobility	Total	Basic Research	AR&D	Total	Human	Nonhuman
1929	1186.2	275.0	272.5	225.8	31.2	15.4	2.6	0.5	2.1	911.1	290.4	620.7
1930	1165.6	276.5	273.9	226.9	32.6	14.4	2.6	0.5	2.1	889.1	284.7	604.3
1931	1066.9	266.1	263.5	219.1	33.2	11.2	2.7	0.6	2.1	800.7	253.5	547.2
1932	946.2	248.5	245.9	205.6	33.3	7.0	2.6	0.6	2.1	697.7	223.1	474.5
1933	918.2	240.2	237.4	198.8	33.6	5.1	2.8	0.6	2.2	678.0	218.2	459.8
1934	979.2	251.0	248.0	207.9	34.7	5.4	3.0	0.6	2.4	728.2	238.9	489.3
1935	1007.5	261.9	258.6	216.6	35.5	6.5	3.3	0.7	2.6	745.6	251.9	493.8
1936	1045.4	272.0	268.4	224.0	36.7	7.7	3.7	0.8	2.9	773.4	258.1	515.3
1937	1123.8	294.4	290.4	243.7	38.4	8.2	4.1	0.9	3.2	829.3	272.7	556.6
1938	1133.0	303.5	299.2	247.9	42.9	8.3	4.4	0.9	3.4	829.5	265.8	563.7
1939	1142.2	308.8	303.9	255.8	40.4	7.7	4.8	1.0	3.8	833.4	266.0	567.4
1940	1182.8	322.6	317.2	267.4	41.9	8.0	5.4	1.1	4.3	860.1	274.8	585.3
1941	1320.3	355.0	348.3	293.7	44.5	10.1	6.7	1.3	5.4	965.3	303.2	662.0
1942	1545.1	411.1	402.7	340.7	48.6	13.3	8.4	1.6	6.8	1134.0	357.7	776.3
1943	1766.8	471.1	460.9	392.4	52.9	15.7	10.1	1.8	8.3	1295.7	403.8	891.9
1944	1932.6	516.2	504.6	432.3	55.9	16.3	11.6	2.1	9.6	1416.4	432.4	984.1
1945	2047.7	558.5	545.7	467.6	58.9	19.2	12.8	2.2	10.5	1489.2	458.3	1030.9
1946	2276.6	626.7	612.7	525.4	64.9	22.4	14.0	2.4	11.6	1649.9	506.9	1143.0

1947	2677.8	720.9	704.1	605.0	74.3	24.9	16.8	2.8	14.0	1956.9	582.8	1374.1
1948	2974.6	803.4	784.2	674.0	83.1	27.1	19.2	3.1	16.1	2171.2	634.1	1537.1
1949	3043.3	852.3	831.0	713.3	89.5	28.3	21.4	3.4	18.0	2190.9	634.4	1556.6
1950	3210.4	910.0	885.5	759.1	95.3	31.1	24.4	3.7	20.7	2300.5	662.0	1638.5
1951	3578.7	1003.9	975.3	833.7	105.8	35.9	28.6	4.3	24.3	2574.8	738.7	1836.0
1952	3814.3	1094.7	1061.8	907.1	115.9	38.9	32.9	4.8	28.1	2719.6	768.8	1950.8
1953	4015.7	1177.6	1139.7	974.4	124.7	40.6	37.9	5.5	32.4	2838.1	792.1	2046.0
1954	4179.7	1251.6	1207.9	1032.1	134.3	41.5	43.7	6.3	37.5	2928.1	817.0	2111.1
1955	4428.0	1347.6	1296.2	1108.0	144.1	44.1	51.4	7.3	44.1	3080.4	841.9	2238.6
1956	4793.5	1477.2	1414.2	1209.4	157.3	47.5	63.0	8.8	54.3	3316.3	878.7	2437.6
1957	5169.5	1608.8	1534.6	1312.8	171.4	50.4	74.1	10.2	64.0	3560.7	936.6	2624.1
1958	5455.0	1724.1	1639.8	1404.2	186.7	48.9	84.3	11.5	72.8	3730.9	992.9	2738.0
1959	5763.5	1861.6	1763.7	1513.1	202.6	48.1	97.9	13.3	84.6	3901.9	1026.1	2875.8
1960	6067.3	1999.0	1888.8	1618.8	219.3	50.7	110.3	15.0	95.2	4068.3	1075.9	2992.3
1961	6334.4	2136.2	2012.6	1724.6	235.2	52.7	123.7	17.2	106.5	4198.2	1121.0	3077.3
1962	6665.1	2289.1	2150.8	1844.3	251.0	55.5	138.3	19.7	118.6	4376.0	1169.9	3206.1
1963	7025.7	2452.6	2298.7	1972.4	268.1	58.2	153.9	22.6	131.3	4573.1	1222.9	3350.3
1964	7523.8	2645.6	2471.4	2123.4	286.4	61.5	174.3	26.0	148.2	4878.2	1271.8	3606.4
1965	7881.5	2844.1	2653.1	2281.3	307.0	64.9	191.0	29.9	161.1	5037.4	1338.2	3699.2
1966	8451.0	3112.4	2900.8	2485.1	335.7	80.0	211.6	34.3	177.3	5338.6	1375.7	3962.9
1967	9091.4	3396.0	3162.7	2709.1	372.3	81.3	233.3	38.8	194.5	5695.4	1442.3	4253.1
1968	9877.8	3747.1	3489.0	2994.6	410.0	84.5	258.0	44.0	214.1	6130.7	1536.8	4593.9
1969	10837.4	4175.9	3889.9	3331.4	460.0	98.5	286.0	49.8	236.1	6661.5	1650.9	5010.6

Table B-15. *Tangible Nonhuman Gross Capital Stocks in Current Dollars, U.S. Domestic Economy* (billions of dollars)

YEAR	Total	Land	Structures	Equipment	Inventories	Addendum: Military Reproducibles
1929	620.7	111.5	304.0	143.8	61.5	11.7
1930	604.3	107.2	299.0	140.2	58.0	9.9
1931	547.2	95.3	274.4	129.2	48.2	8.2
1932	474.5	82.0	236.6	116.1	39.8	6.9
1933	459.8	77.3	236.7	109.3	36.5	6.7
1934	489.3	82.6	256.8	110.9	39.1	6.9
1935	493.8	84.3	259.6	108.9	40.9	6.7
1936	515.3	87.4	273.3	110.8	43.7	6.7
1937	556.6	90.9	297.7	118.3	49.7	7.2
1938	563.7	91.0	304.6	120.4	47.7	6.9
1939	567.4	90.0	310.0	119.8	47.6	7.0
1940	585.3	91.7	322.9	119.5	51.3	9.1
1941	662.0	99.5	360.6	140.9	61.0	14.3
1942	776.3	103.7	410.9	180.8	75.9	43.2
1943	891.9	117.7	453.7	236.0	84.5	100.2
1944	984.1	126.9	480.7	287.1	89.4	145.2
1945	1030.9	135.7	502.8	299.1	93.3	149.1
1946	1143.0	152.2	562.2	321.5	107.1	154.5
1947	1374.1	177.9	687.6	378.0	130.6	176.5
1948	1537.1	197.9	779.2	419.4	140.6	181.8
1949	1556.6	199.9	783.1	438.8	134.8	169.4

Table B-15.   (Completed)

YEAR	Total	Land	Structures	Equipment	Inventories	Addendum: Military Reproducibles
1950	1638.5	211.7	829.9	456.0	140.8	156.7
1951	1836.0	236.7	921.5	511.5	166.3	167.0
1952	1950.8	248.5	977.8	553.8	170.7	182.2
1953	2046.0	253.9	1020.1	597.9	174.0	199.9
1954	2111.1	257.5	1043.2	633.4	176.9	208.0
1955	2238.6	271.5	1105.1	678.7	183.2	217.7
1956	2437.6	291.1	1192.2	756.9	197.3	245.3
1957	2624.1	309.5	1267.5	841.2	205.8	275.5
1958	2738.0	326.7	1313.7	887.2	210.4	283.8
1959	2875.8	352.6	1379.5	925.6	218.2	292.1
1960	2992.3	376.0	1435.0	953.1	228.2	297.8
1961	3077.3	388.2	1484.4	971.6	233.0	298.2
1962	3206.1	412.6	1552.6	999.5	241.3	304.1
1963	3350.3	436.7	1628.4	1033.7	251.4	309.7
1964	3606.4	466.5	1714.6	1162.1	263.3	314.0
1965	3699.2	502.3	1804.9	1111.0	281.0	312.5
1966	3962.9	539.1	1963.5	1157.2	303.1	309.3
1967	4253.1	574.2	2109.4	1242.6	326.9	317.8
1968	4593.9	622.6	2288.3	1342.6	340.5	332.8
1969	5010.6	686.8	2520.6	1447.7	355.4	340.7

Table B-16. *Total Gross Stocks in Constant Dollars, by Sector, U.S. National Economy* (billions of 1958 dollars)

| YEAR | National Total | DOMESTIC CAPITAL STOCKS BY SECTOR | | | | Net Foreign Assets and Monetary Metals |
		Total	Personal	Business	Government	
1929	2647.6	2616.3	1397.5	878.1	340.7	31.3
1930	2713.9	2680.4	1433.3	896.2	350.8	33.5
1931	2752.5	2718.2	1454.6	901.2	362.4	34.3
1932	2762.5	2729.8	1463.2	892.6	373.9	32.7
1933	2761.7	2732.2	1468.8	879.1	384.4	29.5
1934	2773.6	2745.8	1481.1	869.2	395.5	27.8
1935	2801.4	2774.4	1499.7	866.7	408.0	27.0
1936	2842.1	2817.4	1521.8	872.2	423.3	24.7
1937	2893.9	2870.5	1545.7	884.4	440.4	23.4
1938	2943.3	2919.6	1569.2	892.8	457.7	23.6
1939	2988.7	2964.5	1590.8	896.7	477.0	24.2
1940	3054.8	3029.5	1625.9	903.6	500.0	25.4
1941	3148.8	3121.0	1680.0	910.4	530.6	27.9
1942	3292.7	3263.3	1738.9	908.5	615.9	29.3
1943	3481.3	3452.4	1793.7	893.9	764.8	28.8
1944	3637.0	3609.8	1846.8	874.9	888.1	27.1
1945	3703.0	3677.8	1902.8	860.0	915.0	25.2
1946	3761.3	3733.2	1964.1	867.0	902.1	28.2
1947	3863.6	3827.9	2031.2	891.2	905.5	35.7
1948	3963.6	3922.6	2104.9	918.8	898.8	41.1
1949	4052.7	4009.1	2181.6	943.6	883.9	43.6

Table B-16. (Completed)

YEAR	National Total	DOMESTIC CAPITAL STOCKS BY SECTOR				Net Foreign Assets and Monetary Metals
		Total	Personal	Business	Government	
1950	4152.7	4110.3	2264.3	970.4	875.5	42.4
1951	4284.7	4243.9	2350.4	1008.3	885.2	40.8
1952	4439.1	4397.9	2434.8	1042.3	920.8	41.3
1953	4604.5	4562.9	2525.9	1070.2	966.8	41.6
1954	4765.3	4724.2	2623.8	1096.4	1004.0	41.1
1955	4938.8	4898.4	2733.0	1127.7	1037.8	40.4
1956	5136.2	5094.7	2847.4	1164.9	1082.4	41.5
1957	5334.1	5288.8	2955.9	1199.7	1133.2	45.3
1958	5502.2	5455.0	3056.0	1227.2	1171.8	47.2
1959	5673.1	5627.5	3159.2	1255.0	1213.4	45.6
1960	5877.0	5831.5	3273.1	1290.0	1268.5	45.5
1961	6064.9	6017.9	3385.2	1322.6	1310.0	47.0
1962	6264.9	6215.6	3500.3	1357.6	1357.6	49.3
1963	6480.9	6429.3	3623.8	1397.3	1408.2	51.7
1964	6708.7	6654.2	3755.4	1440.3	1458.5	54.5
1965	6952.5	6894.8	3897.5	1493.2	1504.1	57.7
1966	7187.4	7127.9	4014.8	1557.9	1555.2	59.5
1967	7475.2	7414.3	4174.8	1622.6	1616.9	60.9
1968	7760.4	7703.4	4337.6	1683.6	1682.2	57.0
1969	8069.9	8014.1	4518.3	1747.6	1748.2	55.8

Table B-17. *Total Gross Capital Stocks in Constant Dollars, by Type, U.S. Domestic Economy (billions of 1958 dollars)*

YEAR	Grand Total	Intangible Total	HUMAN INTANGIBLES Total	Education and Training	Medical and Health	Mobility	NONHUMAN INTANGIBLES Total	Basic Research	AR&D	TANGIBLES Total	Human	Nonhuman
1929	2616.3	638.7	631.9	529.3	66.1	36.4	6.9	1.3	5.6	1977.6	509.7	1467.9
1930	2680.4	659.6	652.2	548.4	68.9	35.0	7.4	1.4	6.0	2020.8	523.4	1497.4
1931	2718.2	673.3	665.3	564.9	71.4	29.1	7.9	1.5	6.4	2044.9	535.4	1509.5
1932	2729.8	680.3	671.7	578.0	73.5	20.2	8.6	1.6	7.0	2049.5	545.9	1503.6
1933	2732.2	689.5	680.2	589.4	75.3	15.5	9.3	1.8	7.5	2042.7	555.2	1487.4
1934	2745.8	704.5	694.6	601.6	77.1	16.0	9.9	1.9	8.0	2041.3	564.3	1477.0
1935	2774.4	723.5	713.0	615.2	78.9	18.9	10.5	2.0	8.5	2050.9	573.3	1477.5
1936	2817.4	744.6	733.5	630.7	80.8	22.0	11.2	2.2	9.0	2072.7	582.7	1490.1
1937	2870.5	765.1	753.2	647.9	83.0	22.3	11.9	2.3	9.5	2105.4	592.5	1512.9
1938	2919.6	786.1	773.5	665.4	85.1	22.9	12.7	2.5	10.2	2133.5	602.7	1530.8
1939	2964.5	805.5	791.9	683.9	87.3	20.7	13.6	2.7	10.9	2159.0	613.7	1545.3
1940	3029.5	830.7	816.2	705.0	89.9	21.3	14.6	2.9	11.7	2198.7	625.6	1573.1
1941	3121.0	862.8	846.6	729.0	92.6	25.1	16.1	3.1	13.0	2258.2	637.8	1620.4
1942	3263.3	900.7	882.6	758.4	95.3	28.9	18.1	3.4	14.7	2362.6	650.5	1712.1
1943	3452.4	944.0	923.9	795.1	98.3	30.5	20.1	3.7	16.4	2508.4	663.9	1844.5
1944	3609.8	988.8	966.8	835.0	101.6	30.1	22.1	3.9	18.1	2621.0	677.9	1943.1
1945	3677.8	1037.1	1013.0	873.5	105.3	34.2	24.1	4.2	19.9	2640.7	692.5	1948.2
1946	3733.2	1081.2	1054.9	908.0	109.4	37.5	26.3	4.5	21.8	2652.0	708.1	1943.9

1947	3827.9	1122.4	1093.7	941.1	114.1	38.5	28.7	4.8	23.9	2705.5	724.9	1980.6
1948	3922.6	1166.2	1134.6	975.7	119.3	39.6	31.6	5.1	26.5	2756.4	743.0	2013.4
1949	4009.1	1208.1	1173.5	1008.3	124.7	40.4	34.6	5.4	29.2	2801.0	762.1	2038.9
1950	4110.3	1250.6	1213.0	1039.8	130.5	42.7	37.7	5.8	31.9	2859.6	781.9	2077.8
1951	4243.9	1298.4	1257.4	1074.8	136.5	46.1	41.0	6.2	34.8	2945.5	802.8	2142.7
1952	4397.9	1350.1	1305.2	1114.8	142.7	47.7	44.9	6.7	38.2	3047.8	825.2	2222.6
1953	4562.9	1405.3	1355.4	1158.3	149.2	48.0	49.9	7.3	42.6	3157.6	849.0	2308.6
1954	4724.2	1463.2	1407.7	1203.3	156.1	48.2	55.6	8.0	47.6	3260.9	874.2	2386.7
1955	4898.4	1525.4	1463.9	1251.2	163.3	49.3	61.6	8.7	52.8	3373.0	901.3	2471.7
1956	5094.7	1592.0	1523.5	1301.8	170.9	50.9	68.5	9.6	58.9	3502.7	930.6	2572.1
1957	5288.8	1659.8	1583.6	1352.9	178.7	52.0	76.1	10.5	65.6	3629.0	961.4	2667.6
1958	5455.0	1724.1	1639.8	1404.2	186.7	48.9	84.3	11.5	72.8	3730.9	992.9	2738.0
1959	5627.5	1791.5	1698.4	1457.4	194.9	46.0	93.1	12.6	80.5	3836.0	1025.4	2810.6
1960	5831.5	1870.6	1768.3	1517.0	203.9	47.3	102.3	13.9	88.4	3960.9	1061.7	2899.2
1961	6017.9	1951.9	1840.2	1579.0	213.1	48.1	111.7	15.3	96.4	4066.0	1099.5	2966.5
1962	6215.6	2034.0	1912.5	1641.2	222.2	49.1	121.5	17.0	104.5	4181.6	1136.3	3045.3
1963	6429.3	2121.0	1989.2	1707.3	231.7	50.2	131.9	18.9	112.9	4308.2	1174.0	3134.2
1964	6654.2	2213.1	2070.5	1777.6	241.8	51.1	142.6	21.1	121.5	4441.1	1213.3	3227.8
1965	6894.8	2312.5	2158.9	1854.0	252.7	52.2	153.5	23.4	130.1	4582.3	1254.4	3327.9
1966	7127.9	2427.8	2263.0	1939.8	264.3	58.9	164.9	25.9	139.0	4700.1	1255.2	3444.9
1967	7414.3	2548.4	2372.3	2033.4	276.0	62.9	176.1	28.4	147.7	4865.9	1298.2	3567.7
1968	7703.4	2672.4	2485.2	2133.2	287.9	64.1	187.2	30.9	156.3	5031.0	1342.2	3688.8
1969	8014.1	2810.8	2612.7	2241.2	300.4	71.2	198.1	33.5	164.6	5203.3	1387.3	3816.0

Table B-18. *Tangible Nonhuman Gross Capital Stocks in Constant Dollars, by Type, U.S. Domestic Economy* (billions of 1958 dollars)

YEAR	Total	Land	Structures	Equipment	Inventories	Addendum: Military Reproducibles
1929	1467.9	267.2	803.6	284.2	112.8	27.5
1930	1497.4	271.3	821.2	290.6	114.3	25.2
1931	1509.5	273.5	834.1	290.7	111.2	23.0
1932	1503.6	273.9	841.0	284.7	104.0	21.3
1933	1487.4	273.5	842.9	275.5	95.5	19.9
1934	1477.0	273.7	845.3	267.4	90.7	18.7
1935	1477.5	273.7	849.7	262.9	91.3	18.1
1936	1490.1	273.5	858.2	262.8	95.5	17.6
1937	1512.9	274.5	870.0	266.7	101.7	17.1
1938	1530.8	276.1	881.4	268.5	104.9	16.8
1939	1545.3	277.3	894.2	267.7	106.1	17.3
1940	1573.1	278.0	909.4	274.4	111.4	21.9
1941	1620.4	278.4	930.2	290.6	121.2	33.3
1942	1712.1	278.3	958.9	343.6	131.4	92.8
1943	1844.5	277.5	978.2	452.1	136.8	212.0
1944	1943.1	276.5	978.9	548.0	139.7	307.9
1945	1948.2	275.9	975.4	556.4	140.5	312.1
1946	1943.9	277.0	980.5	540.7	145.6	286.5
1947	1980.6	279.4	993.7	557.1	150.4	282.5
1948	2013.4	282.4	1009.3	570.0	151.8	265.4
1949	2038.9	285.9	1027.2	572.4	153.4	236.6

Table B-18. (Completed)

YEAR	Total	Land	Structures	Equipment	Inventories	Addendum: Military Reproducibles
1950	2077.8	289.6	1052.4	578.7	157.1	213.7
1951	2142.7	293.8	1082.0	599.8	167.2	207.5
1952	2222.6	297.5	1109.5	639.3	176.3	221.4
1953	2308.6	301.3	1138.3	686.1	183.0	239.5
1954	2386.7	305.8	1170.2	723.8	186.9	246.6
1955	2471.7	310.7	1205.4	762.6	193.1	250.1
1956	2572.1	315.9	1242.1	812.1	202.1	263.1
1957	2667.6	321.3	1278.2	860.8	207.4	280.7
1958	2738.0	326.7	1313.7	887.2	210.4	283.8
1959	2810.6	332.3	1351.0	909.8	217.5	286.2
1960	2899.2	349.1	1388.7	935.5	226.0	290.7
1961	2966.5	354.7	1425.4	954.9	231.5	291.0
1962	3045.3	360.4	1463.9	982.1	238.8	295.6
1963	3134.2	366.4	1504.9	1014.2	248.8	300.3
1964	3227.8	372.7	1547.3	1048.5	259.4	301.1
1965	3327.9	379.5	1592.3	1084.3	271.9	295.2
1966	3444.8	386.7	1639.0	1130.1	289.2	290.2
1967	3567.7	393.2	1684.3	1186.2	304.2	290.8
1968	3688.8	400.0	1729.8	1245.3	313.7	292.6
1969	3816.0	406.2	1776.5	1309.4	323.9	294.6

Table B-19. *Total Net Capital Stocks in Current Dollars, by Sector, U.S. National Economy* (billions of current dollars)

YEAR	National Total	DOMESTIC CAPITAL STOCKS BY SECTOR				Net Foreign Assets and Monetary Metals
		Total	Personal	Business	Government	
1929	799.2	782.8	449.3	237.7	95.7	16.5
1930	783.0	765.8	440.9	230.6	94.4	17.2
1931	707.5	691.2	396.7	206.0	88.5	16.3
1932	624.7	610.2	350.2	177.6	82.3	14.5
1933	598.9	585.9	332.7	166.6	86.6	13.0
1934	636.2	620.3	353.2	172.9	94.3	15.9
1935	653.0	635.8	362.6	174.7	98.5	17.1
1936	674.2	657.4	373.3	181.2	102.9	16.8
1937	723.3	706.2	399.3	193.9	113.0	17.2
1938	725.3	707.2	397.9	194.2	115.0	18.1
1939	731.1	711.5	398.9	192.5	120.1	19.6
1940	761.7	739.5	413.4	199.3	126.8	22.1
1941	847.0	822.2	458.7	220.0	143.5	24.7
1942	983.9	957.9	535.9	242.1	179.9	25.9
1943	1108.9	1083.0	601.7	257.0	224.3	25.8
1944	1201.2	1176.7	651.2	265.7	259.9	24.5
1945	1269.3	1246.2	694.1	275.1	277.0	23.2
1946	1411.3	1385.2	775.5	307.9	301.8	26.1
1947	1655.2	1622.9	910.2	367.6	345.1	32.3
1948	1838.9	1801.4	1014.6	415.4	371.4	37.6
1949	1884.6	1845.0	1042.7	427.7	374.6	39.6

Table B-19.   (Completed)

YEAR	National Total	DOMESTIC CAPITAL STOCKS BY SECTOR				Net Foreign Assets and Monetary Metals
		Total	Personal	Business	Government	
1950	1993.4	1954.7	1115.2	458.8	380.7	38.8
1951	2227.5	2189.0	1245.8	524.6	418.5	38.5
1952	2372.7	2333.6	1322.0	560.6	451.0	39.1
1953	2497.8	2458.3	1388.6	580.0	489.6	39.5
1954	2599.8	2560.5	1442.8	594.5	523.2	39.3
1955	2750.8	2711.8	1524.3	628.2	559.4	38.9
1956	2971.1	2930.6	1636.7	683.6	610.3	40.5
1957	3196.5	3151.7	1756.3	733.9	661.5	44.8
1958	3377.3	3330.1	1857.3	767.8	705.0	47.2
1959	3574.8	3528.8	1968.2	804.1	756.5	46.0
1960	3774.9	3728.6	2076.6	836.1	815.9	46.3
1961	3950.7	3902.4	2179.4	862.7	860.2	48.4
1962	4170.9	4119.2	2300.7	900.6	917.9	51.7
1963	4415.5	4360.2	2438.1	943.8	978.2	55.3
1964	4695.1	4636.1	2590.8	996.7	1048.6	59.0
1965	5010.6	4947.2	2759.0	1064.4	1123.8	63.4
1966	5425.0	5358.3	2967.3	1168.3	1222.9	66.7
1967	5852.7	5782.5	3197.2	1257.7	1327.5	70.2
1968	6365.1	6297.0	3471.3	1354.7	1471.0	68.1
1969	6989.6	6920.4	3798.9	1476.0	1645.6	69.2

Table B-20. Total Net Capital Stocks in Current Dollars, by Sector, U.S. Domestic Economy (billions of dollars)

YEAR	Grand Total	Intangible Total	HUMAN INTANGIBLES				NONHUMAN INTANGIBLES			TANGIBLES		
			Total	Education and Training	Medical and Health	Mobility	Total	Basic Research	AR&D	Total	Human	Nonhuman
1929	782.8	188.5	186.7	164.1	18.1	4.6	1.7	0.5	1.2	594.3	204.0	390.3
1930	765.8	189.2	187.4	164.6	18.8	3.9	1.8	0.5	1.2	576.7	199.2	377.4
1931	691.2	182.4	180.5	158.3	19.0	3.2	1.8	0.6	1.2	508.8	176.5	332.3
1932	610.2	171.0	169.2	147.8	18.8	2.6	1.8	0.6	1.2	439.2	154.4	284.8
1933	585.9	165.2	163.3	142.2	18.8	2.3	1.9	0.6	1.3	420.8	149.9	270.8
1934	620.3	171.3	169.2	147.7	19.2	2.3	2.1	0.6	1.4	449.0	162.9	286.2
1935	635.8	176.9	174.7	152.8	19.4	2.5	2.2	0.7	1.5	458.9	170.4	288.6
1936	657.4	182.0	179.5	156.9	19.9	2.7	2.5	0.8	1.7	475.5	173.3	302.2
1937	706.2	196.2	193.5	169.8	20.7	3.0	2.7	0.9	1.9	510.0	181.8	328.2
1938	707.2	200.7	197.8	171.8	23.0	3.0	2.9	0.9	2.0	506.5	175.9	330.6
1939	711.5	204.1	200.9	176.4	21.5	3.0	3.2	1.0	2.2	507.4	174.8	332.6
1940	739.5	212.9	209.3	183.7	22.2	3.4	3.6	1.1	2.5	526.6	179.3	347.4
1941	822.2	233.7	229.1	201.1	23.5	4.6	4.5	1.3	3.2	588.6	196.4	392.1
1942	957.9	270.7	264.9	233.1	25.6	6.2	5.8	1.6	4.2	687.2	230.1	457.0
1943	1083.0	310.9	303.8	269.0	27.7	7.2	7.1	1.8	5.3	772.1	258.1	514.0
1944	1176.7	341.1	333.0	296.8	29.2	6.9	8.2	2.1	6.1	835.6	274.8	560.8
1945	1246.2	367.4	358.5	320.9	30.7	6.8	9.0	2.2	6.8	878.7	289.8	588.9
1946	1385.2	410.4	400.6	359.0	33.8	7.8	9.8	2.4	7.4	974.8	319.3	655.6

1947	1622.9	471.4	459.7	411.6	38.8	9.4	11.7	2.8	8.9	1151.5	365.8	785.7
1948	1801.4	525.2	511.9	457.8	43.5	10.6	13.3	3.1	10.2	1276.2	396.9	879.2
1949	1845.0	557.3	542.6	484.4	46.9	11.2	14.7	3.4	11.3	1287.7	396.3	891.4
1950	1954.7	594.9	578.3	516.1	50.1	12.1	16.6	3.7	12.9	1359.8	413.0	946.8
1951	2189.0	656.2	637.0	567.8	55.6	13.6	19.2	4.3	14.9	1532.7	460.7	1072.1
1952	2333.6	715.0	693.0	617.4	61.0	14.6	22.0	4.8	17.2	1618.6	479.6	1139.0
1953	2458.3	767.5	742.0	661.2	65.6	15.3	25.5	5.5	20.0	1690.8	494.8	1196.0
1954	2560.5	812.6	783.0	697.1	70.5	15.3	29.6	6.3	23.3	1747.9	511.4	1236.5
1955	2711.8	870.8	835.8	744.6	75.6	15.6	35.1	7.3	27.8	1841.0	528.4	1312.6
1956	2930.6	952.3	908.9	810.4	82.4	16.0	43.4	8.8	34.7	1978.2	553.8	1424.4
1957	3151.7	1035.4	983.8	877.7	89.8	16.3	51.6	10.2	41.4	2116.3	593.0	1523.3
1958	3330.1	1110.0	1051.0	936.8	97.8	16.4	59.0	11.5	47.5	2220.1	631.6	1588.5
1959	3528.8	1199.6	1131.0	1007.7	106.1	17.2	68.6	13.3	55.3	2329.1	655.9	1673.2
1960	3728.6	1287.4	1210.2	1077.3	114.8	18.1	77.2	15.0	62.1	2441.2	691.2	1750.0
1961	3902.4	1375.2	1289.0	1147.1	123.0	18.8	86.2	17.2	69.0	2527.2	723.8	1803.4
1962	4119.2	1473.8	1378.0	1226.7	131.3	20.0	95.8	19.7	76.1	2645.4	759.4	1886.0
1963	4360.2	1581.0	1475.1	1313.0	140.3	21.8	105.9	22.6	83.2	2779.2	797.9	1981.2
1964	4636.1	1708.7	1589.8	1415.6	150.1	24.2	118.9	26.0	92.9	2927.4	834.1	2093.3
1965	4947.2	1841.8	1712.3	1524.5	161.2	26.7	129.5	29.9	99.6	3105.4	882.1	2223.3
1966	5358.3	2019.2	1876.6	1667.5	176.6	32.5	142.6	34.3	108.3	3339.1	942.1	2397.0
1967	5782.5	2212.2	2056.8	1825.9	195.9	35.0	155.4	38.9	116.6	3570.3	992.9	2577.4
1968	6297.0	2450.6	2281.4	2027.4	215.5	38.5	169.2	44.0	125.3	3846.4	1063.0	2783.4
1969	6920.4	2737.9	2553.0	2267.3	241.7	43.9	184.9	49.8	135.1	4182.5	1146.9	3035.6

Table B-21. *Tangible Nonhuman Net Capital Stocks in Current Dollars, by Type,*
U.S. Domestic Economy (billions of dollars)

YEAR	Total	Land	Structures	Equipment	Inventories	Addendum: Military Reproducibles
1929	390.3	111.5	157.2	60.1	61.5	4.3
1930	377.4	107.2	154.5	57.8	58.0	3.6
1931	332.3	95.3	140.7	48.1	48.2	3.1
1932	284.8	82.0	119.1	43.8	39.8	2.7
1933	270.8	77.3	117.5	39.5	36.5	2.7
1934	286.2	82.6	125.5	39.0	39.1	2.9
1935	288.6	84.3	125.0	38.3	40.9	2.8
1936	302.2	87.4	130.8	40.3	43.7	2.9
1937	328.2	90.9	142.6	45.0	49.7	3.3
1938	330.6	91.0	145.3	46.6	47.7	3.2
1939	332.6	90.0	148.1	46.9	47.6	3.4
1940	347.4	91.7	154.0	50.4	51.3	4.3
1941	392.1	99.5	172.0	59.6	61.0	7.5
1942	457.0	108.7	195.5	76.9	75.9	20.3
1943	514.0	117.7	213.3	98.5	84.5	44.7
1944	560.8	126.9	222.5	122.0	89.4	67.2
1945	588.9	135.7	228.7	131.2	93.3	73.0
1946	655.6	152.2	255.3	141.0	107.1	72.2
1947	785.7	177.9	317.1	160.0	130.6	70.1
1948	879.2	197.9	365.2	175.6	140.6	65.6
1949	891.4	199.9	372.0	184.8	134.8	59.5

Table B-21.   (Completed)

YEAR	Total	Land	Structures	Equipment	Inventories	Addendum: Military Reproducibles
1950	946.8	211.7	399.5	194.7	140.8	54.8
1951	1072.1	236.7	450.2	218.8	166.3	56.9
1952	1139.0	248.5	484.2	235.7	170.7	65.1
1953	1196.0	253.9	511.5	256.5	174.0	79.1
1954	1236.5	257.5	529.3	272.8	176.9	88.1
1955	1312.6	271.5	567.4	290.4	183.2	94.9
1956	1424.4	291.1	619.0	317.0	197.3	103.9
1957	1523.3	309.5	663.9	344.0	205.8	111.6
1958	1588.5	326.7	692.5	358.9	210.4	116.8
1959	1673.2	352.6	732.0	370.5	218.2	122.1
1960	1750.0	376.0	766.2	379.7	228.2	123.9
1961	1803.4	388.2	796.4	385.7	233.0	124.8
1962	1886.0	412.6	837.0	395.1	241.3	127.7
1963	1981.2	436.7	882.2	410.9	251.4	130.5
1964	2093.3	466.5	932.9	430.5	263.3	133.2
1965	2223.3	502.3	986.3	453.7	281.0	134.0
1966	2396.9	539.1	1072.7	482.0	303.1	133.1
1967	2577.4	574.3	1152.8	523.5	326.9	137.6
1968	2783.4	622.5	1250.3	570.1	340.5	146.0
1969	3035.6	686.8	1376.1	617.4	355.3	146.8

Table B-22. *Total Net Capital Stocks in Constant Dollars, by Sector, U.S. National Economy* (billions of 1958 dollars)

YEAR	National Total	DOMESTIC CAPITAL STOCKS BY SECTOR				Net Foreign Assets and Monetary Metals
		Total	Personal	Business	Government	
1929	1741.2	1709.8	911.5	561.5	236.9	31.3
1930	1780.5	1747.0	930.0	571.8	245.2	33.5
1931	1797.8	1763.5	939.2	569.7	254.6	34.3
1932	1793.1	1760.3	940.6	556.2	263.5	32.7
1933	1776.4	1746.9	936.6	539.5	270.8	29.5
1934	1769.2	1741.4	935.7	527.2	278.5	27.8
1935	1775.9	1748.9	940.1	521.6	287.1	27.0
1936	1795.6	1770.8	949.3	523.2	298.3	24.7
1937	1827.3	1803.9	962.2	531.0	310.7	23.4
1938	1854.6	1831.0	973.4	534.8	322.8	23.6
1939	1880.8	1856.6	985.4	534.9	336.3	24.2
1940	1922.0	1896.6	1005.9	539.9	350.8	25.4
1941	1983.0	1955.1	1036.6	548.1	370.4	27.9
1942	2062.0	2032.6	1067.9	549.6	415.1	29.3
1943	2150.2	2121.4	1094.3	539.8	487.3	28.8
1944	2226.5	2199.4	1119.5	527.4	552.5	27.1
1945	2265.0	2239.8	1145.6	519.0	575.3	25.2
1946	2298.0	2269.9	1182.4	528.9	558.6	28.2
1947	2351.0	2315.3	1228.6	551.3	535.4	35.7
1948	2413.1	2372.0	1277.3	573.4	521.3	41.1
1949	2476.7	2433.1	1326.8	590.2	516.2	43.6

Table B-22.   (Completed)

YEAR	National Total	DOMESTIC CAPITAL STOCKS BY SECTOR				Net Foreign Assets and Monetary Metals
		Total	Personal	Business	Government	
1950	2547.4	2505.0	1380.6	607.5	516.8	42.4
1951	2634.9	2594.1	1436.2	634.8	523.1	40.8
1952	2731.9	2690.6	1487.3	657.9	545.4	41.3
1953	2836.4	2794.8	1540.8	675.4	578.6	41.6
1954	2935.9	2894.8	1597.7	689.5	607.6	41.1
1955	3040.6	3000.1	1662.0	707.3	630.9	40.4
1956	3157.0	3115.5	1731.0	731.8	652.8	41.5
1957	3271.9	3226.6	1796.0	753.7	676.9	45.3
1958	3377.3	3330.1	1857.3	767.8	705.0	47.2
1959	3486.8	3441.2	1922.8	782.2	736.2	45.6
1960	3621.5	3576.0	1996.5	803.5	776.0	45.5
1961	3743.3	3696.3	2069.1	821.7	805.5	47.0
1962	3872.4	3823.1	2143.8	841.6	837.7	49.3
1963	4016.6	3965.0	2227.2	865.9	871.9	51.7
1964	4172.0	4117.5	2317.8	892.7	907.0	54.5
1965	4343.2	4285.5	2417.2	927.4	940.9	57.7
1966	4536.4	4476.9	2526.6	971.3	978.0	59.5
1967	4729.8	4668.9	2635.0	1012.8	1021.2	60.9
1968	4917.6	4860.6	2745.0	1048.9	1066.7	57.0
1969	5116.5	5060.7	2864.8	1086.2	1109.7	55.8

Table B-23. *Total Net Capital Stocks in Constant Dollars, by Type, U.S. Domestic Economy* (billions of 1958 dollars)

YEAR	Grand Total	Intangible Total	HUMAN INTANGIBLES				NONHUMAN INTANGIBLES			TANGIBLES		
			Total	Education and Training	Medical and Health	Mobility	Total	Basic Research	AR&D	Total	Human	Nonhuman
1929	1709.8	438.6	434.0	385.1	38.3	10.6	4.6	1.3	3.3	1271.2	358.1	913.1
1930	1747.0	452.2	447.3	398.2	39.8	9.4	4.9	1.4	3.5	1294.8	366.3	928.6
1931	1763.5	462.8	457.5	408.4	40.9	8.2	5.3	1.5	3.8	1300.7	372.8	927.9
1932	1760.3	470.5	464.7	415.5	41.7	7.4	5.8	1.6	4.2	1289.9	377.8	912.1
1933	1746.9	476.5	470.2	421.0	42.3	7.0	6.3	1.8	4.5	1270.4	381.5	888.9
1934	1741.4	483.1	476.4	426.8	42.7	6.8	6.6	1.9	4.7	1258.4	384.8	873.6
1935	1748.9	491.0	484.0	433.6	43.3	7.1	7.0	2.0	5.0	1257.9	387.8	870.1
1936	1770.8	500.7	493.3	441.8	44.0	7.5	7.4	2.2	5.2	1270.1	391.2	878.9
1937	1803.9	512.3	504.5	451.6	44.9	8.0	7.8	2.3	5.5	1291.7	394.9	896.8
1938	1831.0	523.7	515.4	461.5	45.7	8.2	8.3	2.5	5.9	1307.3	398.8	908.6
1939	1856.6	535.6	526.7	472.0	46.6	8.1	8.9	2.7	6.3	1321.0	403.2	917.8
1940	1896.6	551.4	541.7	484.8	47.7	9.1	9.7	2.9	6.8	1345.2	408.1	937.1
1941	1955.1	571.3	560.3	500.1	48.9	11.4	10.9	3.1	7.8	1383.8	413.2	970.7
1942	2032.6	596.5	583.9	520.4	50.1	13.5	12.5	3.4	9.1	1436.2	418.5	1017.7
1943	2121.4	626.3	612.3	546.9	51.5	13.9	14.1	3.7	10.4	1495.1	424.4	1070.7
1944	2199.4	656.8	641.2	575.4	53.1	12.8	15.5	3.9	11.6	1542.7	430.9	1111.8
1945	2239.8	685.4	668.5	601.5	54.9	12.1	17.0	4.2	12.7	1554.4	437.9	1116.5
1946	2269.9	710.4	692.0	621.9	57.0	13.0	18.4	4.5	13.9	1559.5	445.9	1113.6

Year											
1947	2315.3	735.0	715.0	641.0	59.6	14.5	20.0	4.8	15.2	1580.4	455.1	1125.3
1948	2372.0	763.0	741.2	663.2	62.4	15.5	21.8	5.1	16.8	1609.0	465.1	1143.9
1949	2433.1	790.5	766.8	685.3	65.4	16.1	23.8	5.4	18.4	1642.6	476.1	1166.5
1950	2505.0	818.3	792.7	707.5	68.5	16.7	25.6	5.8	19.8	1686.7	487.8	1198.9
1951	2594.1	849.2	821.6	732.4	71.8	17.5	27.6	6.2	21.4	1744.9	500.6	1244.3
1952	2690.6	882.1	852.1	759.1	75.0	18.0	30.0	6.7	23.4	1808.5	514.8	1293.7
1953	2794.8	916.5	883.0	786.5	78.4	18.1	33.5	7.3	26.3	1878.3	530.3	1347.9
1954	2894.8	950.5	912.9	813.1	81.9	17.8	37.7	8.0	29.7	1944.3	547.1	1397.1
1955	3000.1	986.2	944.2	841.1	85.7	17.5	42.0	8.7	33.3	2013.9	565.7	1448.2
1956	3115.5	1026.3	979.1	872.4	89.6	17.2	47.2	9.6	37.6	2089.2	586.5	1502.7
1957	3226.6	1068.0	1015.0	904.6	93.6	16.8	53.0	10.5	42.5	2158.6	608.7	1549.9
1958	3330.1	1110.0	1051.0	936.8	97.8	16.4	59.0	11.5	47.5	2220.1	631.6	1588.5
1959	3441.2	1154.5	1089.3	970.7	102.1	16.5	65.2	12.6	52.6	2286.7	655.4	1631.3
1960	3576.0	1204.6	1133.1	1009.4	106.8	16.9	71.6	13.9	57.7	2371.4	682.0	1689.3
1961	3696.3	1256.2	1178.4	1049.8	111.5	17.2	77.8	15.3	62.5	2440.0	710.0	1730.1
1962	3823.1	1308.9	1224.9	1090.9	116.2	17.8	84.0	17.0	67.0	2514.2	737.6	1776.7
1963	3965.0	1366.3	1275.8	1135.7	121.3	18.8	90.5	18.9	71.6	2598.7	766.1	1832.6
1964	4117.5	1428.2	1331.0	1184.2	126.7	20.1	97.2	21.1	76.1	2689.3	795.8	1893.5
1965	4285.5	1495.8	1392.0	1237.8	132.7	21.5	103.9	23.4	80.5	2789.6	826.8	1962.8
1966	4476.9	1574.6	1463.8	1299.7	139.1	25.0	110.8	25.9	84.9	2902.3	859.6	2042.7
1967	4668.9	1657.3	1540.3	1368.0	145.3	27.0	117.0	28.4	88.5	3011.6	893.7	2117.9
1968	4860.6	1744.1	1621.7	1441.2	151.4	29.1	122.4	30.9	91.4	3116.5	928.4	2188.1
1969	5060.7	1838.2	1710.6	1520.9	157.9	31.8	127.6	33.5	94.2	3222.5	963.8	2258.7

Table B-24. *Tangible Nonhuman Net Capital Stocks in Constant Dollars, by Type,*
U.S. Domestic Economy (billions of 1958 dollars)

YEAR	Total	Land	Structures	Equipment	Inventories	Addendum: Military Reproducibles
1929	913.1	267.2	416.0	117.1	112.8	10.1
1930	928.6	271.3	425.0	118.0	114.3	9.3
1931	927.9	273.5	429.1	114.2	111.2	8.7
1932	912.1	273.9	427.3	106.8	104.0	8.3
1933	888.9	273.5	421.1	98.7	95.5	8.1
1934	873.6	273.7	415.9	93.4	90.7	7.8
1935	870.1	273.7	413.1	92.0	91.3	7.6
1936	878.9	273.5	414.8	95.1	95.5	7.7
1937	896.8	274.5	419.8	100.8	101.7	7.7
1938	908.6	276.1	424.4	103.3	104.9	7.9
1939	917.8	277.3	430.3	104.2	106.1	8.4
1940	937.1	278.0	437.9	109.9	111.4	10.4
1941	970.7	278.4	448.7	122.3	121.2	17.0
1942	1017.7	278.3	462.2	145.8	131.4	43.4
1943	1070.7	277.5	467.4	189.0	136.8	94.6
1944	1111.8	276.5	461.4	234.2	139.7	142.1
1945	1116.5	275.9	453.1	247.0	140.5	152.6
1946	1113.6	277.0	452.8	238.2	145.6	134.0
1947	1125.3	279.4	461.1	234.4	150.4	112.6
1948	1143.9	282.4	473.4	236.3	151.8	95.5
1949	1166.5	285.9	488.6	238.7	153.4	82.7

Table B-24. (Completed)

YEAR	Total	Land	Structures	Equipment	Inventories	Addendum: Military Reproducibles
1950	1198.9	289.6	507.7	244.5	157.1	74.0
1951	1244.3	293.8	529.4	253.9	167.2	70.0
1952	1293.7	297.5	550.0	269.8	176.3	78.3
1953	1347.9	301.3	571.1	292.6	183.0	93.8
1954	1397.1	305.8	593.8	310.7	186.9	103.6
1955	1448.2	310.7	619.0	325.5	193.1	107.9
1956	1502.7	315.9	645.1	339.7	202.1	110.1
1957	1549.9	321.3	669.5	351.8	207.4	113.2
1958	1588.5	326.7	692.5	358.9	210.4	116.8
1959	1631.3	332.3	716.9	364.5	217.5	119.7
1960	1689.3	349.1	741.4	372.8	226.0	120.8
1961	1730.1	354.7	764.6	379.3	231.5	121.9
1962	1776.7	360.4	788.6	388.8	238.8	124.3
1963	1832.6	366.4	814.2	403.3	248.8	126.7
1964	1893.5	372.7	840.3	421.2	259.4	127.7
1965	1962.8	379.5	868.0	443.4	271.9	126.3
1966	2042.7	386.7	895.9	470.9	289.2	125.1
1967	2117.9	393.2	921.0	499.7	304.0	126.4
1968	2188.1	400.0	945.4	529.0	313.5	128.9
1969	2258.7	406.2	970.4	558.6	323.6	129.1

Table B-25. Total Gross Capital Stocks Employed, in Current Dollars, by Type, U.S. Private Domestic Business Economy (billions of dollars)

YEAR	Grand Total	Intangible Total	HUMAN INTANGIBLES				NONHUMAN INTANGIBLES			TANGIBLES		
			Total	Education and Training	Medical and Health	Mobility	Total	Basic Research	AR&D	Total	Human	Nonhuman
1929	576.9	137.1	134.5	108.7	13.4	12.4	2.6	0.5	2.1	439.8	102.1	337.7
1930	552.9	129.4	126.7	103.3	13.3	10.1	2.6	0.5	2.1	423.5	94.4	329.2
1931	488.5	113.1	110.5	91.5	12.6	6.3	2.7	0.6	2.1	375.3	76.7	298.6
1932	423.4	98.2	95.6	80.2	11.9	3.4	2.6	0.6	2.1	325.2	63.2	262.0
1933	408.1	94.9	92.2	77.2	12.0	3.0	2.8	0.6	2.2	313.2	62.3	250.9
1934	437.2	102.7	99.7	83.5	12.6	3.6	3.0	0.6	2.4	334.4	71.4	263.1
1935	458.1	111.6	108.3	90.7	13.3	4.3	3.3	0.7	2.6	346.5	79.4	267.1
1936	480.4	118.8	115.1	95.9	13.9	5.3	3.7	0.8	2.9	361.6	84.0	277.6
1937	520.6	132.2	128.1	107.4	15.0	5.7	4.1	0.9	3.2	388.5	92.3	296.2
1938	518.7	131.8	127.5	105.8	16.2	5.5	4.4	0.9	3.4	386.9	87.6	299.3
1939	523.1	135.8	131.0	109.9	15.4	5.7	4.8	1.0	3.8	387.2	88.8	298.4
1940	543.2	145.4	140.0	117.7	16.2	6.1	5.4	1.1	4.3	397.7	94.8	302.9
1941	617.0	167.8	161.1	135.0	18.0	8.1	6.7	1.3	5.4	449.2	110.4	338.8
1942	706.7	199.1	190.7	159.5	20.2	10.9	8.4	1.6	6.8	507.6	133.7	373.9
1943	777.8	226.5	216.3	181.0	22.3	13.0	10.1	1.8	8.3	551.3	149.9	401.3
1944	815.8	241.3	229.6	192.6	23.5	13.5	11.6	2.1	9.6	574.5	156.1	418.4
1945	854.2	256.6	243.8	203.8	24.4	15.7	12.8	2.2	10.5	597.6	162.5	435.1
1946	966.6	301.3	287.3	241.8	27.3	18.2	14.0	2.4	11.6	665.4	186.9	478.5

Year												
1947	1141.7	365.0	348.3	296.1	31.8	20.4	16.8	2.8	14.0	776.7	223.4	553.3
1948	1269.4	411.1	391.8	334.2	35.6	22.1	19.2	3.1	16.1	858.3	243.8	614.5
1949	1298.9	430.3	408.9	349.2	37.6	22.1	21.4	3.4	18.0	868.7	238.7	629.9
1950	1384.0	462.1	437.7	373.3	40.0	24.4	24.4	3.7	20.7	921.9	248.0	673.9
1951	1546.1	514.2	485.7	412.5	44.4	28.8	28.6	4.3	24.3	1031.8	275.9	755.9
1952	1647.8	560.6	527.7	447.8	48.7	31.2	32.9	4.8	28.1	1087.2	284.4	802.8
1953	1716.5	599.9	562.0	477.2	52.2	32.6	37.9	5.5	32.4	1116.6	289.0	827.6
1954	1769.3	630.6	586.8	499.5	55.6	31.7	43.7	6.3	37.5	1138.7	291.8	846.9
1955	1876.5	685.0	633.7	539.8	59.7	34.2	51.4	7.3	44.1	1191.4	299.3	892.2
1956	2035.3	758.7	695.6	593.4	65.5	36.7	63.0	8.8	54.3	1276.7	312.2	964.5
1957	2176.8	819.0	744.8	636.0	70.4	38.5	74.1	10.2	64.0	1357.8	325.9	1031.9
1958	2271.2	859.3	775.0	664.3	74.6	36.1	84.3	11.5	72.8	1411.9	333.9	1078.1
1959	2395.8	930.1	832.2	715.5	80.6	36.1	97.9	13.3	84.6	1465.7	342.2	1123.6
1960	2512.4	996.0	885.7	761.2	86.5	38.0	110.3	15.0	95.2	1516.4	354.5	1161.9
1961	2610.4	1054.1	930.5	800.0	91.4	39.0	123.7	17.2	106.5	1556.3	362.3	1194.0
1962	2740.1	1127.8	989.5	851.0	97.0	41.5	138.3	19.7	118.6	1612.3	374.0	1238.3
1963	2887.0	1208.9	1055.1	908.5	103.2	43.3	153.9	22.6	131.3	1678.0	388.2	1289.8
1964	3157.9	1313.0	1138.7	982.4	110.4	45.9	174.3	26.0	148.2	1844.9	404.0	1440.9
1965	3285.0	1423.4	1232.4	1064.8	118.8	48.8	191.0	29.9	161.1	1861.6	428.0	1433.6
1966	3583.1	1565.9	1354.3	1164.7	130.0	59.6	211.6	34.3	177.3	2017.2	441.6	1575.6
1967	3859.2	1704.1	1470.8	1266.3	143.8	60.7	233.3	38.8	194.5	2155.1	461.5	1693.6
1968	4212.1	1892.9	1634.9	1411.5	159.9	63.5	258.0	43.9	214.1	2319.2	496.4	1822.8
1969	4659.7	2132.6	1846.6	1589.8	181.8	75.0	286.0	49.8	236.2	2527.1	539.8	1987.3

Table B-26. Total Gross Capital Stocks Employed, in Constant Dollars, by Type, U.S. Private Domestic Business Economy (billions of dollars)

YEAR	Grand Total	Intangible Total	HUMAN INTANGIBLES				NONHUMAN INTANGIBLES			TANGIBLES		
			Total	Education and Training	Medical and Health	Mobility	Total	Basic Research	AR&D	Total	Human	Nonhuman
1929	1324.0	320.2	313.4	255.9	28.4	29.1	6.9	1.3	5.6	1003.7	179.2	824.6
1930	1324.0	310.5	303.1	250.7	28.1	24.3	7.4	1.4	6.0	1013.9	173.5	840.5
1931	1294.3	288.1	280.1	237.1	27.0	16.0	7.9	1.5	6.4	1006.2	162.1	844.1
1932	1261.2	271.5	262.9	227.3	26.3	9.4	8.6	1.6	7.0	989.6	154.7	835.0
1933	1255.6	276.3	267.0	231.6	26.8	8.6	9.3	1.8	7.5	979.3	158.5	820.8
1934	1270.8	292.3	282.4	244.3	28.0	10.1	9.9	1.9	8.0	978.5	168.6	809.8
1935	1298.9	312.2	301.7	259.9	29.5	12.2	10.5	2.0	8.5	986.7	180.8	805.9
1936	1327.9	328.5	317.4	271.9	30.7	14.8	11.2	2.2	9.0	999.3	189.7	809.7
1937	1367.0	346.5	334.7	287.1	32.3	15.3	11.9	2.3	9.5	1020.5	200.5	820.0
1938	1370.8	345.4	332.7	285.8	32.1	14.8	12.7	2.5	10.2	1025.4	198.5	826.9
1939	1391.3	357.3	343.8	295.5	33.1	15.1	13.6	2.7	10.9	1034.0	204.8	829.1
1940	1427.6	377.5	362.9	311.9	34.8	16.3	14.6	2.9	11.7	1050.1	215.8	834.3
1941	1482.6	409.6	393.4	336.0	37.3	20.1	16.1	3.1	13.0	1073.1	232.2	840.9
1942	1524.6	436.6	418.5	355.2	39.6	23.7	18.1	3.4	14.7	1088.0	243.2	844.8
1943	1541.8	453.4	433.3	366.4	41.5	25.3	20.1	3.7	16.4	1088.4	246.5	841.9
1944	1538.1	460.8	438.7	371.1	42.7	25.0	22.1	3.9	18.1	1077.3	244.7	832.6
1945	1542.8	475.0	450.9	379.4	43.5	28.0	24.1	4.2	19.9	1067.8	245.5	822.3
1946	1601.1	519.5	493.2	416.8	46.0	30.5	26.3	4.5	21.8	1081.6	261.1	820.5

Year												
1947	1675.1	569.3	540.6	460.2	48.9	31.6	28.7	4.8	23.9	1105.8	277.9	827.9
1948	1728.6	598.7	567.1	483.8	51.0	32.3	31.6	5.1	26.5	1129.9	285.7	844.3
1949	1760.7	612.4	577.9	493.9	52.4	31.6	34.6	5.4	29.2	1148.2	286.8	861.4
1950	1812.3	637.2	599.5	511.2	54.7	33.6	37.7	5.8	31.9	1175.1	292.9	882.2
1951	1879.4	667.0	626.0	531.6	57.3	37.0	41.0	6.2	34.8	1212.4	299.8	912.6
1952	1937.6	693.7	648.8	550.5	59.9	38.4	44.9	6.7	38.2	1243.9	305.2	938.7
1953	1987.6	718.4	668.5	567.5	62.5	38.6	49.9	7.3	42.6	1269.2	309.7	959.5
1954	2030.6	739.8	684.2	582.8	64.6	36.8	55.6	8.0	47.6	1290.8	312.2	978.5
1955	2098.4	777.0	715.4	609.5	67.7	38.2	61.6	8.7	52.8	1321.4	320.4	1001.1
1956	2177.4	817.5	749.1	638.6	71.2	39.3	68.5	9.6	58.9	1359.8	330.6	1029.2
1957	2236.0	844.6	768.4	655.4	73.4	39.7	76.1	10.5	65.6	1391.4	334.5	1056.9
1958	2271.2	859.3	775.0	664.3	74.6	36.1	84.3	11.5	72.8	1411.9	333.9	1078.0
1959	2334.9	894.2	801.1	689.0	77.6	34.6	93.1	12.6	80.5	1440.7	341.9	1098.7
1960	2407.2	931.5	829.2	713.4	80.4	35.4	102.3	13.9	88.4	1475.6	349.8	1125.8
1961	2468.9	962.8	851.1	732.7	82.8	35.6	111.7	15.3	96.4	1506.1	355.4	1150.7
1962	2542.5	1001.8	880.3	757.8	85.8	36.7	121.5	17.0	104.5	1540.7	363.3	1177.4
1963	2626.6	1045.4	913.5	787.0	89.2	37.4	131.9	18.9	112.9	1581.3	372.7	1208.6
1964	2725.1	1096.5	954.0	822.7	93.2	38.1	142.6	21.1	121.5	1628.6	385.4	1243.2
1965	2843.5	1156.2	1002.6	865.6	97.8	39.3	153.5	23.4	130.1	1687.4	401.2	1286.2
1966	2963.6	1221.8	1057.0	910.6	102.3	44.1	164.8	25.9	138.9	1741.8	402.9	1338.9
1967	3088.5	1281.9	1105.8	952.4	106.6	46.8	176.1	28.4	147.7	1806.6	415.4	1391.2
1968	3228.3	1355.6	1168.5	1008.0	112.3	48.2	187.1	30.9	156.2	1872.7	433.5	1439.2
1969	3386.3	1444.1	1246.0	1073.2	118.7	54.1	198.1	33.5	164.6	1942.2	453.6	1488.6

Table B-27. *Total Net Capital Stocks Employed, in Current Dollars, by Type, U.S. Private Domestic Business Economy* (billions of dollars)

YEAR	Grand Total	Intangible Total	HUMAN INTANGIBLES				NONHUMAN INTANGIBLES			TANGIBLES		
			Total	Education and Training	Medical and Health	Mobility	Total	Basic Research	AR&D	Total	Human	Nonhuman
1929	372.9	90.8	89.0	77.5	7.8	3.7	1.7	0.5	1.2	282.1	60.8	221.3
1930	355.1	85.6	83.8	73.2	7.7	2.8	1.8	0.5	1.2	269.5	55.5	214.0
1931	309.1	75.0	73.2	64.1	7.2	1.9	1.8	0.6	1.2	234.1	44.2	189.9
1932	263.3	65.4	63.6	55.5	6.8	1.3	1.8	0.6	1.2	197.9	35.7	162.2
1933	249.8	63.2	61.3	53.3	6.7	1.3	1.9	0.6	1.3	186.6	35.1	151.5
1934	266.6	68.4	66.3	57.8	7.1	1.5	2.1	0.6	1.4	198.2	40.5	157.7
1935	278.5	73.9	71.7	62.7	7.4	1.6	2.2	0.7	1.5	204.6	45.3	159.3
1936	291.7	78.2	75.7	66.1	7.8	1.9	2.5	0.8	1.7	213.4	48.0	165.4
1937	316.7	87.0	84.2	73.8	8.3	2.1	2.7	0.9	1.9	229.7	52.6	177.1
1938	312.7	86.1	83.2	72.3	9.0	2.0	2.9	0.9	2.0	226.5	49.6	177.0
1939	313.9	88.7	85.5	74.8	8.5	2.2	3.2	1.0	2.2	225.2	50.0	175.2
1940	330.1	95.2	91.6	80.1	9.0	2.6	3.6	1.1	2.5	234.9	53.6	181.3
1941	374.6	109.8	105.3	91.7	9.9	3.7	4.5	1.3	3.2	264.8	62.9	201.9
1942	431.1	129.2	123.4	107.3	11.0	5.1	5.8	1.6	4.2	301.9	75.9	226.0
1943	472.8	144.4	137.4	119.4	12.0	5.9	7.1	1.8	5.3	328.4	83.7	244.7
1944	492.8	151.3	143.1	124.9	12.5	5.8	8.2	2.1	6.1	341.5	85.3	256.2
1945	514.7	159.7	150.7	132.2	12.9	5.6	9.0	2.2	6.8	354.9	87.8	267.1
1946	589.5	191.9	182.1	161.1	14.7	6.3	9.8	2.4	7.4	397.6	101.3	296.3

1947	707.2	238.9	227.3	202.2	17.4	7.7	11.7	2.8	8.9	468.3	121.7	346.6
1948	790.6	271.1	257.8	229.6	19.6	8.7	13.3	3.1	10.2	519.5	132.5	387.0
1949	807.3	283.9	269.2	239.7	20.7	8.8	14.7	3.4	11.3	523.3	128.9	394.4
1950	857.9	303.7	287.0	255.4	22.1	9.6	16.6	3.7	12.9	554.3	133.0	421.3
1951	962.3	335.6	316.5	280.9	24.6	11.0	19.2	4.3	14.9	626.6	146.7	480.0
1952	1021.9	363.3	341.3	302.5	27.0	11.8	22.0	4.8	17.2	658.6	149.5	509.1
1953	1060.3	386.7	361.2	320.0	28.9	12.4	25.5	5.5	20.0	673.6	150.3	523.3
1954	1089.9	405.0	375.3	332.9	30.7	11.8	29.6	6.3	23.3	684.9	150.7	534.2
1955	1155.2	438.4	403.4	358.3	33.0	12.1	35.1	7.3	27.8	716.8	154.4	562.4
1956	1256.0	485.5	442.1	393.5	36.2	12.4	43.4	8.8	34.7	770.5	161.3	609.2
1957	1343.3	523.7	472.1	420.7	39.0	12.4	51.6	10.2	41.4	819.6	168.2	651.4
1958	1401.1	550.4	491.4	437.8	41.5	12.2	59.0	11.5	47.5	850.7	172.0	678.7
1959	1480.8	597.1	528.5	470.7	44.9	12.9	68.6	13.3	55.3	883.7	176.7	707.0
1960	1554.8	639.7	562.5	500.8	48.2	13.5	77.2	15.0	62.1	915.1	183.8	731.3
1961	1615.6	676.8	590.6	525.7	51.0	13.9	86.2	17.2	69.0	938.7	188.5	750.2
1962	1698.5	723.3	627.5	558.4	54.2	15.0	95.8	19.7	76.1	975.1	195.2	779.9
1963	1794.9	776.1	670.2	596.2	57.8	16.3	105.9	22.6	83.2	1018.9	203.5	815.3
1964	1917.3	845.2	726.3	646.3	62.0	18.0	118.9	26.0	92.9	1072.1	213.5	858.6
1965	2065.5	920.1	790.6	703.6	67.0	20.0	129.5	29.9	99.6	1145.4	228.7	916.6
1966	2264.9	1011.7	869.1	771.2	73.6	24.3	142.6	34.3	108.3	1253.2	245.9	1007.3
1967	2445.1	1104.6	949.2	841.9	81.4	25.9	155.4	38.8	116.6	1340.5	258.2	1082.3
1968	2672.3	1230.7	1061.6	942.5	90.4	28.7	169.1	43.9	125.2	1441.6	279.6	1162.0
1969	2955.0	1386.7	1201.8	1065.9	102.6	33.3	184.9	49.8	135.1	1568.3	305.1	1263.2

Table B-28. *Total Net Capital Stocks Employed, in Constant Dollars, by Type, U.S. Private Domestic Business Economy* (billions of 1958 dollars)

YEAR	Grand Total	Intangible Total	HUMAN INTANGIBLES				NONHUMAN INTANGIBLES			TANGIBLES		
			Total	Education and Training	Medical and Health	Mobility	Total	Basic Research	AR&D	Total	Human	Nonhuman
1929	847.3	212.2	207.7	182.6	16.5	8.6	4.6	1.3	3.3	635.1	106.7	528.4
1930	845.2	205.6	200.7	177.7	16.3	6.7	4.9	1.4	3.5	639.6	102.0	537.6
1931	820.1	191.4	186.1	165.9	15.5	4.7	5.3	1.5	3.8	628.7	93.3	535.4
1932	790.9	181.4	175.6	157.2	14.9	3.5	5.8	1.6	4.2	609.5	87.4	522.2
1933	779.6	184.9	178.6	159.8	15.1	3.7	6.3	1.8	4.5	594.7	89.3	505.4
1934	783.8	195.4	188.7	168.8	15.7	4.2	6.6	1.9	4.7	588.4	95.6	492.8
1935	797.5	207.7	200.7	179.6	16.5	4.6	7.0	2.0	5.0	589.9	103.0	486.9
1936	813.4	217.2	209.8	187.6	17.1	5.1	7.4	2.2	5.2	596.2	108.4	487.7
1937	837.8	228.8	221.0	197.4	18.0	5.6	7.8	2.3	5.5	609.0	114.3	494.7
1938	837.5	226.8	218.5	195.4	17.8	5.3	8.3	2.5	5.9	610.6	112.4	498.3
1939	847.6	234.4	225.4	201.2	18.3	5.8	8.9	2.7	6.3	613.2	115.4	497.8
1940	872.4	248.2	238.6	212.3	19.3	6.9	9.7	2.9	6.8	624.2	122.0	502.2
1941	912.6	269.2	258.3	223.7	20.6	9.1	10.9	3.1	7.8	643.4	132.3	511.1
1942	941.5	284.6	272.0	239.4	21.6	11.0	12.5	3.4	9.1	656.9	138.1	518.9
1943	947.8	290.4	276.3	242.5	22.3	11.5	14.1	3.7	10.4	657.4	137.5	519.8
1944	939.0	290.1	274.6	241.3	22.6	10.6	15.5	3.9	11.6	648.9	133.8	515.1
1945	938.6	296.6	279.6	246.6	23.1	10.0	17.0	4.2	12.7	642.0	132.7	509.3
1946	984.4	331.9	313.5	278.1	24.8	10.6	18.4	4.5	13.9	652.5	141.5	511.0

1947	1043.2	373.0	353.0	314.4	26.7	11.9	20.0	4.8	15.2	670.3	151.4	518.9
1948	1081.9	395.0	373.2	332.4	28.1	12.7	21.8	5.1	16.8	686.9	155.3	531.6
1949	1101.3	404.2	380.4	338.9	28.9	12.6	23.8	5.4	18.4	697.1	154.9	542.3
1950	1130.7	419.0	393.3	349.9	30.3	13.2	25.6	5.8	19.8	711.8	157.1	554.7
1951	1171.5	435.5	407.9	362.0	31.8	14.1	27.6	6.2	21.4	736.0	159.4	576.6
1952	1204.9	449.7	419.7	372.0	33.2	14.5	30.0	6.7	23.4	755.2	160.4	594.7
1953	1232.6	463.5	429.9	380.8	34.5	14.6	33.5	7.3	26.3	769.1	161.1	608.0
1954	1255.7	475.4	437.8	388.5	35.7	13.7	37.7	8.0	29.7	780.2	161.3	619.0
1955	1295.7	497.6	455.5	404.6	37.4	13.5	42.0	8.7	33.3	798.1	165.3	632.8
1956	1345.8	523.3	476.1	423.4	39.4	13.3	47.2	9.6	37.6	822.5	170.8	651.8
1957	1381.3	540.1	487.1	433.6	40.7	12.9	53.0	10.5	42.5	841.3	172.6	668.6
1958	1401.1	550.4	491.4	437.8	41.5	12.2	59.0	11.5	47.5	850.7	172.0	678.7
1959	1439.5	574.0	508.8	453.2	43.2	12.4	65.2	12.6	52.6	865.4	176.5	688.9
1960	1484.9	598.3	526.7	469.2	44.9	12.6	71.6	13.9	57.7	886.6	181.4	705.2
1961	1521.9	618.1	540.3	481.4	46.2	12.7	77.8	15.3	62.5	903.8	184.9	718.9
1962	1566.3	642.4	558.3	497.1	48.0	13.3	84.0	17.0	67.0	924.0	189.6	734.4
1963	1620.1	670.8	580.2	516.2	49.9	14.0	90.5	18.9	71.6	949.4	195.4	754.0
1964	1685.2	705.5	608.3	541.0	52.3	15.0	97.2	21.1	76.1	979.7	203.7	776.1
1965	1766.2	746.8	642.9	571.7	55.2	16.1	103.9	23.4	80.5	1019.4	214.4	805.0
1966	1855.0	789.0	678.2	602.3	58.0	17.9	110.8	25.9	84.9	1066.0	224.4	841.6
1967	1937.4	829.4	712.6	632.4	60.3	19.9	116.9	28.4	88.5	1107.9	232.4	875.5
1968	2027.7	879.5	757.2	672.1	63.4	21.7	122.3	30.9	91.4	1148.2	244.2	904.0
1969	2126.3	936.8	809.2	718.2	66.9	24.1	127.6	33.5	94.1	1189.5	256.4	933.1

Table B-29. *Total Gross Capital Stocks Utilized, in Current Dollars, by Type, U.S. Private Domestic Business Economy* (billions of dollars)

YEAR	Grand Total	Intangible Total	HUMAN INTANGIBLES				NONHUMAN INTANGIBLES			TANGIBLES		
			Total	Education and Training	Medical and Health	Mobility	Total	Basic Research	AR&D	Total	Human	Nonhuman
1929	401.7	61.1	58.5	47.3	5.8	5.4	2.6	0.5	2.1	340.6	44.4	296.2
1930	340.7	56.8	54.2	44.2	5.7	4.3	2.6	0.5	2.1	283.9	40.3	243.6
1931	277.5	49.2	46.6	38.6	5.3	2.7	2.7	0.6	2.1	228.2	32.4	195.9
1932	207.9	41.5	38.9	32.6	4.9	1.4	2.6	0.6	2.1	166.4	25.7	140.7
1933	196.1	40.3	37.5	31.4	4.9	1.2	2.8	0.6	2.2	155.8	25.3	130.5
1934	216.0	40.4	37.4	31.3	4.7	1.3	3.0	0.6	2.4	175.6	26.7	148.9
1935	241.0	44.8	41.5	34.7	5.1	1.7	3.3	0.7	2.6	196.3	30.4	165.8
1936	274.8	49.0	45.3	37.8	5.5	2.1	3.7	0.8	2.9	225.8	33.1	192.7
1937	307.6	55.7	51.6	43.3	6.0	2.3	4.1	0.9	3.2	251.9	37.2	214.7
1938	284.0	54.1	49.8	41.3	6.3	2.1	4.4	0.9	3.4	229.9	34.2	195.8
1939	303.4	56.9	52.0	43.7	6.1	2.2	4.8	1.0	3.8	246.6	35.3	211.3
1940	326.1	61.0	55.6	46.7	6.4	2.4	5.4	1.1	4.3	265.2	37.6	227.5
1941	402.0	71.6	64.9	54.4	7.2	3.3	6.7	1.3	5.4	330.4	44.5	286.0
1942	477.1	87.2	78.8	65.9	8.3	4.5	8.4	1.6	6.8	389.9	55.2	334.6
1943	544.5	101.5	91.3	76.4	9.4	5.5	10.1	1.8	8.3	443.0	63.3	379.7
1944	594.1	109.3	97.7	81.9	10.0	5.8	11.6	2.1	9.6	484.8	66.4	418.4
1945	608.2	114.2	101.4	84.7	10.1	6.5	12.8	2.2	10.5	494.0	67.6	426.4
1946	642.8	127.6	113.7	95.7	10.8	7.2	14.0	2.4	11.6	515.1	73.9	441.2

222

1947	734.6	151.4	134.6	114.4	12.3	7.9	16.8	2.8	14.0	583.2	86.3	496.9
1948	810.6	168.8	149.5	127.5	13.6	8.4	19.2	3.1	16.1	641.8	93.1	548.7
1949	796.2	177.7	156.3	133.5	14.4	8.4	21.4	3.4	18.0	618.5	91.3	527.3
1950	874.5	189.8	165.3	141.0	15.1	9.2	24.4	3.7	20.7	684.7	93.7	591.0
1951	988.3	211.1	182.5	155.0	16.7	10.8	28.6	4.3	24.3	777.2	103.7	673.5
1952	1041.3	230.7	197.7	167.8	18.3	11.7	32.9	4.8	28.1	810.7	106.6	704.1
1953	1101.4	246.1	208.2	176.8	19.4	12.1	37.9	5.5	32.4	855.2	107.1	748.2
1954	1073.0	259.4	215.7	183.6	20.4	11.7	43.7	6.3	37.5	813.6	107.3	706.3
1955	1198.9	287.2	235.8	200.9	22.2	12.7	51.4	7.3	44.1	911.7	111.4	800.3
1956	1300.9	320.3	257.3	219.5	24.2	13.6	63.0	8.8	54.3	980.6	115.5	865.1
1957	1370.6	346.5	272.3	232.5	25.7	14.1	74.1	10.2	64.0	1024.1	119.2	905.0
1958	1349.2	364.9	280.5	240.4	27.0	13.1	84.3	11.5	72.8	984.4	120.8	863.5
1959	1490.1	402.9	305.0	262.2	29.5	13.2	97.9	13.3	84.6	1087.2	125.4	961.8
1960	1544.7	434.3	324.1	278.5	31.6	13.9	110.3	15.0	95.2	1110.4	129.7	980.6
1961	1573.6	462.6	339.0	291.4	33.3	14.2	123.7	17.2	106.5	1111.0	132.0	979.1
1962	1681.2	500.4	362.1	311.4	35.5	15.2	138.3	19.7	118.6	1180.8	136.9	1043.9
1963	1779.5	539.8	385.9	332.3	37.7	15.8	153.9	22.6	131.3	1239.7	142.0	1097.7
1964	1989.9	591.2	417.0	359.7	40.4	16.8	174.3	26.0	148.2	1398.6	147.9	1250.7
1965	2093.6	645.5	454.5	392.7	43.8	18.0	191.0	29.9	161.1	1448.1	157.8	1290.2
1966	2339.2	708.6	497.0	427.4	47.7	21.9	211.6	34.3	177.3	1630.6	162.1	1468.5
1967	2464.1	767.3	534.0	459.7	52.2	22.1	233.3	38.8	194.5	1696.8	167.5	1529.3
1968	2710.5	851.5	593.5	512.4	58.0	23.1	258.0	43.9	214.1	1859.6	180.2	1678.8
1969	3001.2	950.8	664.8	572.3	65.5	27.0	286.0	49.8	236.2	2050.4	194.3	1856.1

Table B-30. *Total Gross Capital Stocks Utilized, in Constant Dollars, by Type, U.S. Domestic Private Business Economy* (billions of 1958 dollars)

YEAR	Grand Total	Intangible Total	HUMAN INTANGIBLES				NONHUMAN INTANGIBLES			TANGIBLES		
			Total	Education and Training	Medical and Health	Mobility	Total	Basic Research	AR&D	Total	Human	Nonhuman
1929	944.3	143.2	136.3	111.3	12.3	12.7	6.9	1.3	5.6	801.1	77.9	723.2
1930	833.0	136.9	129.6	107.2	12.0	10.4	7.4	1.4	6.0	696.1	74.2	621.9
1931	748.2	126.1	118.1	100.0	11.4	6.8	7.9	1.5	6.4	622.1	68.3	553.7
1932	626.9	115.6	107.0	92.5	10.7	3.8	8.6	1.6	7.0	511.3	62.9	448.4
1933	609.2	117.9	108.6	94.2	10.9	3.5	9.3	1.8	7.5	491.3	64.5	426.8
1934	637.3	115.7	105.8	91.5	10.5	3.8	9.9	1.9	8.0	521.6	63.2	458.4
1935	695.8	126.0	115.5	99.5	11.3	4.7	10.5	2.0	8.5	569.7	69.2	500.5
1936	772.8	136.2	125.0	107.1	12.1	5.8	11.2	2.2	9.0	636.6	74.7	561.9
1937	822.1	146.8	134.9	115.7	13.0	6.2	11.9	2.3	9.5	675.3	80.8	594.5
1938	760.8	142.5	129.9	111.5	12.5	5.8	12.7	2.5	10.2	618.3	77.5	540.8
1939	818.5	150.1	136.5	117.4	13.2	6.0	13.6	2.7	10.9	668.4	81.4	587.0
1940	870.9	158.7	144.1	123.8	13.8	6.5	14.6	2.9	11.7	712.2	85.7	626.6
1941	977.9	174.6	158.5	135.4	15.0	8.1	16.1	3.1	13.0	803.2	93.6	709.7
1942	1047.6	191.0	172.9	146.7	16.4	9.8	18.1	3.4	14.7	856.6	100.5	756.1
1943	1103.5	203.0	182.9	154.7	17.5	10.7	20.1	3.7	16.4	900.5	104.1	796.4
1944	1145.3	208.6	186.6	157.8	18.1	10.6	22.1	3.9	18.1	936.7	104.1	832.6
1945	1119.6	211.6	187.5	157.8	18.1	11.6	24.1	4.2	19.9	908.0	102.1	805.9
1946	1081.2	221.4	195.2	164.9	18.2	12.1	26.3	4.5	21.8	859.8	103.3	756.5

Year											
1947	1088.5	237.7	209.0	177.9	18.9	12.2	28.7	4.8	23.9	850.9	107.4	743.4
1948	1111.0	248.0	216.5	184.6	19.5	12.3	31.6	5.1	26.5	862.9	109.0	753.9
1949	1086.2	255.5	220.9	188.8	20.0	12.1	34.6	5.4	29.2	830.7	109.6	721.0
1950	1148.5	264.1	226.5	193.1	20.7	12.7	37.7	5.8	31.9	884.4	110.7	773.7
1951	1202.0	276.2	235.2	199.8	21.5	13.9	41.0	6.2	34.8	925.8	112.7	813.1
1952	1225.6	288.0	243.1	206.3	22.5	14.4	44.9	6.7	38.2	937.6	114.4	823.2
1953	1279.7	297.6	247.7	210.2	23.1	14.3	49.9	7.3	42.6	982.1	114.7	867.4
1954	1237.9	307.1	251.5	214.2	23.7	13.5	55.6	8.0	47.6	930.9	114.8	816.1
1955	1345.0	327.8	266.2	226.8	25.2	14.2	61.6	8.7	52.8	1017.2	119.2	897.9
1956	1391.0	345.5	277.0	236.2	26.3	14.5	68.5	9.6	58.9	1045.5	122.3	923.2
1957	1406.3	357.1	281.0	239.6	26.8	14.5	76.1	10.5	65.6	1049.2	122.3	926.9
1958	1349.2	364.9	280.5	240.4	27.0	13.1	84.3	11.5	72.8	984.3	120.8	863.5
1959	1452.5	386.7	293.6	252.5	28.4	12.7	93.1	12.6	80.5	1065.8	125.3	940.5
1960	1483.9	405.7	303.4	261.0	29.4	13.0	102.3	13.9	88.4	1078.2	128.0	950.2
1961	1494.8	421.8	310.0	266.9	30.2	13.0	111.7	15.3	96.4	1073.0	129.5	943.6
1962	1569.2	443.6	322.2	277.3	31.4	13.4	121.5	17.0	104.5	1125.5	132.9	992.6
1963	1630.8	466.0	334.1	287.9	32.6	13.7	131.9	18.9	112.9	1164.8	136.3	1028.5
1964	1712.1	491.9	349.3	301.2	34.1	14.0	142.6	21.1	121.9	1220.2	141.1	1079.1
1965	1828.8	523.3	369.8	319.2	36.1	14.5	153.5	23.4	130.1	1305.5	148.0	1157.5
1966	1948.8	553.0	388.2	334.3	37.6	16.3	164.8	25.9	138.9	1395.8	147.9	1247.9
1967	1984.5	577.5	401.4	345.8	38.7	16.9	176.1	28.4	147.7	1407.0	150.8	1256.2
1968	2094.2	611.3	424.2	365.9	40.8	17.5	187.1	30.9	156.2	1482.9	157.4	1325.5
1969	2200.2	646.6	448.5	386.3	42.7	19.5	198.1	33.5	164.6	1553.6	163.3	1390.3

Table B-31. Total Net Capital Stocks Utilized, in Current Dollars, by Type, U.S. Private Domestic Business Economy (billions of dollars)

YEAR	Grand Total	Intangible Total	HUMAN INTANGIBLES				NONHUMAN INTANGIBLES			TANGIBLES		
			Total	Education and Training	Medical and Health	Mobility	Total	Basic Research	AR&D	Total	Human	Nonhuman
1929	261.0	40.5	38.7	33.7	3.4	1.6	1.7	0.5	1.2	220.6	26.5	194.1
1930	219.7	37.6	35.8	31.3	3.3	1.2	1.8	0.5	1.2	182.1	23.7	158.4
1931	175.9	32.7	30.9	27.0	3.0	0.8	1.8	0.6	1.2	143.2	18.6	124.6
1932	129.3	27.7	25.9	22.6	2.7	0.5	1.8	0.6	1.2	101.6	14.5	87.1
1933	119.9	26.9	25.0	21.7	2.7	0.5	1.9	0.6	1.3	93.1	14.3	78.8
1934	131.4	26.9	24.8	21.6	2.6	0.6	2.1	0.6	1.4	104.4	15.2	89.3
1935	145.9	29.7	27.5	24.0	2.8	0.6	2.2	0.7	1.5	116.3	17.3	98.9
1936	166.0	32.3	29.8	26.0	3.1	0.7	2.5	0.8	1.7	133.7	18.9	114.8
1937	186.3	36.7	34.0	29.8	3.4	0.8	2.7	0.9	1.9	149.6	21.2	128.4
1938	170.5	35.4	32.5	28.2	3.5	0.8	2.9	0.9	2.0	135.1	19.3	115.8
1939	181.1	37.2	34.0	29.7	3.4	0.9	3.2	1.0	2.2	143.9	19.9	124.0
1940	197.4	40.0	36.4	31.8	3.6	1.0	3.6	1.1	2.5	157.4	21.3	136.2
1941	242.7	47.0	42.4	36.9	4.0	1.5	4.5	1.3	3.2	195.7	25.3	170.4
1942	290.4	56.8	51.0	44.3	4.6	2.1	5.8	1.6	4.2	233.6	31.4	202.2
1943	331.9	65.1	58.0	50.4	5.1	2.5	7.1	1.8	5.3	266.8	35.3	231.5
1944	361.5	69.0	60.9	53.1	5.3	2.5	8.2	2.1	6.1	292.5	36.3	256.2
1945	369.9	71.7	62.7	55.0	5.4	2.3	9.0	2.2	6.8	298.2	36.5	261.7
1946	395.1	81.8	72.1	63.7	5.8	2.5	9.8	2.4	7.4	313.3	40.1	273.2

1947	457.8	99.5	87.8	78.1	6.7	3.0	11.7	2.8	8.9	358.3	47.0	311.2
1948	507.8	111.7	98.4	87.6	7.5	3.3	13.3	3.1	10.2	396.1	50.6	345.6
1949	497.0	117.6	102.9	91.6	7.9	3.4	14.7	3.4	11.3	379.4	49.3	330.1
1950	544.8	125.1	108.4	96.5	8.4	3.6	16.6	3.7	12.9	419.7	50.2	369.4
1951	620.9	138.1	118.9	105.5	9.3	4.1	19.2	4.3	14.9	482.8	55.1	427.7
1952	652.4	149.9	127.9	113.4	10.1	4.4	22.0	4.8	17.2	502.5	56.0	446.5
1953	688.1	159.3	133.8	118.6	10.7	4.6	25.5	5.5	20.0	528.7	55.7	473.1
1954	668.5	167.6	138.0	122.3	11.3	4.3	29.6	6.3	23.3	500.9	55.4	445.5
1955	747.1	185.2	150.1	133.3	12.3	4.5	35.1	7.3	27.8	561.9	57.5	504.5
1956	813.0	206.9	163.5	145.5	13.4	4.6	43.4	8.8	34.7	606.1	59.6	546.5
1957	857.0	224.2	172.6	153.8	14.3	4.6	51.6	10.2	41.4	632.8	61.5	571.3
1958	842.7	236.9	177.9	158.5	15.0	4.4	59.0	11.5	47.5	605.9	62.3	543.6
1959	932.3	262.3	193.7	172.5	16.4	4.7	68.6	13.3	55.3	670.0	64.7	605.2
1960	967.4	283.0	205.8	183.2	17.6	4.9	77.2	15.0	62.1	684.4	67.2	617.2
1961	985.2	301.4	215.2	191.5	18.6	5.1	86.2	17.2	69.0	683.9	68.7	615.2
1962	1054.4	325.5	229.7	204.3	19.8	5.5	95.8	19.7	76.1	728.9	71.5	657.5
1963	1119.3	351.0	245.1	218.1	21.1	6.0	105.9	22.6	83.2	768.3	74.5	693.8
1964	1208.3	384.9	265.9	236.6	22.7	6.6	118.9	26.0	92.9	823.5	78.2	745.3
1965	1330.5	421.1	291.6	259.5	24.7	7.4	129.5	29.9	99.6	909.3	84.4	825.0
1966	1490.6	461.6	319.0	283.1	27.0	8.9	142.6	34.3	108.3	1029.0	90.2	938.8
1967	1571.0	500.0	344.6	305.5	29.6	9.5	155.4	38.8	116.6	1071.0	93.7	977.3
1968	1726.3	554.6	385.5	342.2	32.8	10.5	169.1	43.9	125.2	1171.7	101.5	1070.2
1969	1907.1	617.4	432.5	383.7	36.9	11.9	184.9	49.8	135.1	1289.7	109.8	1179.9

Table B-32. Total Net Capital Stocks Utilized, in Constant Dollars, by Type, U.S. Private Domestic Business Economy (billions of 1958 dollars)

YEAR	Grand Total	Intangible Total	HUMAN INTANGIBLES				NONHUMAN INTANGIBLES			TANGIBLES		
			Total	Education and Training	Medical and Health	Mobility	Total	Basic Research	AR&D	Total	Human	Nonhuman
1929	604.7	94.9	90.3	79.4	7.2	3.7	4.6	1.3	3.3	509.8	46.4	463.4
1930	532.1	90.7	85.8	76.0	7.0	2.9	4.9	1.4	3.5	441.4	43.6	397.8
1931	474.4	83.8	78.5	69.9	6.5	2.0	5.3	1.5	3.8	390.6	39.3	351.2
1932	393.2	77.3	71.4	64.0	6.1	1.4	5.8	1.6	4.2	316.0	35.5	280.4
1933	378.1	78.9	72.7	65.0	6.1	1.5	6.3	1.8	4.5	299.2	36.3	262.8
1934	392.1	77.4	70.7	63.3	5.9	1.6	6.6	1.9	4.7	314.7	35.8	278.9
1935	425.6	83.8	76.9	68.8	6.3	1.8	7.0	2.0	5.0	341.8	39.5	302.3
1936	471.2	90.0	82.6	73.9	6.7	2.0	7.4	2.2	5.2	381.2	42.7	338.5
1937	501.6	96.9	89.1	79.6	7.2	2.2	7.8	2.3	5.5	404.7	46.1	358.7
1938	463.3	93.6	85.3	76.2	7.0	2.1	8.3	2.5	5.9	369.7	43.9	325.9
1939	496.8	98.5	89.5	79.9	7.3	2.3	8.9	2.7	6.3	398.3	45.8	352.5
1940	529.9	104.4	94.7	84.3	7.6	2.8	9.7	2.9	6.8	425.6	48.4	377.1
1941	599.7	115.0	104.1	92.1	8.3	3.7	10.9	3.1	7.8	484.7	53.3	431.4
1942	646.4	124.9	112.4	98.9	8.9	4.5	12.5	3.4	9.1	521.4	57.0	464.4
1943	680.6	130.7	116.7	102.4	9.4	4.9	14.1	3.7	10.4	549.8	58.1	491.8
1944	704.3	132.3	116.8	102.6	9.6	4.5	15.5	3.9	11.6	572.0	56.9	515.1
1945	687.6	133.2	116.3	102.5	9.6	4.2	17.0	4.2	12.7	554.3	55.2	499.1
1946	669.6	142.4	124.0	110.0	9.8	4.2	18.4	4.5	13.9	527.2	56.0	471.2

Year												
1947	680.9	156.4	136.5	121.5	10.3	4.6	20.0	4.8	15.2	524.5	58.5	465.9
1948	698.2	164.3	142.4	126.9	10.7	4.8	21.8	5.1	16.8	534.0	59.3	474.7
1949	682.3	169.2	145.4	129.6	11.0	4.8	23.8	5.4	18.4	513.1	59.2	453.9
1950	720.0	174.2	148.6	132.2	11.4	5.0	25.6	5.8	19.8	545.8	59.3	486.4
1951	754.5	180.8	153.3	136.0	11.9	5.3	27.6	6.2	21.4	573.6	59.9	513.7
1952	769.0	187.3	157.3	139.4	12.4	5.4	30.0	6.7	23.4	581.7	60.1	521.6
1953	802.1	192.8	159.3	141.1	12.8	5.4	33.5	7.3	26.3	609.3	59.7	549.7
1954	774.1	198.6	160.9	142.8	13.1	5.0	37.7	8.0	29.7	575.5	59.3	516.2
1955	840.7	211.6	169.5	150.6	13.9	5.0	42.0	8.7	33.3	629.2	61.5	567.6
1956	871.1	223.3	176.1	156.6	14.6	4.9	47.2	9.6	37.6	647.8	63.2	584.6
1957	880.6	231.1	178.1	158.5	14.9	4.7	53.0	10.5	42.5	649.5	63.1	586.4
1958	842.7	236.9	177.9	158.5	15.0	4.4	59.0	11.5	47.5	605.9	62.3	543.6
1959	906.1	251.7	186.5	166.1	15.8	4.5	65.2	12.6	52.6	654.4	64.7	589.7
1960	925.9	264.3	192.7	171.7	16.4	4.6	71.6	13.9	57.7	661.6	66.4	595.2
1961	931.5	274.6	196.8	175.4	16.8	4.6	77.8	15.3	62.5	656.9	67.4	589.5
1962	976.8	288.4	204.3	181.9	17.6	4.9	84.0	17.0	67.0	688.5	69.4	619.1
1963	1015.9	302.8	212.2	188.8	18.3	5.1	90.5	18.9	71.6	713.1	71.5	641.6
1964	1068.1	319.9	222.7	198.1	19.2	5.5	97.2	21.1	76.1	748.2	74.6	673.6
1965	1144.6	341.0	237.1	210.8	20.3	5.9	103.9	23.4	80.5	803.6	79.1	724.5
1966	1226.5	359.7	248.9	221.0	21.3	6.6	110.8	25.9	84.9	866.8	82.4	784.4
1967	1250.4	375.5	258.6	229.5	21.9	7.2	116.9	28.4	88.5	874.9	84.4	790.5
1968	1318.4	397.2	274.9	244.0	23.0	7.9	122.3	30.9	91.4	921.2	88.6	832.6
1969	1382.7	418.9	291.3	258.5	24.1	8.7	127.6	33.5	94.1	963.8	92.3	871.5

C

An Extension of Selected Total Investment and Wealth Estimates through 1973.

As this manuscript was going to press the author had occasion to update key estimates through 1973 in a paper for the Joint Economic Committee of Congress.[1] The summary tables from the Joint Committee print are reproduced in this appendix. Figures for earlier key years, although shown elsewhere in this volume, have been left in the tables in order to facilitate comparison of the recent changes with earlier trends. Estimates for the year 1966 have also been included in these tables.

Although 1966 was not a major cycle peak, it did precede the "minirecession" of 1967 and is a "subcycle" peak year. More importantly, with the perspective gained by the subsequent decade, 1966 appears to mark the beginning of a new epoch or subperiod of American economic history. It saw the beginning of a marked acceleration in the growth rate of the labor force, a deceleration of productivity advance, an acceleration of inflation, and, as we shall see, the beginning of a decline in the ratio of total investment to adjusted GNP which continued from 1969 through 1973 (the most recent cycle peak year).

Instead of reproducing the text of the Joint Committee print, which repeats the description of earlier trends contained in this volume (and has a policy orientation), we shall merely call attention to the more important tendencies between 1966 and 1973 in the formation and stocks of total capital and associated variables.

Table C-1 shows the conventional gross investment estimates in

1. See footnote 14, p. xxv.

230

relation to GNP, in current and constant dollars, on the old as well as the revised bases. Whereas the ratio of gross investment to product dropped between 1966 and 1969, it recovered between 1969 and 1973. On the revised basis, the investment ratio was slightly above 1966 in both current and constant dollars.

For calculating the ratio of total investment to GNP, it was necessary to extend the adjustments of GNP for consistency with the expanded investment estimates through 1973. As shown in Table C-2, adjusted GNP from 1969 to 1973 continued its prior upward trend in relation to the official GNP estimates. In constant dollars, the ratio leveled out at around 132 percent.

The total gross investment estimates are presented in Table C-3. In the first column, it is shown that after rising from around 43 percent of adjusted GDP in 1929 and 1948 to 50.5 percent in 1966, the total gross domestic investment ratio dropped to 49.0 percent in 1969 and further to 48.5 percent by 1973. The decline from 1966 to 1969 was concentrated in the tangibles, but from 1969 to 1973 it was the intangibles that pulled the aggregate ratio down further—particularly the relative decline in outlays for R&D and education and training.

With regard to the sectoral composition of gross domestic investment, the relative decline after 1966 came in the business and public sectors, as shown in Table C-4. In the business sector, the ratio of disposable income (cash flow) to gross product dropped from 12.5 percent in 1966 to 9.3 percent in 1973, reflecting declining profit margins due to macroeconomic policies designed to combat accelerating inflation. Although net business borrowing increased substantially over this period, it was not enough to counteract the decline of internally generated funds, and the ratio of business total investment to adjusted GNP dropped by almost one percentage point. The disposable income of governments (revenues less transfers) also declined between 1966 and 1973, by 2½ percentage points, reversing its prior upward trend. Since the ratio of total public investment to disposable income was only fractionally higher in 1973 than in 1966, the investment/product ratio dropped by more than a percentage point.

Disposable personal income reversed its decline as a fraction of GNP in 1966, rising from 63 percent to almost 69 percent in 1973. But households and nonprofit institutions reduced the proportion of disposable income devoted to total investment, and the investment/product ratio remained quite steady at around 26½ percent.

Reflecting the lagged effect of investment on stocks of capital, the rate of increase in real total gross national wealth reached a high point in the 1966–1969 subperiod with an average annual rate of 4.0 percent. (See Table C-5.) This exceeded fractionally the rate of increase in real adjusted GNP, bringing to a halt the downward trend in the national wealth coefficient. In the 1969–1973 subperiod, the average rate of increase in real total GNP slowed a bit to 3.8 percent a year. But the growth rate of real adjusted GNP also slowed, and the real total GNW/GNP ratio rose fractionally from 8.4 to 8.5. This suggests that the growth in total capital productivity declined after 1966. But, as explained in the text, it is more meaningful to compute productivity ratios for the private domestic economy than for the total.

Looking at real product in relation to real tangible capital alone for the business economy (Table C-6, line 6), it can be seen that the average rate of increase in "tangible capital productivity" decelerated drastically from 1.7 percent a year in 1948–1966 to 0.2 percent in 1966–1973. The deceleration was not due to a slower growth of intangible capital relative to that of tangible capital, however. As shown in line 5 of the table, the ratio of total to tangible capital continued to increase after 1966 at about the same rate as before. And, as shown in Table C-7, the share of intangible capital in total wealth continued its upward trend, rising from almost 37 percent in 1966 to near 40 percent in 1973. In fact, when real gross product is related to real total gross wealth in the business sector, "total capital productivity" actually declined during 1966–73, in contrast to the one percent a year average rate of increase from 1948 to 1966!

The marked deceleration in productivity, based on this and other measures, appears to be due to a number of factors, as noted in the Joint Committee print (p. 9). The slower rate of growth after 1966 meant fewer opportunities for economies of scale, of course. The bulge in labor force growth after 1965 reduced the average experience of workers and slowed the growth of real product per worker for the time being, since compensation and value added are below average for young workers.

The rate of utilization of the labor force was lower in 1973 than in 1966 (4.9 percent unemployment versus 3.6 percent, respectively); yet there were capacity bottlenecks in many basic industries, e.g., steel, aluminum, paper, and petroleum. This suggests inadequate business tangible investment in the earlier years, and possibly some misallocation of investment. The inadequate amount, in view of the rapid growth of the labor force, is related to a declining net rate of return on investment, especially when adjustments to profits are made for revaluation of book depreciation charges to replacement cost. The declining rate of return reflects the use of macroeconomic policies to combat the accelerating inflation which, on balance, held increases in the price level below increases in unit costs. Some misallocation of investment probably resulted from the wage and price control programs from August 1971 to April 1974.

Further, the increasing amounts of investment required for environmental protection and occupational health and safety reduced the proportion available for direct productive purposes. Since the benefits of these programs are not reflected in real product while the investments are reflected in the real capital measures, the programs tend to reduce increases in productivity as measured.

It also seems probable that the relative decline of research and development investments and the leveling out of the relative R&D stock (see Table C-7) tended to slow down productivity growth, since R&D is the fountainhead of scientific and technological advance.

Finally, there were various negative social tendencies, particularly in the latter 1960s, that probably reduced productivity growth. Examples are increasing drug use and crime, increased antiestablishment and antibusiness sentiment and a possible loosening of the work ethic. However, the development of social indicators has not yet reached the point where it permits quantification of the economic impacts of these and other social developments.

Table C-8 shows that both the gross and net rates of return on total capital stocks employed in the business economy declined significantly between 1966 and 1973. It will be recalled that the rates of return dropped from the high levels reached in 1948, which had reflected postwar capital shortages, until 1960. Then there was a temporary reversal between 1960 and 1966, although the 1966 rates were still well under the 1948 rates. But after 1966 the gross rates of return declined from 11.8 percent to 10.4 percent in 1973, while the net rates fell from 11.4 percent to 10.0 percent. The 1973 rates were back approximately at the level estimated for 1929. The rates of return on human capital continued to remain above those on nonhuman capital in the 1966–1973 subperiod. However, it is noteworthy that the rates of return on human capital continued their decline from 1969 to 1973, whereas the returns on nonhuman capital appeared to stabilize. As indicated in Table C-7, this was associated with an increase in the human proportion of total gross domestic wealth from 51.1 percent in 1969 to 52.3 percent in 1973—a stronger relative growth than in the preceding subperiod. Evidence of a decline in rates of return on specific types of human capital in recent years has been adduced in other studies.[2]

The decline in tangible, nonhuman investment between 1973 and 1975 is shown in Table C-1. If past experience is any guide, it is doubtful if intangible and human investment dropped at all during the recession. But our estimates of the formation and stocks of total capital end with 1973, so analysis of the current cycle must await another occasion.

2. See, for example, Richard R. Freeman, "Overinvestment in College Training?" in *The Journal of Human Resources*, X-3, 1975.

Table C-1. *Investment in Relation to Gross National Product*

Year	GROSS NATIONAL PRODUCT		GROSS INVESTMENT (DOMESTIC PLUS FOREIGN)		RATIOS	
	Unrevised (1)	Revised (2)	Unrevised (3)	Revised (4)	(3) ÷ (1) (5)	(4) ÷ (2) (6)
			(billions of current dollars)			
1929	103.1		17.0		16.5	
1948	257.6	259.1	47.9	47.8	18.6	18.4
1957	441.1	442.8	71.2	72.8	16.1	16.4
1966	749.9	753.0	123.9	126.1	16.5	16.7
1969	930.3	935.5	137.9	144.2	14.8	15.4
1973	1,294.9	1,306.3	209.4	220.2	16.2	16.9
(1975)		1,499.0		209.5		13.1
		(billions of constant, 1958 and 1972, dollars)				
1929	203.6		42.0		20.6	
1948	323.7	487.7	62.8	86.0	19.4	17.6
1957	452.5	680.9	72.3	102.7	16.0	15.1
1966	658.1	981.0	111.4	163.4	16.9	16.7
1969	725.6	1,078.8	109.7	170.3	15.1	15.8
1973	839.2	1,233.4	138.2	207.1	16.5	16.8
(1975)		1,186.4		149.1		12.6

NOTE: The estimates contained in the Joint Committee print and in the rest of the present volume were based on the unrevised BEA estimates. Revised estimates appeared in the January 1976 *Survey of Current Business,* and the constant dollar revised estimates were shifted from a 1958 to a 1972 base. Both sets of estimates are shown here for the overlapping years.

Table C-2. *Adjustments of Commerce Department Estimates of GNP for Consistency with Total Investment and Capital Estimates* (in billions of dollars)

	1969	1973
Current dollars:		
GNP commerce concept	929.1	1,294.9
Plus:		
Personal sector imputations:		
Student compensation	92.3	148.1
Frictional unemployment	16.0	24.1
Rentals on household capital	100.1	138.5
Rentals on institutional capital	5.7	8.5
Business: Investments charged to current account:		
Tangible	2.3	3.3
Intangible	35.4	45.6
General governments: Imputed rentals on public capital	67.0	91.2
Equals: Adjusted GNP	1,247.9	1,754.3
Ratio to Commerce GNP	1.343	1.355
Constant 1958 dollars:		
Commerce GNP	724.7	839.2
Adjusted GNP	957.2	1,104.5
Ratio	1.321	1.316

Table C-3. *Total Gross Investment, by Type, U.S. Domestic Economy* (in billions of dollars and percentages; selected years)

	Grand Total	Intangible Investments					Tangibles Total
		Total	Education and Training	Health and Safety	Mobility	R&D	
Billions of current dollars:							
1929	55.0	15.7	11.0	1.9	2.5	0.3	39.2
1948	139.9	45.0	31.0	5.2	6.6	2.4	94.9
1951	272.0	92.7	61.4	10.6	10.5	10.3	179.2
1966	495.8	198.1	137.4	21.4	17.0	22.3	297.7
1969	611.7	267.8	192.4	27.9	21.3	26.2	344.0
1973	851.0	369.6	262.6	45.9	31.0	30.1	481.4
Percent distribution of total gross investment:							
1929	43.1[a]	28.5	20.0	3.5	4.6	.5	71.5
1948	42.7[a]	32.1	22.0	3.7	4.7	1.6	67.9
1957	47.6[a]	34.0	22.5	4.0	3.8	3.8	66.0
1966	50.5[a]	40.0	27.7	4.3	3.4	4.5	60.0
1969	49.0[a]	43.8	31.5	4.6	3.5	4.3	56.2
1973	48.5[a]	43.4	30.9	5.4	3.6	3.5	56.6

[a]Percent of adjusted GNP.

Table C-4. *Total Gross Investment, by Domestic Sector, in Relation to Gross Product and Sectoral Disposable Income* (percentages, selected peak years, 1929–73)

	1929	1948	1957	1966	1969	1973
Persons:						
DI/GNP	78.8	70.4	68.5	63.0	67.0	68.8
Inv./DI	33.2	35.2	37.3	41.9	39.4	38.5
Inv./GNP	26.1	24.8	25.5	26.4	26.5	26.5
Business:						
DI/GNP	10.0	10.2	10.1	12.5	9.5	9.3
Inv./DI	124.4	123.8	109.5	102.4	123.9	128.0
Inv./GNP	12.4	12.6	11.1	12.8	11.8	11.9
Governments:						
DI/GNP	10.4	18.7	20.9	24.2	23.4	21.7
Inv./DI	44.3	28.6	52.2	46.3	48.1	46.5
Inv./GNP	4.6	5.2	10.9	11.2	11.3	10.1

Note: DI = Disposable income of each sector, equals gross income earned from current production plus transfers (including taxes, in the case of governments) received from other sectors less transfer (and tax) payments. Inv. = Total gross investment, both tangible and intangible, of each sector. GNP = Sum of disposable income of each sector (including rest-of-the-world, not shown here) plus the statistical discrepancy between income and product.

Table C-5. *Total U.S. Gross National Wealth and Product, Selected Years, 1929–73* (dollar amount in billions)

	Current	Price Deflators (indexes, 1958=100)	Constant
	A—Absolute levels		
Adjusted GNP:			
1929	$127	50.5	$252
1948	328	77.9	421
1966	983	114.8	856
1969	1,248	130.4	957
1973	1,754	158.8	1,105
Total GNW:			
1929	1,203	45.4	2,648
1948	3,012	76.0	3,964
1966	8,518	118.5	7,187
1969	10,907	135.2	8,070
1973	15,641	166.7	9,383

(cont.)

Table C-5.   (Completed)

	Current	Price Deflators (indexes, 1958=100)	Constant
B—Average annual percentage rates of change			
Adjusted GNP:			
1929–73	6.1	2.7	3.4
1929–48	5.1	2.3	2.7
1948–66	6.4	2.3	4.0
1966–69	8.3	4.3	3.8
1969–73	8.9	5.1	3.6
Total GNW:			
1929–73	6.0	3.0	2.9
1929–48	4.9	2.7	2.1
1948–66	6.0	2.6	3.3
1966–69	8.6	4.5	4.0
1969–73	9.4	5.4	3.8
C—Ratios, GNW/GNP			
Total GNW/GNP:			
1929	9.4	.90	10.5
1948	9.2	.98	9.4
1966	8.7	1.03	8.4
1969	8.7	1.04	8.4
1973	8.9	1.05	8.5

Table C-6.   *Major Components of U.S. Economic Growth* (private domestic business economy, average annual percentage rates of change)

	1948–66	1966–73
1. Real adjusted gross product	4.1	3.5
2. Real gross capital stock—total	3.1	4.1
3. Tangible capital	2.4	3.3
4. Intangible capital	4.1	5.2
5. Ratio: real total capital over real tangible capital (2–3)	.7	.8
6. Tangible capital productivity (1–3)	1.7	.2
7. Total capital productivity (1–2)	1.0	−.6

Table C-7. *Composition of Total Gross Domestic Wealth* (by type and by sector; selected years)

Year	TANGIBLE CAPITAL			INTANGIBLE CAPITAL		
	Total	Human	Nonhuman	Total	Human	Nonhuman (R&D)
A. Percentage distribution by major type:						
1929	76.8	24.5	52.3	23.2	23.0	0.2
1948	73.0	21.3	51.7	27.0	26.4	0.6
1957	68.9	18.1	50.8	31.1	29.7	1.4
1966	63.2	16.3	46.9	36.8	34.3	2.5
1969	61.5	15.2	46.2	38.5	35.9	2.6
1973	60.2	15.1	45.1	39.8	37.2	2.6

Year	Personal	Business	Governments	Addendum: Net Foreign Claims as Percent of GDW
B. Percentage distribution, by major sectors:				
1929	58.0	30.6	11.4	1.4
1948	56.2	22.4	21.4	1.3
1957	55.9	22.6	21.4	.9
1966	55.4	21.9	22.7	.8
1969	54.9	21.6	23.5	.6
1973	55.5	21.3	23.2	.4

Table C-8. *Rates of Return on Total Capital Stocks Employed—U.S. Private Domestic Business Economy* (in percentages; selected peak years)

Year	Total	Human	Nonhuman
A. Cross rates of return:			
1929	10.2	11.7	9.2
1948	12.1	12.2	12.0
1953	12.1	13.5	10.8
1957	11.4	12.7	10.1
1960	10.0	12.3	9.7
1966	11.8	12.2	11.4
1969	10.8	11.7	9.9
1973[a]	10.4	10.8	10.1
B. Net rates of return:			
1929	10.0	10.1	10.0
1948	13.4	12.6	14.2
1953	13.1	14.8	11.4
1957	11.6	13.4	9.9
1960	11.0	12.9	9.2
1966	11.4	12.8	10.7
1969	10.6	12.2	8.9
1973[a]	10.0	11.2	8.8

[a]Preliminary.

Bibliography

ABRAMOVITZ, MOSES. *Resource and Output Trends in the United States since 1870*. New York: NBER, 1956.

AMERICAN ASSOCIATION OF UNIVERSITY PROFESSORS. "The Economic Status of the Profession." *AAUP Bulletin* 50 (1964).

American Economic Review 51 (1961): 1–17.

AMERICAN MEDICAL ASSOCIATION. *The Cost of Medical Care*. General Report, vol. 1 (1964).

ARNOW, KATHRYN S. "Indicators of Price and Cost Change in Research and Development Inputs." In *1966 Proceedings, Business and Economic Statistics Section, American Statistical Association*. Washington, D.C.: American Statistical Association, 1966.

BACHMAN, GEORGE W. AND ASSOCIATES. *Health Resources in the United States*. Washington, D.C.: Brookings Institution, 1952.

BARGER, HAROLD. *Outlay and Income in the United States, 1921–1938*. New York: NBER, 1942.

BECKER, GARY S. *Human Capital*. New York: NBER, 1975.

———. "Investment in Human Capital: A Theoretical Analysis." *Journal of Political Economy* 70, supplement (1962): 9–49.

BLAI, JR., BORIS. "Worker Turnover Bites into Profits." *Personnel Journal* 31 (1953): 367–372.

BLAUG, MARK, ED. *Economics of Education*, vol. 1. Baltimore: Penguin Books, 1968.

BOWMAN, MARY JEAN. "Economics of Higher Education." *HEW Bulletin* 5 (1962).

BRIGHT, MARGARET L. and THOMAS, DOROTHY S. "Interstate Migration and Intervening Opportunities." *American Sociological Review* 6 (1941): 773–783.

241

BRUNNER, E. D. *The Cost of Basic Research Effort: Air Force Experience, 1954–1964*. RM-4250-PR. Santa Monica: The RAND Corporation, 1965.

BURGESS, W. RANDOLPH. *Trends of School Costs*. New York: The Russell Sage Foundation, 1920.

BUSH, VANNEVAR. *Science, The Endless Frontier, A Report to the President on a Program for Postwar Scientific Research*. Washington, D.C.: 1945.

CANFIELD, GRANT W. "How to Compute Your Labor Turnover Costs." *Personnel Journal* 37 (1959): 414.

DEARBORN, DeWITT C.; KNEZNEK, ROSE W.; and ANTHONY, R.N. *Spending for Industrial Research, 1951–1952*. Boston: Harvard University, Graduate School of Business Administration, 1953.

DENISON, EDWARD F. *The Sources of Economic Growth in the United States and the Alternatives before Us*. New York: Committee for Economic Development, 1962.

———. "Theoretical Aspects of Quality Change, Capital Consumption, and Net Capital Formation." In *Problems of Capital Formation*. New York: NBER, 1957.

DEWHURST, J. FREDERICK and ASSOCIATES. *America's Needs and Resources, A New Survey*. New York: Twentieth Century Fund, 1955.

DISNEY, FRANCIS M. "Employee Turnover Is Costly." *Personnel Journal* 33 (1954): 97.

DUPREE, A. HUNTER. *Science in the Federal Government*. Cambridge, Mass.: Belknap Press of Harvard University Press, 1957.

EPSTEIN, LENORE A. "Consumers' Tangible Assets." In *Studies in Income and Wealth*, vol. 12. New York: NBER, 1950.

Federal Reserve Bulletin, various issues.

FISHER, IRVING. *The Nature of Capital and Income*. New York: Macmillan, 1930.

FRIEDMAN, CHARLES S. "The Stock of Automobiles in the United States: Its Size and Value in the Postwar Period." *Survey of Current Business* 45 (October 1965): 21–27.

———. "Stocks of Durable Consumer Goods Other than Automobiles, 1946–1965." Unpublished.

GALLMAN, R. E. "Commodity Output, 1839–1899." In *Trends in the American Economy in the Nineteenth Century*. Princeton: Princeton University Press for NBER, 1960.

———. "Gross National Product in the United States, 1834–1909." In *Output, Employment, and Productivity in the United States after 1800*. New York: NBER, 1966.

GLICK, PAUL. *American Families.* New York: John Wiley, 1957.

GOLDSMITH, RAYMOND W. *The National Wealth of the United States in the Postwar Period.* Princeton: Princeton University Press for NBER, 1962.

———. *A Study of Saving in the United States.* Princeton: Princeton University Press, 1955–1956.

GOLDSMITH, RAYMOND W. and LIPSEY, ROBERT E. *Studies in the National Balance Sheet of the United States,* vol. 1. Princeton: Princeton University Press for NBER, 1963.

GOLDSMITH, RAYMOND W., ED. *Institutional Investors and Corporate Stock: A Background Study.* New York: NBER, 1973.

GORMAN, JOHN A. "Nonfinancial Corporations: New Measure of Output and Input." *Survey of Current Business* 52 (March 1972).

GREBLER, LEO; BLANK, DAVID M.; and WINNICK, LOUIS. *Capital Formation in Residential Real Estate.* Princeton: Princeton University Press for NBER, 1956.

GROAT, THEODORE. "Internal Migration Patterns of a Population Subgroup: College Students, 1887–1958." *American Journal of Sociology* 69 (1964): 383–394.

GROSE, LAWRENCE; ROTTENBERG, IRVING; and WASSON, ROBERT C. "New Estimates of Fixed Business Capital in the United States." *Survey of Current Business* 46 (December 1966): 34–40.

HAMEL, HARVEY H. "Educational Attainment of Workers, March 1966." *Special Labor Force Report* 83, U.S. Department of Labor (1967).

HICKS, J. R. *Capital and Time.* Oxford: Oxford University Press, 1973.

HOLLAND, MAURICE and SPRARAGEN, W. *Research in Hard Times.* Washington, D.C.: National Research Council, 1933.

HUDDLESTON, EDITH M. and SULKIN, NAOMI A. "Comprehensive Report on Enrollment in Higher Education, First Term 1961–62 and Summer Sessions 1961." *Circular* 743, U.S. Department of Health, Education, and Welfare, OE-54302 (1964).

HUNT, JR., IRA A. "National Security Contribution to Post-World War II U.S. Economic Growth." Ph.D. dissertation, The George Washington University, 1964.

"Industrial Investment in Manpower." *New England Business Review* (February 1964): 1–5.

JOHNSON, HARRY G. "Comments on Mr. John Vaizey's Paper." *The Residual Factor and Economic Growth.* Paris: OECD, 1964.

JOHNSTON, DENIS F. "Educational Attainment of Workers, March 1962." *Special Labor Force Report* 30, U.S. Department of Labor (Reprint 2416 from *Monthly Labor Review* 86, May 1963).

JUSTER, F. THOMAS. *Household Capital Formation and Financing, 1897–1962.* New York: NBER, 1966.

KAPLAN, DAVID L. and CASEY, M. CLAIRE. "Occupational Trends in the United States: 1900 to 1950." *Working Paper* 5, U.S. Department of Commerce, Bureau of the Census (1958).

KENDRICK, JOHN W. *Productivity Trends: Capital and Labor.* New York: NBER, 1956.

———. *Productivity Trends in the United States.* Princeton: Princeton University Press for NBER, 1961.

———. "Comments on Mr. John Vaizey's Paper." *The Residual Factor and Economic Growth.* Paris: OECD, 1964.

———. "Restructuring Economic Accounts for Growth Analysis." *Statistisk Tidskrift* (Stockholm, 1966).

———. *Economic Accounts and Their Uses.* New York: McGraw-Hill, 1972.

———. "The Treatment of Intangible Resources as Capital." *Review of Income and Wealth* 18 (March 1972).

———. *Postwar Productivity Trends in the United States, 1948–1969.* New York: NBER, 1973.

———. "The Accounting Treatment of Human Investment and Capital." *Review of Income and Wealth* 20 (December 1974).

KIKER, B. FRAZIER. "Human Capital: In Retrospect." *Essays in Economics* 16, University of South Carolina, Bureau of Business and Economic Research (June 1968).

KLEIN, LAWRENCE R. and SUMMERS, ROBERT. *The Wharton Index of Capacity Utilization.* Philadelphia: University of Pennsylvania, Wharton School of Finance and Commerce, 1966.

KUZNETS, SIMON. *Capital in the American Economy, Its Formation and Financing.* Princeton: Princeton University Press for NBER, 1961.

———. *Commodity Flow and Capital Formation,* vol. 1. New York: NBER, 1938.

LANDIS, BENSON Y., ED. *Yearbook of American Churches,* Edition for 1960. New York: National Council of Churches of Christ in the U.S.A., 1959.

LEBERGOTT, STANLEY. *Manpower in Economic Growth: The American Record since 1820.* New York: McGraw-Hill, 1964.

LONG, CLARENCE D. *Wages and Earnings in the United States, 1860–1890.* Princeton: Princeton University Press for NBER, 1960.

LOS ALAMOS SCIENTIFIC LABORATORIES. *National Survey of Professional Salaries in Private Industry,* annual reports, 1948–1965.

MCCLURE, LOIS V. "Weekday Religious Education at the High School Level." *Religious Education* 46 (1951): 349.

MACHLUP, FRITZ. *The Production and Distribution of Knowledge in the United States*. Princeton: Princeton University Press, 1962.

MANVEL, ALLEN D. "Trends in the Value of Real Estate and Land, 1956 to 1966." In *Three Land Research Studies*. Washington, D.C.: National Commission on Urban Problems, 1968.

Media/Scope, various issues.

MERRIAM, IDA C. "Social Welfare Expenditures." *Social Security Bulletin*, various issues.

MILLER, HERMAN P. and HORNSETH, RICHARD A. "Present Value of Estimated Lifetime Earnings." *Technical Paper* 16, U.S. Department of Commerce, Bureau of the Census (1967).

MINCER, JACOB. "On-the-Job Training: Costs, Returns, and Some Implications." *Journal of Political Economy* 70, supplement (1962): 50–79.

MUSHKIN, SELMA J. "Health as an Investment." *Journal of Political Economy* 70, supplement (1962): 129–157.

NADIRI, M. ISHAQ. "Some Approaches to the Theory and Measurement of Total Factor Productivity: A Survey." *Journal of Economic Literature* 8 (1970): 1137–1177.

NATIONAL INDUSTRIAL CONFERENCE BOARD. *The Economic Almanac*, various issues.

———. *Vacation and Holiday Practices*. New York: NICB, 1964.

NATIONAL RESOURCES COMMITTEE. "Relation of the Federal Government to Research." *Research—A Natural Resource*, vol. 1 (Washington, D.C., 1938).

NATIONAL SCIENCE FOUNDATION. *Basic Research, Applied Research and Development in Industry, 1965*. NSF67-12 (1967).

———. "Federal Funds for Separately Budgeted Research and Development." In *Scientific Research and Development in Colleges and Universities—Expenditures and Manpower, 1953–54*, NSF 19-10 (1959).

———. *Federal Funds for Research, Development and other Scientific Activities*, vol. 15, NSF 66-25, various years.

———. *Funds for Research and Development in Industry, 1957, 1958, and 1959* (NSF 60-49, NSF 61-32, and NSF 62-3, respectively).

———. *National Patterns of R & D Resources, 1953–1968*, NSF 67-7 (1967).

———. *R & D Activities in State Government Agencies, Fiscal Years 1964 and 1965*, NSF 67-16 (1967).

———. *Reviews of Data on Research and Development* 33, NSF 62-9 (1962).

———. *Science and Engineering in American Industry, Report on a 1956 Survey*, NSF 59-50 (1959).

The National Underwriter, August 7, 1959.

NELSON, RICHARD R. "Recent Exercises in Growth Accounting: New Understanding or Dead End?" *American Economic Review* 63 (June 1973).

NORDHAUS, WILLIAM and TOBIN, JAMES. "Is Growth Obsolete?" *Economic Growth,* Fiftieth Anniversary Colloquium V. New York: NBER, 1972.

OFFICE OF SCIENTIFIC RESEARCH AND DEVELOPMENT. *Cost Analysis of Research and Development Work and Related Fiscal Information, June 1940–November 1945.* Washington, D.C.: National Research Council, May 1, 1947.

OGBORN, WILLIAM F. "The Financial Cost of Rearing a Child." In *Standards of Child Welfare,* sec. 1, Children's Bureau Conference Series No. 1, Washington, D.C., 1919.

ORGANIZATION OF ECONOMIC COOPERATION AND DEVELOPMENT. *Proposed Standard Practice for Surveys of Research and Development.* Paris: OECD, n.d.

ORNATI, OSCAR. *Poverty amid Affluence.* New York: Twentieth Century Fund, 1966.

ORSHANSKY, MOLLIE. "Counting the Poor: Another Look at the Poverty Profile." *Social Security Bulletin* 28 (January 1965): 3–29.

PERAZICH, GEORGE and FIELD, PHILIP M. *Industrial Research and Changing Technology.* Philadelphia: U.S. Works Project Administration, National Research Project, 1940.

REES, ALBERT. *Real Wages in Manufacturing.* Princeton: Princeton University Press, 1961.

RUGGLES, NANCY and RICHARD. *The Design of Economic Accounts.* New York: NBER, 1970.

SAMMON, ROBERT. "Foreign Investment Aspects of Measuring National Wealth." In *Studies in Income and Wealth,* vol. 12. New York: NBER, 1950.

SCHULTZ, THEODORE W. "Capital Formation by Education." *Journal of Political Economy* 68 (1960): 571–583.

———. "Human Wealth and Economic Growth." *The Humanist* II, 19 (1959): 71–81.

———. "Investment in Human Capital." Reprinted in E. S. Phelps, *The Goal of Economic Growth.* New York: Norton, 1969.

SEARLE, ALLAN D. "Measuring Price Change in Research and Development." In *1966 Proceedings, Business and Economic Statistics Section, American Statistical Association.* Washington, D.C.: American Statistical Association, 1966.

SHAW, WILLIAM H. *Value of Commodity Output Since 1869.* New York: NBER, 1947.

SIMON, KENNETH A. and GRANT, W. VANCE. *Digest of Educational Statistics.* U.S. Department of Health, Education, and Welfare, Office of Education, Bulletins 1964 (OE-10024-64), 1965 (OE-10024-65), and 1966 (OE-10024-66).

SMITH, VERNON L. "The Measurement of Capital." In *Measuring the Nation's Wealth.* New York: NBER, 1964.

SOLOW, ROBERT. "Technical Change and the Aggregate Production Function." *Review of Economics and Statistics* 39 (1957): 312–320.

SPRIEGEL, WILLIAM R. and JAMES, VIRGIL A. "Trends in Training and Development, 1930–1957." *Personnel* 36 (January-February 1959): 60–63.

STEELMAN, JOHN, chairman, the President's Scientific Research Board. *Science and Public Policy, A Report to the President.* Washington, D.C.: 1947.

STIGLER, GEORGE. "Information in the Labor Market." *Journal of Political Economy* 70, supplement (1962): 94–105.

TARVER, J. D. "Costs of Rearing and Educating Farm Children." *Journal of Farm Economics* (February 1956): 144–153.

TERBORGH, GEORGE. *Realistic Depreciation Policy.* Chicago: Machinery and Allied Products Institute, 1954.

TERLECKYJ, NESTOR. "Effect of R&D on the Productivity Growth of Industries." Washington, D.C.: National Planning Association, 1974.

———. *Research and Development: Its Growth and Composition.* Studies in Business Economics 82. New York: National Industrial Conference Board, 1963.

U.N. DEPARTMENT OF ECONOMIC AND SOCIAL AFFAIRS, Statistical Office. *A System of National Accounts and Supporting Tables.* Studies in Methods, Series F, No. 2, Rev. 2. New York: United Nations, 1964.

U.S. BUREAU OF THE BUDGET. *The Budget of the U.S. Government,* annual issues.

U.S. CIVIL SERVICE COMMISSION. *Annual Report,* various issues.

———. "Monthly Trend of Accessions and Separations of Federal Employees, by Type of Personnel Action." *Annual Reports,* various issues.

U.S. DEPARTMENT OF AGRICULTURE. "Family Income and Expenditures." Consumer Purchase Study, miscellaneous publication 465, 1941.

———. *Family Economics Review,* April 1964.

———. *Major Uses of Land and Water in the United States, Summary for 1959.* Economic Research Service, Agricultural Economic Report 13, 1962.

————. *Major Uses of Land and Water in the United States with Special Reference to Agriculture, Summary for 1964*. Agricultural Economic Report 149, 1968.

————. *Reports of Agricultural Research Stations*, 1920–1965, released annually.

U.S. DEPARTMENT OF COMMERCE. "Age of Gainful Workers." News Release, Population U.S. 41 (September 1932).

————. *The Balance of International Payments of the United States, 1946–1948* (1950).

————. *Balance of Payments, Statistical Supplement to the Survey of Current Business* (1963).

————. *Business Statistics, 1965*. Biennial Supplement to the *Survey of Current Business* (1965).

————. *Business Statistics, 1967*. Biennial Supplement to the *Survey of Current Business* (1967).

————. *Census of Population: 1930* (Fifteenth), vol. 4, *Characteristics of Age*, Part I (United States Summary).

————. *Census of Population: 1940* (Sixteenth), vol. 14, *Characteristics of Age*, Part I (United States Summary).

————. *Census of Population: 1940* (Sixteenth), vol. 3, *The Labor Force*, Part I (United States Summary).

————. *Census of Population: 1950*, vol. 2, *Characteristics of the Population*, Part I (United States Summary).

————. *Census of Population: 1950*, vol. 4, Special Reports. *Education* (P-E No. 5B); *Occupational Characteristics* (P-E No. 1B).

————. *Census of Population: 1960*, vol. 1, *Characteristics of the Population*. Part 1 (United States Summary); Part 3 (Alaska); and Part 13 (Hawaii).

————. *Census of Population: 1960*, Subject Reports. *Educational Attainment* (Final Report PC (2)-5B); *Mobility for States and State Economic Areas* (Final Report PC (2)-2B); and *Occupational Characteristics* (Final Report PC (2)-7A).

————. *Censuses of Population and Housing: 1960, 1/1,000 National Sample*, punched card file, 1964.

————. *City Finances: 1952*, G-CF 52, No. 2.

————. *Construction Review* 11, February 1965.

————. *Current Population Reports, Consumer Income*. Series P-60, various issues.

————. *Current Population Reports, Population Estimates*. Series P-25: Estimates of Age, Color, and Sex: 1950 to 1960 (No. 310); Estimates of Single Year of Age, Color, and Sex: 1900 to 1959 (No. 311); 1960 to 1964 (No. 314); July 1, 1960 to 1965 (No. 321); and July 1, 1966 (No. 352).

————. *Government Finances in 1963*, Series G-GF 63, No. 2, 1964.

————. *Historical Review of State and Local Government Finances,* State and Local Government Special Studies No. 25.

————. *Historical Statistics on Government Finances and Employment,* Census of Government: 1962, vol. 6, No. 4.

————. *Historical Statistics of the United States, Colonial Times to 1957* (1960); Continuation to 1962 and Revision (1965).

————. *School Attendance of the Civilian Population,* October 1945, Series P-S, No. 9.

————. *School Enrollment of the Civilian Population,* Series P-20. October 1949 (No. 30), October 1950 (No. 34), and October 1964 (No. 148).

————. *Statistical Abstract of the United States,* 1947–1969.

————. *Survey of Current Business, 1936 Supplement.*

U.S. DEPARTMENT OF DEFENSE. *The Growth of Scientific Research and Development.* Washington, D.C.: 1953.

————. *Research and Development,* Thirty-Second Report by the (House) Committee on Government Operations (1958).

————. *Selected Manpower Statistics* (April 11, 1966).

U.S. DEPARTMENT OF HEALTH, EDUCATION, AND WELFARE. *Biennial Survey of Education in the United States,* 1918–1930, various issues.

————. *Financial Statistics of Institutions of Higher Education, 1959–1960* (1964).

————. *Vital Statistics of the United States,* Vol. II, *Mortality,* Part A, various years.

————. *Vital and Health Statistics,* Series 10, No. 27 (1965).

U.S. DEPARTMENT OF THE INTERIOR. *Minerals Yearbook,* various issues.

————. *Report of the Commissioner of Education for the Year of 1872.* Washington, D.C.: 1873.

U.S. DEPARTMENT OF JUSTICE, IMMIGRATION AND NATURALIZATION SERVICE. *Annual Report,* various issues.

U.S. DEPARTMENT OF LABOR. *Consumer Price Indexes for Selected Items and Groups,* special releases.

————. *Employment and Earnings and Monthly Report on the Labor Force* 12, No. 8 (February 1966).

————. *Employment and Earnings Statistics for the United States, 1909–1964* (Bulletin 1312) and *1909–1965* (Bulletin 1312-3).

————. *The Extent and Nature of Frictional Unemployment.* Study Paper No. 6 (November 1959).

————. *Handbook of Labor Statistics 1967,* Bulletin 1555.

————. *Indexes of Output per Man-Hour for the Private Economy, 1947–1966* (March 1967).

————. *Monthly Labor Review* 87 (June 1964).

————. *National Survey of Professional, Administrative, Technical, and Clerical Pay,* various issues.

————. *The Operation of Severance Pay Plans and Their Implications for Labor Mobility,* Bulletin 1462 (January 1966).

————. *Scientific Research and Development in American Industry, A Study in Manpower and Costs,* Bulletin 1148 (1953).

————. *Severance Pay and Layoff Benefit Plans,* Bulletin 1425-2 (March 1965).

————. *Training of Workers in American Industry.* Research Division Report No. 1 (1964).

————. *Trends in Output per Man-Hour in the Private Economy, 1909–1958,* Bulletin 1-49 (1959).

————. *Wages and Related Benefits, Part II: Metropolitan Areas, United States and Regional Summaries, 1963–64,* Bulletin 1385-82 (June 1965).

U.S. HOUSE OF REPRESENTATIVES, COMMITTEE ON POST OFFICE AND CIVIL SERVICE. *Severance Pay Benefits for Federal Employees* (advance edition), Civil Service Commission Regulations (January 1966).

U.S. IMMIGRATION COMMISSION. *Annual Report of the Commissioner General of Immigration,* 1897–1933.

U.S. PRESIDENT. *Economic Report of the President,* transmitted annually to the Congress.

————. *Manpower Report of the President,* transmitted annually to the Congress.

U.S. TREASURY DEPARTMENT. *Annual Report of the Director of the Mint,* various issues.

————. *Bulletin "F"* (January 1942).

————. *Internal Revenue Bulletin,* No. 1965-20 (May 17, 1965).

————. *Treasury Bulletin* (1967).

WALSH, J. R. "Capital Concept Applied to Man." *Quarterly Journal of Economics* (February 1935).

WANN, MARIE D.; WOODWARD, MARTHINE V.; and FOSTER, E. M. *Participation in Adult Education.* Washington, D.C.: Department of Health, Education, and Welfare, 1959.

WASSON, ROBERT C. "Some Problems in the Estimation of Service Lives of Fixed Capital Assets." In *Measuring the Nation's Wealth.* New York: NBER, 1964.

"Wealth Inventory Planning Study," The George Washington University. In *Measuring the Nation's Wealth.* New York: NBER, 1964.

WERTHEIMER, R. F. *The Monetary Rewards of Migration within the United States.* Washington, D.C.: The Urban Institute, 1970.

Index

Note: The symbol (M) denotes citations on microfiche.

251

DATE DUE

MAY 13 '80			